I0893487

Praise for *Organizing Life*

McClure crafts a pastoral vision for religious leadership that is desperately needed in our time. Those who seek to center the flourishing of individuals, organizations, and our world—and that should include all of us who are leaders—would do well to heed the practical wisdom that McClure so generously offers.

—Kristina Lizardy-Hajbi,
associate professor of leadership and formation,
Iliff School of Theology

Barbara J. McClure's *Organizing Life: Leadership and Human Flourishing* arrives at just the right moment, offering both an analysis of and a guide to religious leadership in this threatening time. McClure's practical direction for transformational religious leaders who feel called to create positive change based on the deepest values inherent in our faith traditions is an important text for scholars and practitioners alike.

—William Goettler, associate dean,
Ministerial and Social Leadership,
Yale Divinity School

McClure's *Organizing Life* arrives at a critical moment when both religious institutions and higher education desperately need a leadership paradigm centered on human flourishing. As someone who straddles both worlds—training future Islamic chaplains at Hartford International University while serving in campus engagement leadership at Williams College—I find this work uniquely valuable. McClure transcends the typical leadership manual by offering a deeply theological, yet practical, framework that speaks directly to the complex challenges my chaplaincy students will face in their life and service in diverse settings. At the same time, this book provides invaluable insights for navigating institutional structures in higher-education student experience. Her nuanced exploration of organizational thriving, contextual constraints, and self-leadership offers a paradoxical approach to both roles. This book belongs on the essential reading list for every chaplaincy program and in the hands of every campus leader committed to creating communities where all can genuinely flourish.

—Bilal Ansari, associate professor of pastoral theology
and director of the Islamic Chaplaincy Program,
Hartford International University; and
assistant vice president of campus
engagement, Williams College

This book immediately went on my list of foundational texts for leading with hope into the current religious, sociopolitical, and ecological crisis. Grounding our vocation in the created impulse to flourish, Dr. McClure provides a gorgeous vocabulary for success, defined not by the marketplace but by resurrection.

—Bradley E. Schmeling, senior pastor,
Gloria Dei Lutheran Church, St. Paul, Minnesota

Grounded in the convictions that we are bound up in our interconnectedness and that the Divine desires all creation to flourish, McClure summons members of faith communities to engage in truly transformational leadership that has at its core the care and well-being of humanity. She challenges us to resist the destructive goals of rapacious power and wealth, and to cultivate spaces where justice and hope are foundational, because it is only in recognizing the dignity and the image of God in each other that we can survive and thrive.

—Laura VanDale, Associate for Justice Ministries,
Presbytery of the Western Reserve

ORGANIZING LIFE

ORGANIZING LIFE

LEADERSHIP AND HUMAN FLOURISHING

BARBARA J. MCCLURE

FORTRESS PRESS
Minneapolis

ORGANIZING LIFE
Leadership and Human Flourishing

Copyright © 2025 Fortress Press. All rights reserved. Except for brief quotations in critical articles or reviews, no part of this book may be reproduced in any manner without prior written permission from the publisher. Email copyright@fortresspress.com or write to Permissions, Fortress Press, PO Box 1209, Minneapolis, MN 55440-1209.

30 29 28 27 26 25 1 2 3 4 5 6 7 8 9

Library of Congress Control Number: 2025000704 (print)

Cover design: Marti Naughton
Cover image: Abstract painting art background multiple colored brushstrokes, from undefined undefined/Getty Images

Print ISBN: 978-1-5064-8110-4
eBook ISBN: 978-1-5064-8111-1

To all who find ways to nurture life,
if only in small spaces

CONTENTS

PREFACE

Religious leaders typically understand themselves as called to serve others, to care, to create a positive legacy, and to make a significant and positive difference in the lives of those in their communities. Religious leadership, ideally, is funded by seeing and understanding the world in ways different than others do. Religious leaders in a variety of contexts, from not-for-profit organizations to congregations and beyond, lean into the best of their religious traditions—their highest values—creating places where people can feel welcome, included, and dignified and where they can be offered real hope. Religious leaders ideally see and understand themselves, others, their wider contexts clearly and accurately and proclaim God's presence amid it all: Clarity boosts morale for both leaders and followers, even if the news is difficult.

All leadership is contextual. Leaders rise out of specific circumstances, environments, and contexts. For this reason, leadership is not a one-size-fits-all quality or a set of behaviors that work universally. The ways power is exercised, the strategies employed, and the practices engaged depend on the situations in which one leads, the culture leaders seek to address, and the people they seek to influence and how.[1] To be transformational toward the good of others, leaders must consider the needs, motivations, skills, and personalities of those they are leading and adapt their approach depending on the leadership goals they hold. Goals can be short term (even urgent) and long term, which may influence the style a leader adopts: For example, crisis leadership may require quick decisions, whereas long-term visions invite a transformational leadership style. Economic, political, and social forces can affect leadership styles, and what leaders choose to focus on will inevitably shape their approach.

Religious leadership in the twenty-first century is in the context of the global economic and political dynamics of neoliberalism, a broad force that has eroded democratic values and institutions.[2] Briefly, neoliberalism is a form of governance that shapes everything from personal subjectivity and experience to social relations and the fundamental institutions that organize our peoples' lives. Neoliberalism promotes a model of society where everything—people, organizations, even governments—is treated as a market, an opportunity for profit. This transforms all individuals into "entrepreneurs of the self," focused on self-management, competition, and the maximization of personal capital, no matter the cost to themselves and others. Neoliberalism represents the efforts to intensify US military capacity, increase US global hegemony, dismantle the welfare state, retrench civil liberties, eliminate women's right to health, eschew affirmative action, re-Christianize the state (in very specific and limited ways), deregulate corporations, gut environmental protections, reverse progressive taxation, reduce education spending while increasing prison budgets, and "feather the nests of the rich while criminalizing the poor"—not just in the United States but globally.[3] Neoliberalism, under the guise of efficiency and rationality, has progressively weakened democratic institutions and degraded people's trust in them. Neoliberal capitalism, by design, breaks apart communities because collectives can be powerful sources of resistance.[4] Neoliberal perspectives understand each person as an island adrift in a sea of "freedom," responsible to tread water themselves to stay afloat.

Rather than fostering active, engaged citizenship, neoliberalism encourages apathy, disenchantment, and a focus on individual success, everyone else be damned. Neoliberalism's emphasis on privatization and deregulation reduces the scope of citizen's power and weakens democratic accountability.[5] Neoliberalism has contributed to the rise of authoritarianism around the world because growing inequality creates desperation among what I call the treading-water and underwater classes.[6] Growing inequality and job insecurity for the middle and under classes have given rise to populist and right-wing political movements that exploit the alienation, fear, and anger caused by neoliberal reforms and offer simple, often authoritarian solutions that reject democratic principles. Neoliberalism has further eroded any sense of responsibility for the common good by undermining the rule of law and governance, emphasizing legal and institutional frameworks to consolidate power in the hands of a wealthy few, and pursuing political leaders' agendas for their own enrichment and at the expense of those with the least.[7]

People feel the pain of living in a neoliberal age, but they often do not understand its sources. The false promises of neoliberalism—including growth, freedom, and prosperity for all—have not been realized, and thus they have created conditions ripe for political instability and the rise of autocratic leaders who challenge democratic values. Desperate for relief in a system rigged against them, for example, voters put their trust in authoritarian leaders who claim to offer a way out. These leaders embody in unique and highly effective ways the neoliberal ideal: They flame the fear that treading- and underwater classes carry because of their plight, and these leaders' rise to power has been because of their commitments to authoritarian and self-serving policies. This is a model of leadership that rests in one person (or one group), as they claim that only they can fix the suffering that they and other neoliberalists helped create. But the neoliberal fix offers a gilded cage.[8] Though the promises are shiny, they do not bear fruit in terms of genuine alternatives to the current situation; they feed fear and hide the greed- and power-mongering under the guise of helping others. The lure for the drowning of being saved by someone else is so powerful that people are attracted to these commanding and controlling leaders' machismo and bluster, and in the United States, even people who consider themselves Christian are willing to overlook egregious, criminal, and dangerous behaviors by leaders unconcerned with anyone outside the financial elite. Viewing money, power, and the market as a savior, neoliberal leaders such as these manipulate the markets for their own gain, generate mass amounts of disinformation to hide what they are doing and ensure their success, and cozy up to billionaires and oligarchs, offering the rest of us help in the form of paper towels in a catastrophic storm.

Neoliberal perspectives and the capitalist systems they have generated and continue to fuel have infiltrated religious communities as well. The fact that success is often measured primarily in terms of budgetary numbers and membership growth in congregations has created deep levels of anxiety among religious leaders in a time when formal religious institutions are declining. Religious leaders, often too stressed themselves by the effort for their own lives to pay close attention, struggle to meet the goals set by neoliberal values and despair about their own roles in shrinking communities.[9] There are possibilities for resistance, however, and reimagining religious leadership is one way to do so. Religious leaders are enjoined to care for the widow and the orphan. The powerful do not give up control easily, but there are ways to reclaim some forms of it. To eschew the "free" market as a god, to reimagine what genuine and authentic care can look like, and to "re-member" communities that live out the best of religious values are vital roles for religious leaders in the twenty-first century.[10]

Religious leaders can step into the breach and help create an alternative to what the most powerful leaders promise but only if they clearly understand the context in which they are working, identify the religious telos of their leadership, and reimagine their practices to create places where genuine care, justice, and hope can be found, even in a sea of violence and despair. Creating these kinds of spaces requires understanding self and others, leaning in to God's longing for all of creation, and inviting change in ways that are not authoritarian and lead toward flourishing. Religious leaders can develop communal and organizational practices that resist the fragmentation, competition, suffering, and despair that neoliberalism engenders. By holding fast to the vision God has for God's world, there is a different way of leading, and religious leaders who seek to nurture the flourishing of all are well positioned to model a new way. The current economic, political, and cultural situation, dominated by neoliberal capitalism and the individualization it engenders, offers some "affordances," or opportunities, for religious communities and their leaders to step into the breach and make a real difference in people's lives.[11] Religiously oriented communities will always continue, even if they change, because God longs to be known and because God is still speaking and acting in the world.

While others will need to mine their own religious traditions for wisdom, the bedrock of mine is that the promise of God is found in a vulnerable man, born of an impoverished and marginalized woman, who died under an oppressive system and whose commitments and values continue to live despite the systems designed to eradicate them. My own faith affirms that the way of salvation and redemption is found in following the community building, inclusive, caring, prophetic ways of Jesus of Nazareth.[12] This Christ does not promise to save us from struggle and death, which are, after all, part of the human condition, but to be with us in them as we are to be with one another. It is religious leaders in their roles as priests, prophets, pastors, and leaders who will help guide the way by creating spaces—"islands of sanity"—for people to be deeply and genuinely human together as they find their way.[13]

Part I of this project puts religious leadership in context, laying out the unique purpose of religious leadership and highlighting the challenges leaders face. Part II explores implications of this context for religious leaders. In addition to perspectives on contemporary leadership, this second part offers practices to guide religious leaders in cultivating thriving organizations and their members.

ACKNOWLEDGMENTS

With thanks to Brite Divinity School for granting me the research leaves needed to conduct this work and to the Center for Theological Inquiry in Princeton, New Jersey, where I was a fellow for two years, for providing critical time and support for the luxury of deep scholarship related to the program's theme, "Thriving in Diverse Contexts."

Thank you to Carey Newman and all those at Fortress Press who helped bring this book to the shelf.

A profound thanks to Steve Olson, professor of leadership and executive education—my colleague, conversation partner, and friend for almost twenty-five years. Quite simply, without Steve, this book would not be.

With deepest thanks for those in my life and around the globe who continue to find ways to resist the life-limiting realities of our common experience and for finding ways to nurture the flourishing of all that is. You may not be able to change the world, but you might be able to change your world.

With gratitude every day for Tim, Anna, Miriam, Isaac, and Lydia and for my sisters, parents, and close friends for love that sustains, especially through darkness.

Part I

Contexts

CHAPTER 1

Religious Leadership Toward Human Flourishing

THERE IS AN enormous deficit of life-giving leadership in positions both up and down the hierarchy of all types of organizations from businesses to not-for-profits and houses of worship. The crisis is not because there are untalented or uncommitted people in leadership positions but that "far too few" are providing the leadership that is increasingly needed everywhere for people's lives to be sustainable, even flourishing.[1] The problem is not one of style but about peoples' core behavior on the job; it is not about the "surface detail and tactics, but a core that changes little over time, across different cultures, or in different industries."[2] The world is ready for a new understanding of leadership. However, some of the challenges in leadership may result from confusion about what, exactly, leaders do and what sets them apart from managers. Indeed, even though leadership is one of the most talked about social phenomena on earth, it is also one of the least understood.[3]

People in formal leadership positions often conflate leadership and management and, as a result, end up managing rather than leading. Managing can be understood as having the power to direct people to complete certain tasks. Managers do not necessarily hold a vision beyond completing specific tasks, and they do not necessarily have to understand the work they are doing as contributing to flourishing. Rather, managers typically are most concerned with getting tasks completed. Managers tend to be responsible for directing people and resources in ways that align with a leader's vision. Managers focus on executing functions and maintaining daily operations. They help ensure that the systems, processes, and structures of an organization run efficiently. Managers delve into the specifics of tasks and take steps toward larger goals, often defined by their leader; managers tend to stay within the parameters that have been arranged by others. Clearly, some managers can exhibit leadership qualities, and some leaders manage on occasion, but the perspective differs between managers and leaders. Some leaders also manage, but not all managers are leaders.

Ideally, leadership and management share the goals of personal, team, and organizational thriving, though they may have different means of effecting it. Leaders have a responsibility to help imagine what could be and support developing ways toward it; they bring a broader perspective and understand how to bring others along. Effective leaders gain the confidence of those who would be involved in bringing the vision to fruition. Leading implies that others are willing to follow into unknown territory, to enact change, and to face the complex challenges of life together.

Leaders bring together the best of organizational analysis and human development; they understand how to motivate people and how to effect change. Leadership implies movement. It suggests action; it requires transitions. Leaders see things from a high-level perspective and share with others what they see. They help set new directions for people and for their organization and help facilitate the processes of change. More specifically, *transformational* leaders innovate and inspire engagement and change toward something positive, keeping in mind the common good. Transformative leaders nurture growth in individuals, relationships, and organizations.

Transformational religious leaders prioritize people and motivate individuals and teams toward common and life-giving goals. Transformative religious leaders are highly differentiated, confident, humble, and collaborative.[4] Transformative religious leaders diagnose the conditions—the values expressed in the organization and its members—and cultivate more life-giving ways to function. Transformative leaders want to change something for the better and effect the processes to do so. Transformational religious leaders do not have all the answers, but they bring people together around a problem and pose powerful questions that get members thinking and working together toward answers and new practices. Transformational religious leaders hold important conversations, ask probing questions, and frame challenges in helpful ways, widening the frame of perspective so that challenges become opportunities. Knowing that traditional leadership models of command, control, and coercion are not effective in the long run, nor do they support genuine human flourishing, a true leader influences and guides people without coercion, rallying them around a shared vision that will motivate them to participate—even sacrifice—for the cause.

There are thousands of definitions of *leadership*, but one of the simplest and most meaningful definitions proposed is "a leader is anyone who wants to help."[5] The operative definition of *leadership* here is that leaders are those who want to help and do so by enlivening and directing the energies and sense of meaning, purpose, and values of those willing to join them in order to get the good that needs doing accomplished. Leaders can occupy any role and be in any level of an organization. It can include a formal position or not. In fact, leadership is a set of behaviors, not a role. Anyone whom others are willing to join can be a leader. Those who align themselves with the best of their religious tradition to nurture the flourishing of those around them in and through the organizations of which they are part are religious leaders who help cultivate human flourishing.

Transformational leaders create a positive change, including the creation of a vision to guide that change, or a strategy.[6] They enliven and empower others to make the vision happen despite obstacles, and they create coalitions of energy and momentum that can move meaningful and positive change forward.[7] Management is often understood as setting out to achieve organizational goals by implementing processes, such as budgeting, organizational structuring, and staffing. While some religious leaders must attend to these tasks, they also think ahead and capitalize on opportunities, persuading (not coercing) others of the importance of change and guiding the implementation of it. Both leadership and management are vital, both have an appreciation of what motivates people to behave the ways they do, and both seek to bring out the best in others to accomplish a goal. The most effective leaders, however, attend to the big picture as well as the details, the long view as well as what is happening in the moment. Managers can sometimes lead, and leaders sometimes manage, but that is not their primary focus. An operative definition of a good leader is a person who has others' trust and can motivate them to come together to undertake meaningful and positive work. In fact, leaders can *only* lead if they have the trust of their would-be followers: Leaders cannot lead if others will not join them.

While it is true that sometimes some members of organizations are motivated to follow because of someone's role or position, true leadership happens because members of an organization (a house of worship, a not-for-profits, etc.) are motivated by the values inherent in the vision the leader holds up. They want to be a part of it, and they trust the leader to leverage the resources in the organization to accomplish positive goals for one and all. In fact, people do not follow roles; they follow people. This means leaders can exist at any level of an organization. They can fill any role, paid or volunteer. Their leadership might be formal, but often it is not. *Generative* and transformational leadership captures the spirit of what is ideal.[8]

The term *generative* comes from psychologist and developmental theorist Erik Erikson, who described the last stage of life as the generative stage. This term refers to an adult who was able to generate growth in human beings (i.e., tend to others' formation), as well as generate new ideas and practices. Generative adults continue to invest in their own growth and attend to their ongoing maturation and integration as well. Generative adults care for self, others, and the whole at the same time.[9] One might say the kind of person a leader is and what they stand for are more important than anything else they do.[10] Generative leadership transforms people and organizations.

Generative and transformative leadership is the leadership that has care at its center. It is motivated by care and enacted with care. Generative adults possess many positive characteristics, including good cultural, sociopolitical knowledge and a healthy, critical relationship to the world.[11]

Generative leaders understand what the organization needs to be for it to live more fully into flourishing, and they know how to cultivate flourishing in their own and others' lives. Transformative and generative leaders have a vision of where they are leading the organization and its members and why. Without a vision, people perish—perhaps because vision is related to hope: hope for change, for something better, for something more life-giving.[12] Generative leaders are mature leaders who pursue flourishing in their own lives and in the lives of all others, the organization they are leading, and the communities of which they are all a part. Generative and transformative leaders seek to nurture human thriving.

Flourishing, however, is not something that is ever fully accomplished; rather, it is pursued, cultivated, nurtured. Flourishing is more a process than an accomplishment, and the journey is not a straight line.[13] Thriving is a by-product of acting generatively. Furthermore, flourishing is something people will likely achieve momentarily, as it is not a static state; thriving is not something that can be grasped and held on to but the result of living in a particular way in a particular moment. Leading toward the flourishing of oneself, others, and the organization that one is leading is a complex task that requires the capacity to understand multiple levels in an organization and attend to many simultaneously operating intrapsychic, interpersonal, and systemic dynamics.

Generative and transformative leaders enliven and direct the energy, sense of meaning, purpose, and values of those willing to follow them to do the good work that must be done. Religious leaders who seek to transform do not have all the answers, but they do raise the important, insightful, courageous questions and create formal and informal opportunities for the organization's members to discuss them. This helps members understand what is important and how it relates to the mission of the organization. It helps them understand where challenges lie. Leaders are responsible to hold information-sharing meetings that help members understand each other's perspectives. Good leaders—generative and transformational leaders—help others see and diagnose what is happening at multiple levels; they ask incisive questions and frame conversations in ways that help others understand what is working and what is not, and they empower members to brainstorm how to move through challenges. Transformative leaders frame situations and events in helpful ways, a skill that takes insight, wisdom, and experience. They are clear about what they seek to change an organization *from* and what they want to change it *into*. This includes its processes and the life of its members.

Generative, transformational leaders understand that change is a constant in personal and organizational life, and they intentionally manage and direct the changes already underway, guiding them toward what is more positive and life-giving. These leaders are light on their feet, always open to learning. Indeed, learning agility is one of the most important qualities and skills a leader can have. Learning agility is a set of complex skills that enable someone to learn something new in one place and then apply it elsewhere in a wholly different situation. Learning agility is "our ability to learn, adapt, unlearn, and relearn to keep up with constantly changing conditions."[14] Learning agility dictates whether a leader will figure out a way through a new situation without knowing quite what to do. Learning-agile leaders use past and present experiences to make sense of uncertain situations. They are open to new ideas and innovate rather than relying on outdated information and practices. When one is an agile learner, one is comfortable being uncomfortable. Agile learners seek out new challenges, ask for feedback from others to learn and grow, and are reflective. Agile learners have a positive and hopeful mindset that allows them to continually develop their understanding, to grow, and to use new strategies they have learned along the way, ready to successfully navigate any future problems. Not surprisingly, learning agility is one of the key differentiators between those who lead organizations that succeed and even thrive and those who do not.[15] Fortunately, such agility can be learned at any stage in life, and like a muscle, if one wants this skill to grow stronger, one needs to constantly work at it. Being an agile learner is not about what one has previously accomplished; it is about the potential to accomplish future tasks with creativity and wisdom.

Religious leaders of values-driven communities are called to be generative, transformational leaders, concerned about the members of the organization as well as the thriving of the organization itself. In addition, religious leaders are called to imagine how their organization can support the flourishing of the members of its local and global communities. Learning to assess the values of an organization and its leaders, holding information-sharing meetings, and having learning agility as a shared expectation can help leaders in these capacities.[16] Although there is an "enormous vacuum" of leadership today—in business, politics, government, education, and religious and nonprofit organizations, there is no shortage of people with the capacity for leadership. The problem is that most people operate with a wrongheaded notion of what constitutes a leader, driven by an obsession with leaders at the top.[17] A new paradigm of leadership is needed because "leadership" is misunderstood and corrupted, because the old paradigm is too small a container for new knowledge or is no longer practicable, and because the problems people are currently experiencing are so complex that they can no longer be solved with the same level of thinking or the same practices that created them.[18]

CHAPTER 2

The *Why* of Religious Leadership

EVEN A GLANCE at today's headlines tells of a world in crisis. Anxiety, depression, and rage are common emotions, and suicide rates are rising, especially among youths. Violence seems the dominant mode of dealing with differences. Genuine community is harder and harder to find.[1] Those in power play on fear and intentionally generate reactivity through blame, harsh criticism, promised instant solutions, and disinformation. Social media can amplify the worst in people and create trouble where it might not otherwise exist. Divisiveness has become the norm, and cooperation on any front is difficult to achieve. Membership is declining in voluntaristic organizations such as communities of faith and civic organizations, and workers everywhere are quiet quitting.[2] Children are suffering in families, education systems, and neighborhoods not designed to meet their needs. Adults are drinking more to cope with a world they no longer understand and cannot manage, and drug addiction is on almost every corner.

The world needs leaders who can bring people together and create places of refuge and authenticity. The world needs thoughtful, genuine, courageous, and responsive leaders to join people together, creating a community that is life-giving and meaningful.[3] But even religious leaders do not have all the answers. Religious leaders are expected to address these ills without always having the tools, perspective, or support necessary to engage in this challenging work. Complexifying the challenge is that the days of command-and-control leadership, where leaders coerce others into compliance or create hierarchies where the leader is in charge and tasked with "fixing" the organization's problems, are gone. That form of leadership never did work very well, especially in the long run, but now those leadership styles are a recipe for disaster; people leave toxic or even merely ineffective leaders in search of something more humane, dynamic, and life-giving.[4] If they can, most people will find ways to opt out of organizations that are led by toxic command-and-control leaders. In this environment, many leaders feel confused: Old models of leadership are not life-giving or effective in the long term, but alternative models require different perspectives and learning new practices.

It is no wonder that the subject of leadership has been exploding in literature—both academic and popular—for decades now. This is in part because leadership has a significant impact on people's lives and on the well-being and functioning of the organization they are responsible to guide. For example, the leadership of a business affects its capacities to generate profits, the leadership of a university affects its capacities to attract and keep high-quality teachers and students, and the leadership of a not-for-profit organization affects its capacities for attracting funders and living out its mission. The leadership of a sports team affects its ability to build cooperation and coordination among its members and effect a winning strategy, and the leadership of a house of worship affects its capacities to create a genuine community of people, to nurture caring and just relationships, to explore together the meanings of sacred texts and cultivate shared values, and to embody the vision their God is calling them to live.

The explosion of literature on leadership is also because effective leadership is a complex and difficult task that requires understanding the organization itself, its members (both as individuals and as a collective, with a history), oneself as a leader, and the dynamic relationships among all of these as they change over time. Being an effective leader is challenging, and it is easier to fail at it than it is to succeed.

There are fundamental perspectives that will help orient life-giving leadership. For example, despite the chaos and suffering and confusion all around, it is a useful starting place to assume that people need to belong, to be seen and accepted for who they are, to be valued and dignified, to be cared for, and to find support as they seek to make meaning and find purpose in their lives. People who seek out membership in a religiously oriented organization do so in part to meet their basic need of connection to others, to hear a theological reflection on their lives as they are, to get help making meaning of their quotidian experiences, and to find a sense of purpose. Cultivating communities that meet these needs is a more difficult task than it might seem on the surface, but that is the mission of religious communities.

It makes sense, then, that there is such a market for books designed to help leaders succeed; it is understandable that the subject of being effective in a role with such challenges, as well as significant and important implications for so many—whether they have a formal leadership position or not—would garner as much attention and sell as many pages as it does. Generative, transformational leadership has become popular, with many books written about it, programs that train people in it at prestigious universities, and workshops designed to cultivate such leaders. But few of these books, programs, or workshops articulate explicitly what leaders are transforming, why they are transforming it, and *from* what *to* what they are to be leading others. Few programs both widen the scope of the art of leadership enough and explore the implications of it on a sufficiently small and detailed scale. In addition, there are many books about leadership on the Amazon website or the shelves of Barnes & Noble that suggest the *telos*, or end goal, of leadership, though the goal is often more shortsighted or vaguer than it could be. Some focus on one theme (such as "lead like Jesus"), while others overview the most common tasks of leadership or specific skills needed for effective leadership (e.g., "leading change" and "leading with heart"). Among the topics usually included are certainly some of the most challenging tasks of leadership: developing and using emotional intelligence to understand others, developing practices toward careful listening, knowing how to have difficult conversations that maintain relationships and are productive, having a strategic vision and recognizing how to implement and persuade others to adopt it, motivating members of the organization to do the work that needs doing, managing poor performers, and leading in ways that others will want to follow.

Each of these qualities and tasks of leadership is made more challenging in contexts such as a community of faith, for example, in which many members of the organization's workforce are volunteers. A volunteer workforce requires a leader to have even more effective skills, as volunteers can quit more easily than paid employees who depend on the position for their livelihood. This raises difficult challenges such as how to motivate people, including volunteers, to meaningfully engage in an organization; how to manage poor performers or deal with toxic members when they do not have to be there; and how to shift the dominant values among members of the organization.[5] It invites reflection on how to attend to the emotions operating in themselves, in others, and through the organization itself; how to effect change when there is a strong pull to maintain the status quo; how to guide others toward right actions; and how to help build a sustainable and viable organization.

Religious leaders are not always clear on the *purpose* or *end goal* of their leadership. This is true even though books related to religious, spiritual, and Jesus-centered leadership abound. This raises the question of what sets religious leadership apart from leadership in nonreligious organizations. Many leaders of religious communities have studied best practices used in nonreligious leadership and tried to apply them to their own religious contexts; many of those books, however, simply appropriate leadership principles from the business sector with a thin veneer of, say, "Christianity" over them. They do not often specify what is "Christian" or "religious" or even particularly "Jesus-centered" about the way of leading the author is discussing.[6] There is much on the *how* of religious leadership, the tips and tricks of it, just as there is in nonreligious literature, but there is not often a thorough enough reflection on the *why* of religious leadership, or its chief missional goals. In addition, when there might be a *why* laid out, it is rarely sufficient. A study of religious leadership is ideally set within a worldview—a cosmology, even—that is broad enough to adequately describe the realities of human existence and inform the values and practices to imagine that existence most meaningfully.

There is more to religious leadership than learning to think strategically or knowing how to manage change (as important as both those skills are). Leaders of values-driven communities are called to something different than leaders of for-profit organizations (though leaders in those contexts would do well to expand and deepen their perspectives as well). This should give religious leaders' understanding of their role, its challenges, and its practices a different framework than the one used by, say, Andy Jassy, the current CEO of Amazon.[7]

Religious leadership has a unique character and mission that ideally inform the work. The unique goals of religious leadership must be grounded in a clear understanding of the context of one's leadership, what effective leadership in that context would look like, what the mission is, what its particular challenges are, and how to address them as informed by their religious tradition. Different from other leaders, religious leaders are called explicitly to cultivate God's vision of flourishing for the earth and its people through the work of communities of faith—a critical task that deserves focused attention and generous support.[8]

Because religious leaders should be explicitly informed by the values of their religious tradition, it is important to clarify those values. Typical books on leadership do not challenge the dominant status quo of the sociopolitical and economic order, for example. Nor do they always analyze the use and abuse of power or offer holistic and inclusive visions of flourishing. They do not typically hold the leaders themselves, their behaviors or organizations (or teams or individuals), as accountable to human flourishing. Texts on leadership do not often assign leaders the explicit role of managing their own flourishing, the flourishing of the members of their organization, the flourishing of the communities of which they are a part, and the flourishing of all God's creation. Religious leadership, then, must be driven by unique purposes, often through countercultural practices, and with a group of people whose membership and meaningful participation in the organization and its mission are largely voluntary and thus must be nurtured in particular ways. It is not an exaggeration to say that leadership in faith-based contexts is often understood to be a life-and-death matter; one might say people's very lives are at stake—or at least their *thriving* lives are at stake. To say that effective religious leadership is a crucial vocation only underscores the fact that it is a uniquely challenging task deserving special attention, careful reflection, meaningful insight, and useful guidance. Religious leaders have a *faith-based* or *values-based* responsibility to attend to and lead in the primary spheres of human life; addressing people's personal pain and attending to organizational culture, systems, and processes are important ways to care for God's created order.

Foci of Religious Leadership

Care of People

Religious leaders are called to nurture others' flourishing. They do not bracket people's experience or subjectivity; they centralize it. They take seriously people's lives, and this means attending to what is happening at the individual, personal level, understanding that personal pain is also embedded in wider social, cultural, ecological, political, and economic spheres that create suffering.[9] Religious leaders connect human experience to the complex realities of the day, caring for people as they also help them make meaning of their experiences, resist injustice, and grieve losses.

At the individual level, usually in what is called *spiritual* or *pastoral care*, religious leaders attend to the spiritual/religious, emotional/psychological, physical, and experiential qualities of human life to help lead a person from floundering—perhaps even suffering—toward flourishing. This is most often done in one-on-one meetings, attending to the other by offering them presence (broadly defined as being fully attentive, setting aside one's own internal "static," and joining with the other person's agenda).[10] Through the practice of presence, religious leaders explore the concerns expressed in relation to the parishioner's goals, putting aside the religious leader's own assumptions, listening carefully to the stories the person is sharing, helping another person create meaning by rewriting their stories, helping them develop a sense of larger purpose, and aiding the person in understanding themselves and their experiences, others, and God in new ways.[11] *Presence* also suggests paying attention to the ways the sacred, or divine is present in the situation. Often, the Sacred—God—is experienced in compassion from another, in practices of careful listening, in a trustworthy word, in the reading of a sacred text, or in the performance of a symbolic ritual.[12] Religious leaders accompany people's meaning-making processes, tending carefully to another's unique experiences and helping them create a more complex and nuanced understanding of themselves, of the world, and of their God. Religious leaders support people's meaning-making processes by offering a worldview and theological interpretations that are supported by sacred Scripture, experience, wisdom, and tradition.[13]

Religious leaders help others create a sense of meaning, value, belonging, and even purpose through the prayers that aid in expressing their experiences, their felt needs, and their cries for help, love, grace, and hope. Religious leaders also draw on the symbols, sacred texts, and stories that ground people in their community, and they facilitate rituals that help people and their communities gain a sense of their place in the historical story of God in relation with them and with all of creation. When people are at their most vulnerable, when life seems uncertain, when positive and healthy relationships seem impossible, and when flourishing seems elusive or not deserved, religious leaders walk alongside to reframe and help reconstruct a person's experiences, holding hope when others cannot; helping them imagine a better life; and listening deeply to others as they share their own articulation of their goals, dreams, and solutions they have within themselves.[14] Religious leaders help name the human condition and seek out and name the sacred within it even as they resist what impedes human flourishing.

Religious leaders walk with people when they are suffering.[15] Religious leaders hold and help nurture a sense of hope and belonging even amid the suffering that threatens to pull apart people and communities. Suffering can destroy people's sense of dignity and their worth, and some forms of suffering are often difficult to describe and understand. Because human beings are, at their core, meaning-making creatures and because crises, grief, pain, and struggle are endemic to the human condition, religious leaders are often asked to join people as they seek to make meaning of those experiences.[16] Drawing on the sacred texts, the stories and symbols of a faith, and the rituals that have developed to help people make sense of their lives is the work of religious leaders. By engaging in these practices, religious leaders are understood to embody, represent, and mediate the divine. Most religious leaders understand that a significant part of their responsibility is caring for individual people and their community, especially in times of loss, grief, transition, suffering, and relational rupture. Religious leaders guide others through suffering by helping them shift perspective, access their own wisdom, find motivation for change, and see a way forward. Transformative and generative religious leaders learn new ways to stand in solidarity with those who suffer.

Care of Organizations

People naturally form organizations and live their lives through them. Partnerships, families, villages, states, nations, and global systems structure human life and mediate social, political, economic, and cultural patterns. Individuals, their families, and their communities live their lives within organizations that mediate and manage the dynamics of life together. Each person and community is affected by micro- (individual and familial), meso- (organizational/institutional) and macro- (city, state, national, global) level systems that embody and mediate the values that bind them together. Effective religious leaders, if they wish to cultivate human flourishing, strive to understand people's lived experiences as relayed through the institutions and organizations of which they are a part. For those especially interested in the well-being of others, such as transformational religious leaders, the relationship among sociopolitical systems, organizations, and the well-being of people is necessarily a focus of attention.

One of the defining features of modern life has been the emergence of large-scale organizations that increasingly have come to structure contemporary life. In highly differentiated societies like those in the industrialized world, organizations operate by their own goals and logic by which those goals are achieved. In most cases, the goals and logic of for-profit organizations follow the rationality of the marketplace. Individuals are often viewed as resources to help the organization and its stakeholders achieve their goal, often primarily understood as financial gain. However, not all organizations are intended to be driven by the values of the market (and even people who work in organizations within that frame express the desire for work that is meaningful).[17] In other words, the desire for a sense of vocation—or a sense of deep purpose—is still alive, even in for-profit organizations, and most people want to spend their time in work that they feel has a positive meaning for them.[18] Adults spend most of their time in organizations, and much human satisfaction and dissatisfaction derive from their experiences in the various organizations in which they participate. Organizations, therefore, are elemental to people's flourishing, and yet large systems and the smaller organizations within them can easily be the cause of much human suffering. This suggests that it is not only the religious leader's organization that invites attention but organizations outside the congregation as well.

The organizations in and through which people live can be (and often are) contexts of human suffering.[19] Toxic work relationships, racist and sexist practices, unjust policies, and ineffective leadership can exploit those with less power. On the other hand, when organizations are led and run well and when they are oriented around values beyond the financial bottom line, they can also be contexts within which their members can thrive. As such, organizational systems and their leadership are appropriate sites for theological attention. There are other reasons for religious leaders' attention to organizations—both the one(s) they lead and others as well: The Sunday/Monday gap, despite what it seems, is not as wide as one might assume.[20] Parishioners bring workplace struggles, anxieties, and ambitions with them into congregations, pastoral offices, and their places of volunteer labor—when they show up at all. They are looking for understanding, care, belonging, and purpose.

The good news is that because they want to belong and need to be cared for, they may be more open to transformative, generative pastoral imagination and leadership that provide them a way forward.

Because religious leaders are (or, at least, ought to be) focused on values beyond the financial success of their organization, it is important to explore the principles that will ideally drive religious leadership. One of the unique challenges religious leaders must face, for example, is what vision of success they hold for their organization and by what practices and tools they seek to cultivate that goal. If change is a fundamental quality of leadership, then the question *from* what *to* what do religious leaders seek to compel people, groups, and their organization, and to which they are responsible, is important. Effective religious leaders reflect on how they will accomplish their mission. Especially for faith-based leaders, these are fundamental questions that need to be answered if they want to avoid falling prey to the critique that they are no different than nonreligious leaders, appropriating uncritically nonreligious and unspiritual (e.g., market-driven) goals, values, and means of ensuring financial success of their organizations.[21] Religious leaders have a responsibility to listen for the values and the beliefs expressed in their sacred texts and traditions that ideally will help develop and support a life-giving culture in the organization that extends to its people.[22] Not all values are religiously congruent, and leaders in these contexts have a responsibility to speak out for the cardinal religious values such as love, justice, courage, and temperance/moderation as well as the theological values of faith, hope, charity, compassion, kindness, humility, gentleness, patience, tolerance, and forgiveness.

Religious leaders are charged, too, with stewarding organizations *qua* organizations—that is, stewarding the whole that is more than the sum of its parts. This is the vocation of religious leaders: They are called to care for the flourishing of the whole as they are called to care for its individual members. Many examinations of religious leadership are focused primarily on reconciling individuals to God and to the church, often with the hope of deepening people's spiritual lives and/or increasing church membership. Religious leaders ideally will continue to support these efforts while also making significant contributions to the understanding and practices of caring for the body, even as they have an eye on the context within which the community and its members are embedded.

Care of Worlds

Religious leadership is a practice and a discipline that seeks to promote the well-being—even flourishing or thriving—of individuals and their communities.[23] The underlying conviction of generative, transformational religious leaders is that the divine intends creation—all of creation, from individuals to communities and even the earth and its ecosystems—to flourish. Religious leaders' attention to people who are hurting and their overriding concern for well-being are grounded in a theological vision of a loving God who wills that all participate in the divine (broadly understood)—or flourishing—life.[24] This is a reasonable description of the project of religious leadership: promoting the flourishing of all that is. A central preoccupation of religious leadership, then, is to resist the impediments to the full participation in the life of God.[25] In short, religious leaders are called to ameliorate people's distress and address the alienating dimensions of human life as embodied in the systems and organizational structures in and through which people live. Religious leaders seek to identify, analyze, and help overcome the challenges to human flourishing. Historically, this has primarily meant focusing on people's individual psyches and giving spiritual and psychological/emotional care, but religious leaders must also care for others by resisting what creates suffering, by speaking out and being active against the evils that people, organizations, and larger systems can perpetuate. Nurturing the thriving of individuals requires attention to the worlds they inhabit.[26]

Religious Leadership as Public Theology

Insofar as religious leaders give their primary attention to caring for others, their organizations, and all of God's creation, leadership is a pastoral theological endeavor.[27] This framing understands religious leadership as a form of pastoral *public* theology, a term that implies that caring for others includes attending to the organizational system and the values embodied in the organization's processes and culture.[28]

The term *public theology* is an expansive one, but fundamentally it indicates an effort to bring religious claims and modes of analysis and interpretation into public discourse, to speak to and about the public square. It is a critical and constructive religious reflection on public life and assumes that religious organizations have something to say about the right ordering of society. Religious leaders as public pastoral theologians not only speak to and about the public square; they also create practices that resist the toxic and life-limiting patterns in that public square and the organizations that inhabit it.

Leadership as a public pastoral theological vocation understands all ministry as a form of shepherding, or the "disposition or readiness" for an "attitude of tender and solicitous concern for person or group with whom one is dealing."[29] At its best, religious leadership is a form of care. The readiness to care is always available and presents itself when the need arises. But this tender and solicitous concern extends beyond individual people. Religious leaders must think on multiple levels. Religious leadership is defined as "that branch or field of theological knowledge and inquiry that brings the shepherding perspective to bear upon all the operations and functions of the church and [its leader], and then draws conclusions of a theological order from reflection on these observations."[30] In this framework, religious leadership has three discrete functions: shepherding as caring (healing, sustaining, and guiding), communicating the good news (educating, celebrating, evangelizing), and organizing (nourishing, protecting, relating to the organization one is leading—in other words, ecclesiastical leadership).[31] Whatever one's diagnosis of the present cultural climate—the age of anxiety, the paradoxical trends toward conformity and fragmentation, confusion about moral standards, or the cult of success—"the deepest need is to come somehow to a valid sense of meaningfulness."[32] This is what is meant by shepherding an organization in its three functions. But the details of how one shepherds and to what one attends must be current and relevant to connect with people's lived experiences and help them make meaning amid confusion and suffering. In the culture in which the shepherding metaphor was first developed, "the single shepherd, with his crook to guide and redirect the strays, took his sheep into green pastures by day and at night brought them to the safety of home. [However], the spiritual shepherd of today has as much obligation as the literal shepherd to bring his [or her] methods up to date in order to meet the peculiar needs and dangers of our time."[33] Because all leadership is contextual, even situational, religious and spiritual leadership today requires the development of new knowledge, skills, tools, and perspectives to bear on the work of caring and even healing.[34] Religious leadership today requires the equivalent of the shepherd "knowing how to prevent the grass from disappearing from a green pasture through knowledge of irrigation, crop rotation, and tree planting."[35] Religious practices—including those that attend to the care and leadership of an organization—need to be grounded in theological perspectives, and theological perspectives need to be evaluated for their ability to cultivate human flourishing.

In their work of caring in and for organizations, religious leaders often aid in conflict management, increasing diversity and the full inclusion of a diverse membership, devising new decision-making processes, and holding the organization and its members to religious values such as love, justice, care, and the thriving of all in the organization and the community of which the congregation is a part. This work requires clear communication, advocacy for the "least of these," and attention to both the individuals and the systems that are foundational to that organization. To be effective toward flourishing, religious leaders must be able to make trusting connections with others, practice empathy (and even interpathy), and understand and navigate the systems they seek to lead.[36] But even that is not enough.

Fortunately, religious leaders usually have some basic tools for understanding group dynamics and the role of values in corporate lives. As they hone their capacities to communicate through speaking and writing, to evaluate the operative values in people and organizations and the world, and to articulate ways of being together that are different from the dominant culture, transformative religious leaders nurture flourishing for both individuals and organizations. Especially now, though, generative, transformational religious leaders must constantly increase their skill at leading amid social disruption, disinformation, violence, moral crises, fragmentation of communities and epidemics of loneliness, rising rates of despair, general malaise, confusion, and hopelessness. As they tune their ears to human experience in a dysfunctional and chaotic world, transformative religious leaders also hone the skills of interpreting sacred texts in response to the realities people and their communities are facing and develop wisdom for diagnosing, naming, and resisting contemporary impediments to flourishing.

Organizations can be a primary part of the fabric that can support human flourishing; however, this is dependent on how organizations function, how they are led, and whether and how organizations continue to evolve and develop in ways that are life-giving, not just for their members but also to the wider communities in which they are embedded. Transformative leaders observe how their organization is functioning, whether and how they and the teams they lead are held accountable, and to what extent. While growth is often understood as an individual process, organizations, too, change continually, and good leaders can help them grow in positive ways.[37] Religious leaders who cultivate their own flourishing as well as that of the individuals within their organization and the organization itself consistently explore their *why* and seek to live into that more fully. They hold their organizations to the values in historically religious themes, such as salvation and wholeness.[38]

To this end, religious leaders have unique responsibilities to engage in conversations about the moral implications of their organization's official and unofficial policies and to think with an organization's leadership about its purposes and ends. While many professionals are called on to do this kind of organizational development outside of religious contexts (organizational psychologists, leadership consultants, management coaches, and human resource officers come to mind), most of these are not trained to reflect deeply, critically, or theologically about the worldview and even cosmology that an organization embodies, about the nature of the good or the definition of success that a particular organization seeks to promote.[39] The most generative religious leaders have and continue to develop deep commitments to and capacities for caring for others in their "concrete contingencies and problems," stimulating and enabling people's life of faith and their practical knowledge of God.[40] Transformative and generative religious leaders help their organization pay attention to its operative values (and perhaps shift them) and nurture policies and practices that contribute to a healthy community in which all can flourish.

Religious leaders are responsible to make significant contributions to human flourishing in their work of caring, advocacy, and activism, even as the focus of their attention widens from caring for individuals and leading their organization toward flourishing to include the broader public sphere. Religious leaders are called to be prophets at times, agitating for their organization but also the world outside it, and to be more mindful of access to basic human rights such as dignity and inclusion, love, financial stability, physical and mental health, and a just society. Religious leaders have much to offer in terms of redeeming and transforming organizational culture, and attending to organizations will even more significantly help the individuals and families in their midst for whom they already care. An approach to these practical concerns undertaken with "religious seriousness and theological perspective" may be precisely what is needed for helping Western civilizations "develop more humanly rich and fulfilling traditions of the art of life," beyond the superficial moral and religious perspectives that currently prevail.[41]

To do this work, transformational religious leaders speak to a public realm that often has shallow, competing, consumerist, and individualistic visions of the good. Values are always operative in every endeavor, but not all values are consistent with the idea of religious leadership as being developed here or with human flourishing. Failure to engage the world with a well-considered theological imagination, and failure to nurture systems that support the thriving of people and organizations, risks ceding those spaces to other ideologies or practices and their underlying values, which are often dehumanizing and directly counter to human flourishing.

Religious leaders have a unique responsibility to facilitate a frequent review of the values that are operating in the people, teams, and organizations they seek to lead. Religious leadership invites an examination of the ways people and organizations make meaning and the dominant worldviews they espouse. Religious leaders must be able to interpret personal experiences as well as systems' functioning and actively resist any ways those systems do not align with religious and spiritual values and traditions. Religious leaders are responsible to bring uniquely religious values to questions of meaning and purpose and to the organizations humans have constructed. They are not to be driven primarily by the financial bottom line but by the commitment to emphasize the inherent dignity and value of each person and to hold operational systems and cultures that make organizations accountable to the care and justice for, as well as the flourishing of, all.[42]

Navigating the bureaucratic processes, history, and practices that operate within an organization is a key capacity required of religious leaders who seek to cultivate human flourishing.[43] Teambuilding, conflict management, values-based deliberation, and change facilitation are all skills needed in religious leaders. If religious leaders are responsible to nurture the thriving of the people and organizations they serve, they must understand and attend to interpersonal dynamics, the intersection of persons and systems, the ways that power and privilege flow and are leveraged in the organization, and how the whole affects the one and the one affects the whole. To be transformational, religious leaders need to be able and willing to speak to systemic and public ills, to the patterns of injustice, and to the ways that systems create suffering. Through rituals and ceremonies, pastoral care encounters, and preaching and education, religious leaders help mediate transcendent meanings and provide safe (and often brave) spaces where pain can be expressed and is held in trust with compassion and care. Transformative religious leaders bear witness to the realities of what is and attend to life's transitions, holding experiences of crisis, trauma and loss, and pain and suffering in tension with a vision of wholeness and flourishing. Through it all, transformative religious leaders name what is broken, help imagine what can be and accompany the processes of meaning making and practices of hope in it all.

Walking with others and shepherding organizations, people, and communities through the quotidian experiences of life is a sacred trust. A reflection on religious leadership will include some hints and tips of leadership, of course. It will also include a theology of human flourishing, the perspectives needed to nurture it, and a clear-eyed account of impediments to flourishing.

Religious Leadership for the Thriving of All

Healing understood from a religious perspective is dependent, in part, on understanding and resolving the dynamics of a "sick soul."[44] But because religious leadership is always contextual and situational, practices of care have also included creating communities of faithful people who attend to stories, provide sanctuary, and offer support to parishioners struggling to endure the challenges of life.[45] In recent years, religious leaders have also seen the need to attend to the sociopolitical, economic, and cultural systems that affect people's well-being by drawing on theologies that help make sense of what is happening and provide hope for ways forward. For example, feminist theorists and other scholars from outside the dominant cultural, class, and power structures have contributed to redirecting religious attention to systems of exclusion and oppression that create so much suffering.[46] Black theologians, including James Cone, Archie Smith Jr., Willie J. Jennings, and Jay-Paul Hinds, and womanist theologians, from Delores Williams to Keri Day and Emily Townes, have clearly articulated the ways sexism and racism have created systems of suffering that have become reified in organizational life.[47] Latinx, Asian, and African perspectives illumine the geographical and cultural particularities of suffering. For example, Ghanaian pastoral theologian Emmanuel Lartey's work on the indigenization of theological and theoretical resources and practices has challenged religious leaders to rethink the sources of suffering and grace, and Black pastoral theologians Lee Butler and Chanequa Walker-Barnes have highlighted the ways colonial and neocolonial (which is entangled with neoliberalism) practices have engendered particularly trenchant forms of suffering for those whose land and lives have been taken over by dominant groups.[48] Latinx scholar Rubem Alves and anti-racist scholar Ryan Lamothe have explored radical political theologies and their relationship to the suffering of the created order, and queer pastoral theologians including Cody Sanders, Joretta Marshall, and John Blevins have focused on the unique needs of queer folk and their communities.[49] Only by hearing the experiences of those in minoritized, underrepresented, and underwater groups, and only by studying the suffering, disease, and alienation as experienced in nondominant cultural and class contexts, can religious leaders begin to understand the ways an overly individualistic and universalized understanding of human experience misses many of the sources of distress, its consequences, and its remedies.[50] These scholars understand, at least implicitly, that flourishing is not just the absence of sickness but an active wholeness for one and all and that this is part of the sacred responsibility of religious leaders.[51]

These perspectives have broadened the terrain for religious leadership and redirected its attention to the "reciprocal relationship" among the brokenness of people's lives, the brokenness of the communities in which they live, and the brokenness of the world.[52] As pastoral theologian Larry Graham puts it, "Behind every personal problem is a cluster of societal problems."[53] He adds that suffering is best understood as a crisis in one or more arenas (including self, God, neighbor, justice, and ecological harmony) and that the symptoms of division, dismissiveness, denial, blame, and diminishing others reflect unjust power arrangements at multiple levels throughout the system.[54] The underlying insight from this is that, in Graham's perspective, care of selves entails care of the worlds in which those selves live. Care of worlds and care of persons go together; in fact, care of selves *requires* care of the worlds in which those selves live, including the civic and political worlds—perhaps even especially those worlds. It affirms religious leadership as a form of public theology, as it attends to the experiences of life, faiths, and human beings. The first step in transformational religious leadership is understanding people's lived realities, even before interpreting them in light of theological commitments.[55]

From the perspective of transformative religious leadership, the turn to public theology is motivated by a therapeutic—or healing—sensibility. If human beings and the communities they live in (including the earth's ecological communities) are to realize the thriving life God intends for them, then it is not enough to address a person's unique psychological and spiritual dynamics. A genuinely transformative leader will necessarily critically engage the systems that both create and limit human potential. A focus on public theology is grounded in religious leaders' awareness that suffering and the possibilities of human flourishing are not simply matters of individual concern. More broadly, the turn to public theology also rejects the compartmentalization of religion as a personal or private matter. Instead, public theology recognizes the role of theological voices in the conversation about what makes a good society and how societies effect people's flourishing or floundering. Religious leaders recognize that if they want to offer adequate care in the present moment, they will need to become as knowledgeable about the wider systems that are affecting the health of people and communities as they are about practices for spiritual care.[56]

The range of pastoral concern thus expands from the narrower concern for the salvation of an individual soul before God to the wider cultural and political frames that focus on the structural dimensions of human suffering.[57] Transformative religious leaders are aware that it is not enough to simply attend to the separate or individualized self (as if such a thing exists); they attend to selves in context.

* * *

Religious organizations and their leaders are called to promote flourishing. This will require articulating a vision of flourishing that is grounded theologically, and it will require speaking out against what impedes flourishing. Faithful leaders are to be in but not of the world, and faith-based organizations and their members are to be public witnesses to what is true about the world and people's lives. They can be models of what can be (and what God longs for) and guides toward how to achieve these sacred goals. Those who wish to transformatively lead religious organizations do not bracket human experience; they centralize it, and they see human experience in the context of social, political, and cultural dynamics. They seek to lead organizations into more life-giving cultures and processes, knowing that organizations mediate the wider world to the personal level. Transformative religious leaders know that attending to lived experience is the only way to change processes and systems and that understanding personal experiences is at the heart of broader changes. Faithful leaders draw from the wisdom of their traditions to respond to contemporary situations for this work, and as transformational religious leaders, they hold out hope and are open to a vision of a different future. They help find the sacred amid the ordinary.[58]

Transformational religious leaders can identify the intersections of economic, political, social, and cultural systems that are mediated through organizations and can see and name the suffering these create. They can help make meaning out of chaos; guide people toward life, not death; and lean into the sacred that imbues all of life.[59] Transformational religious leaders bring insights into the suffering that people are experiencing, and they act in faith, hope, and determination to make positive changes to cultivate better human and communal flourishing. Transformational religious leaders bring practical wisdom and knowhow to navigate and even change the webs that support life. Transformational and generative religious leaders know that spiritual care must attend to all dimensions of human relationality: the personal, social, communal, and economic as well as the theological, religious, and spiritual dimensions of life, both in the pain and in the growth and change. Transformative religious leaders are committed to the flourishing that God longs for, and they can envision the flourishing that they, their organization, and all people are called to. They know how to nurture that vision and work to make it a reality. Transformative and generative religious leaders are committed to their own growth, and they know how to cultivate the growth of others and of their organization. Generative and transformative religious leaders are fueled by a commitment to the flourishing of all by attending to the needs and growth of people, organizations, the wider community, the world, and themselves.

CHAPTER 3

Envisioning a Flourishing World

RELIGIOUS LEADERS ARE responsible to promote and nurture the well-being of those they seek to serve. This conviction is supported by the fact that much of the Judeo-Christian sacred texts are about flourishing in one way or another, and it can be argued that the flourishing of all is God's deep desire.[1] For this reason, one might say that cultivating flourishing is religious leaders' vocation. However, clarifying what flourishing is, how people experience it, and how to effect it is no easy task. As one biblical scholar notes, the Judeo-Christian Bible "provides direction for—but does not formulate—a doctrine of happiness [well-being, or flourishing]."[2] Thus, important questions are: What is meant by *flourishing*, and how might religious leaders effect it?

Understanding Human Flourishing

Understanding what it means for individuals, groups, and organizations to flourish has garnered much attention for thousands of years up to the present moment. Many months into the COVID-19 pandemic, the *New York Times* published a series of articles on flourishing as well as languishing that got the attention of readers, as demonstrated by the subsequent comments. Those articles were followed by a "flourishing quiz" and a list of "simple activities" that "can lead to marked improvement in overall well-being."[3] Not only had the *Times* tapped into the sense that people around the world were struggling to flourish, but the series also identified the increased interest across many disciplines (from philosophy to religion and psychology) and policy institutes to understand flourishing and how to effect it. This interest is not new.

Philosophies of Human Flourishing

Ancient Greek philosophers were preoccupied with the question of human flourishing, asking what it looked like and what it required.

The Greeks used the word *eudaimonia*, translated as *flourishing*, *well-being*, and even *happiness*, and their exploration of the topic laid the groundwork for much of the fields of ethics and the study of flourishing by exploring the relationship among human desires, human virtues, and the use of reason and wisdom in pursuit of the good life. Their insights, especially those of Socrates and Plato, the Stoics, Aristotle, and the early Christians who responded to their thinking, continue to influence the study of human flourishing to this day.

Many (though not all) early Greco-Roman philosophers reflected on human flourishing through the dominant worldview of their time: a dualistic perspective that set earthly matters apart from cosmic, heavenly, or spiritual ones.[4] In their view, flourishing primarily had to do with one's manner, character, and understanding. Socrates, one of the founders of Western philosophy, argued that well-being is intricately related to moral virtue, that wisdom is a virtue, and that leading a virtuous life comes from wisdom and leads to deeper wisdom. Plato, Socrates's student and scribe, extended Socrates's work and argued that happiness is the result of a "calm character": A happy or thriving person is one who develops virtues such as courage, kindness, and humility and their capacities for reason to hone the wisdom to know when and how to apply the virtues.[5]

The Stoics, a group of Greek philosophers famous for their asceticism, believed that people are happy when they use their reason to nurture the virtues of "negative freedoms" such as freedom from need, want, desire, personal or social success, and material well-being. The Stoics deemed the material world vastly inferior to the cosmic realm and developed practices around self-control and poverty. They promoted a repudiation of societal conformity to diminish the material world's effect on their lives. Well-being in the Stoics' view is cultivated by internal discipline; the dismissal of conventional morality; and eschewing "common" values such as patriotism, the pursuit of wealth, "courtesies and refinements," fame, honor, reputation, and sexuality.[6] They thought people who seek flourishing should be ruled by reason, rationally indifferent to both joy and grief, accepting with calm the vicissitudes of life in the material world, and focusing on what was beyond. The Stoics argued that common things people desire such as love, honor, good health, a "congenial" family life, and personal freedom all depend too much on external circumstances beyond individuals' control and should be held with indifference.[7] By living according to nature, elevating reason over the passions, and nurturing good habits—especially of self-control, right belief, and right behavior—people can free themselves from the desire to change the unalterable and be indifferent to both pleasure and pain. In other words, the Stoics understood well-being as freedom from human desire and the achievement of inner peace.

Others, such as the ancient philosopher Epicurus, also valued cultivating the virtues as fundamental to thriving, or well-being, though he argued against the Stoics, saying that desire and pleasure *are* the highest goods and, indeed, the ultimate goals of life. However, only *certain* pleasures are worthy, according to Epicurus, namely the simple, life-sustaining ones. Worthy pleasures do not include the "tortured trinity" of wine, sex, and song.[8] Rather, right pleasures prevent suffering and produce a serene spirit; these "pleasures" include health, self-control, independence, moderation, simplicity, cheerfulness, friendship, prudence, intellectual and aesthetic values, peace of mind, and conscience. The calm, tranquil, and harmonious life, then, is the happy or good life for the Epicureans.[9] Because humans are beset by a condition of wanting more and more, they can become addicted to pleasure (and unworthy pleasures) and not practice self-control, allowing themselves too much of the wrong things and not contemplating higher and worthier goals.[10]

The early Greek philosopher Aristotle has had perhaps the most significant impact on the examination of flourishing in the West, especially in relation to the cultivation of virtues. Aristotle valued the earthly realm more than his predecessors did; consequently, his position differed significantly from those of the thinkers he followed in that happiness or well-being in Aristotle's schema does not come as the result of separating oneself from the material world but rather as an activity of the soul in accord with *excellence in the pursuit of one's highest capacities* in the world. Aristotle heralded well-being (flourishing, or, in Greek, *eudaimonia*) as the greatest good because it is desired for its own sake, not for the sake of anything else, and because it is the end toward which all other goods aim.[11] For Aristotle, *eudaimonia, or happiness,* is not simply a mental state or disposition. Because Aristotle was not as strict a dualist as Plato, he did not believe the soul can be a separate entity from the body. Thus, he argued that well-being requires, among other things, fulfilling the needs of the body, both individual and corporate bodies (what he called the *polis*). Aristotle argued that at the individual level, components that comprise well-being include some level of physical and psychological safety and security and some measure of material stability, which implies equal access to required resources.

Aristotle argued that *eudaimonia* (happiness, thriving, flourishing) requires living well and faring well. *Living well* means that a person understands and acts on the virtues: the pursuit of truth, understanding, prudence, courage, temperance, and generosity.[12] These virtues are predicated on the rules found in practical and moral wisdom—"the judgement of the enlightened."[13] Thus, Aristotle believed that living virtuously out of the discerned wisdom of careful reflection is the highest value and a requirement for well-being. However, living well, while necessary for well-being, is not sufficient to achieve it: Aristotle's understanding of well-being also requires *faring well*.

For Aristotle, faring well encompasses a host of practical matters: a measure of material stability, a good family life, friends, leisure time for contemplation, personal freedom, and health.[14] Aristotle also thought that a well-ordered and supportive community was necessary to provide the opportunities and preconditions for happiness. Thus, his understanding of thriving was more complex than others': Well-being, or flourishing, requires contemplation on what is the highest good, the development of intellectual and moral virtues to support personal and social well-being, and a society that supports the faring well of its citizens. As Aristotle defined it, *eudaimonia* requires knowledge, wisdom, courage, temperance, justice, and the pursuit of truth. It also requires a state that supports these virtues in its citizens.[15] In his account, there are both internal and external goods that relate to well-being: Internal goods relate to the mind and the body, one's *self* or *character*, and external goods include some sense of freedom, good friends, financial security, and the respect of others, all of which are to be supported by a stable and supportive community.

Aristotle argued that everything has a *telos*, or an intended purpose, and that happiness, or flourishing, is the highest good for human beings. As noted above, flourishing or well-being has to do with cultivating the virtues in one's life. In Aristotle's view, the good or flourishing life is one in which one's most important interests are safeguarded, and citizens can become wise; that is, they develop the knowledge of what is right and good, and they can hold to it without (and despite) external influence. Aristotle understood flourishing to belong to both the immaterial world and the material one. First, he thought, people should seek the knowledge of first principles, by which he meant scientific knowledge, or knowledge about nature and truth, what is most basic, right, and true.[16] Second, Aristotle argued, people should seek the knowledge that is derived from applying the first principles and, in so doing, develop their character, or their ability to exercise moral virtues. Though Aristotle thought contemplation and learning are important, people must use that knowledge to act rightly. People's behaviors must be in line with the truth they discerned in their contemplation.

Happiness is neither a mood nor an emotion in Aristotle's thinking. Rather, it is the *activity toward well-being* that comes when people put virtues into action. *Eudaimonia* is understood to be an objective condition—a state—that arises from leading a certain type of life, achieved only through the development of a virtuous character and the establishment of effective social and political systems. Though Plato had imagined true well-being as fully achievable only when one eschews earthly matters, Aristotle understood happiness in more earthly terms.

Psychologies of Human Flourishing

The study of happiness has exploded outside of philosophical and religious discourse and received much attention from psychologists and social theorists who, like Aristotle, are more interested in earthy flourishing than otherworldly salvation. For example, psychoanalyst Sigmund Freud suggested that his aim was to enable his clients to love and work well, crucial ingredients of happiness, he thought.[17] Twenty-first-century clinical psychotherapists seek to support life-giving relationships—with oneself and others—and self-actualization, even though they have historically been reluctant to describe or formulate what genuine flourishing might entail. Prominent research psychologist Martin Seligman has spent decades studying what constitutes happiness and how people achieve it, founding the Positive Psychology Center at the University of Pennsylvania to provide a place for the "scientific study of the strengths that enable individuals and communities to thrive."[18] The field of positive psychology, sometimes referred to as the *science of happiness*, assumes that people want to lead meaningful and fulfilling lives, to cultivate what is best within themselves, and to "enhance their experiences of love, work, and play."[19] Seligman argues that "the gold-standard for measuring well-being is flourishing," by which he meant "to be filled with positive emotion and to be functioning well psychologically and socially" or "a state in which all aspects of a person's life are good."[20]

It is out of the positive psychology field that the PERMA and the PERMA+4 models emerged in an attempt to understand what comprises happiness or well-being.[21] The PERMA model outlines the "components that constitute well-being" or the "building blocks of well-being."[22] These building blocks are the experience of positive emotions such as joy and gratitude; engagement, in which one fully utilizes one's skills, strengths, and attentions for accomplishing something meaningful; positive relationships in which one feels valued and supported by others; a sense of meaning, whereby one feels one has purpose and direction in life and that life is valuable and worth living; and accomplishments in which one feels a sense of mastery and achievement.[23] Four additional elements were added by another team of research psychologists to include physical health; a future-oriented and growth mindset; a physical environment that supports well-being, including access to nature; and economic security, through which one is able to meet one's own needs.[24] In one psychological research study, people interviewed mentioned five factors they deemed critical for their flourishing: social support, a stable source of income, a sense of identity and self-worth, family, and meaningful work.[25]

Most of the psychological approaches have defined flourishing in terms of individual psychological factors, implying that efforts to promote flourishing must concentrate on individual, psychological well-being. These approaches have not always provided substantive attention to the broader social and political structures and dynamics that support and impede flourishing or even the possibility of it. Historical, economic, sociocultural, and environmental factors are not always considered. Nor have they included religious perspectives on flourishing. This is a serious oversight: Unless leaders consider and engage, for example, inequities in housing, food, education, health care, safety, access to resources, and opportunities, flourishing as a religious mission and a leadership goal will fall short.

Other approaches have tried to be more comprehensive. For example, the World Health Organization defines flourishing as "a state of complete physical, mental and social well-being and not merely the absence of disease or infirmity."[26] While a more complex framing, this definition, as perhaps all definitions, is not specific enough to be actionable.[27] A useful definition of flourishing must be "plastic enough to adapt to local needs and constraints . . . yet robust enough to maintain a common identity across sites."[28] Understanding flourishing and developing practices that support it must be both broadly philosophical and concrete and practical.

From a psychological and personal perspective, flourishing includes "striving toward excellence [of character] based on one's unique potential."[29] The pursuit of flourishing may be informed by shared values and expectations, but it is also a deeply personal matter shaped by individual efforts to live in keeping with those values and life commitments that are ingrained "so deep" to who people are that they "would not know themselves without them."[30] People's ability to reach their full potential depends not just on internal factors but also on the structural, material, political, social, and ideological environments in which they live.[31] In other words, "for individuals to flourish, they must be situated in societies that promote their flourishing."[32] Taking this idea further, it is worth noting that "hostile environments thwart flourishing; [just and inclusive] environments promote it."[33] Flourishing requires environments that provide basic needs and access to opportunities. Justice is a critical component of flourishing because the latter must apply to all, not just a chosen few. However, this is often missed in happiness theories. As one scholar puts it, "It is not an accident that the assumed understanding of human flourishing has been determined by what improves the well-being of those who are the most privileged in society and in a way that legitimizes their privileged position . . . [This assumption] has elided structural inequalities that advantage them and disadvantage others."[34] Furthermore, the understandings of flourishing that are static (i.e., flourishing as a condition or a state) "neglect the dynamic and contextually-specific ways [flourishing] is imagined, pursued, and experienced in everyday settings—including possibilities of flourishing in one domain but not in others."[35] Similar to what Aristotle argued, "*flourish* is a verb, and as such expresses action. To flourish is to *do* something."[36] Understood this way, flourishing is an active pursuit that involves choice making and action, even under some conditions of restraint, over time. Consistent with Aristotle and more contemporary happiness/well-being scholars, "this 'active pursuit' is no solo endeavor; rather it is 'informed by cultural expectations and social relationships.'"[37]

Flourishing as a construct refers to something "dynamic, aspirational, and frequently elusive."[38] As one team of researchers stated, if flourishing is fundamentally a matter of being able to realize one's potential, as Aristotle and others have argued, then "we cannot ignore the fact that people are—and inevitably will be—hard-pressed to reach their potential in environments of scarcity or risk, oppression, misrecognition, or violence. Without confronting these critical insights head-on, efforts to promote flourishing will inevitably miss the mark."[39]

Religious Perspectives on Human Flourishing

One of the most significant early Christian theologians, Augustine of Hippo, agreed that salvation is the *telos* (or end goal) of human life and added that people's desire for salvation is an instinct "implanted" by God to draw them toward God. For this reason, Augustine argued, salvation understood as joining completely with God *is* the greatest good.[40] Augustine defined happiness/salvation as the satisfaction of desire, though, as with Epicurus, it matters which desires one is talking about. Happiness cannot involve a "treadmill" of satisfying humans' desire after desire; rather, happiness comes with the satisfaction of *all* deepest and most fundamental desires and liberation from the cycle of desiring. The logic of happiness/salvation for Augustine, then, suggests that similar to the Stoics, only *freedom from* "worldly" need and want can produce genuine happiness; humans are created to desire God alone and thus are naturally drawn to the extinction of all otherworldly desires. Because happiness is the fulfillment of all desire and can be found only in God, real happiness cannot be attained in this world, nor can well-being/salvation be destroyed by the contingencies of life.

Like those before him, Augustine emphasized the importance of wisdom, which requires self-awareness in the pursuit of the good life. When people know themselves deeply, Augustine thought, they would recognize their dependence on God; he wrote in the *Confessions*, "Our hearts are restless until they rest in thee, Oh Lord."[41] Augustine believed that love is the highest virtue and the motivation for all moral action and that the love of God is above all else. Influenced by Greek philosophers who had come before him, Augustine's understanding of flourishing meant union with God: He contrasted the earthly city with its temporary pleasures and the heavenly city, or the eternal kingdom of God, and concluded that flourishing can only be achieved through a life of faith, virtue, and, in his tradition, devotion to God through Christ.[42]

A religious (Christian) understanding of thriving is therefore different from nonreligious perspectives. A religious view understands that the abundant life means having love, grace, mercy, and compassion in abundance: "It means life in abundance, not abundance in life."[43] It means having more life in God, not having more stuff.[44] A religious view of flourishing as living life to the full in God is different than a life with abundance. Abundance *of* life is participation in God's love and mercy.[45]

Many explorations of human flourishing in religious treatises have focused on individual happiness, though sometimes their focus extended to communal health and, more rarely, to the health of the *polis*—the community or state. The assumptions on which many theories of flourishing are based are indebted to a dualistic worldview that allows for an individual to be understood separately from their environment. However, the relatively new science of quantum physics is giving rise to a different perspective of the universe: that rather than there being discrete and separate entities (including people) in the world, it is possible that the world and everything in it are radically entangled.[46] Quantum mechanics suggest a radically interconnected and interdependent world, at least at the subatomic and cosmic levels. Such a different view significantly changes the account of flourishing and what it takes to effect it. Understanding human flourishing from this perspective directly relates the flourishing of one to the flourishing of all that is. Transformational religious leadership begins with understanding what is to promote human flourishing in a new cosmology.

Understanding the Cosmos

The conviction that flourishing for one is intimately related to the flourishing of all is based on the possibility that everything in the world is "entangled," interconnected, and affected by what happens elsewhere. Developed out of the new physics, this worldview is centered on evidence that the universe is a single, integrated whole, providing a metaphor for understanding that all is interconnected in the web of existence.[47] This worldview is increasingly supported by empirical research in such disparate fields as quantum physics, ecological studies, and biology, and even some integrated psychologies.[48] It is also a philosophical and spiritual idea found in various religious and philosophical traditions, including Hinduism, Buddhism, Taoism, process thought and theologies, and certain interpretations of mysticism in Christianity, Judaism, and Islam.

As scientists in the twentieth and twenty-first centuries sought to identify the basic building blocks of life and tested Newton's theories considering quantum theories, they found that subatomic particles are not *things* per se; rather, they are bundles of energy potential that became visible only in relationship. Similarly, in biology, the search for genes as causal and specific on/off switches yielded the realization that genes are but one actor among DNA's "ensemble of actors."[49] What were once thought to be independent and separate entities, including living beings, are now suspected to be entangled in mysterious ways.

It is now believed that rather than separate entities, the universe consists only of relationships, energy, and information. In fact, some physicists argue that *relationships between energy and information are all there is to reality*.[50] In other words, everything that exists comes to be as a network of interactions between particles (which only exist as ephemeral interactions with other energy sources or potential energy sources until they are paired). All matter is the result of energy sources combining to build larger particles that network with other particles, which are themselves only a network of energetic interactions. These networks and particles do not exist on their own but only in interaction with other energy sources. Physicists have developed quantum theory as the way things are in the universe and the world, at least as far as they can test it. There are several key principles in quantum mechanics that have radically changed the ways Isaac Newton and Newtonian physics understood it and relate to a more adequate theology of flourishing.

For Sir Isaac Newton in the seventeenth century, the universe was understood to be a static, infinite space filled with matter that is distributed evenly. Newton thought that space and time were absolute and that there were independent objects within them; those discrete objects interact with each other in predictable ways. Newton understood the universe, and our earth within it, to be mechanistic, deterministic, and material, with laws that are inflexible, static, and inviolable. Newton's cosmos operated much like a clock: God was the cosmic clockmaker who set the machine (world) in motion, who started and followed the laws of nature, only to retire to the celestial Sun City and return whenever the clock needed repair: "On the one hand, God was a distant, retired deity for whom there was really no need; on the other hand, when God needed to repair the clock, God would intervene supernaturally, 'from the outside,' external to the ways of the universe."[51] However, contemporary physicists have argued that "the determinism that lies at the heart of classical mechanics [such as Newton's and the theologies that were developed within the same God-world understanding] leaves no room" for making sense of the new science that points to a creative, chaotic, yet self-organizing, constantly changing world.[52]

Against the deterministic, classical understandings of physics and cosmology that dominated in the seventeenth to nineteenth centuries, scientists now understand that solid objects are not solid at all: They are made up of molecules and atoms extended in space and time.[53] Objects are nothing but tiny energy events, invisible even to powerful microscopes. What seems solid to the human eye, objects (including people) are made of a myriad of these energy events, "throbbing, dynamic, interrelated, and interacting, extended in space and time, with varying degrees of complexity of organization."[54] In a phenomenon called *quantum tunneling*, particles can pass through energy barriers that they should not be able to penetrate due to their wavelike structure, and particles can become entangled with other particles, meaning that the state of one particle is dependent on the state of another, no matter the distance between them.[55]

Relational and process-oriented scientists, philosophers, and even theologians extrapolate, that reality itself—everything that is deemed "real"—is fundamentally open, not fixed, dynamic, social, or relational; characterized by processes of random change[56]; and that becoming and perishing characterize all that is rather than there being any static, solid, unchanging state.[57] Everything is dynamically interrelated to and with everything else in the universe.[58] The phenomenon of quantum correlations, together with the mathematics of quantum entanglement, implies "a peculiar kind of macroscopic wholeness—a strange sort of nonseparability of macroscopically separated parts of the universe . . . [an] intrinsic connectedness of Nature that is alien to the classical notion [derived from ordinary experience] that spatial separation entails intrinsic separation."[59] As another scientist puts it, "Quantum wholeness . . . is a fundamentally new kind of togetherness, undiminished by spatial and temporal separation. No causal hookup, this new quantum thing, but a true mingling of distant beings that reaches across the galaxy as forcefully as it reaches across the garden."[60] Human beings "are not like balls on a billiard table that simply bounce around against one another according to the laws of external relations."[61] And the billiards metaphor is no more adequate for the physical and cosmic worlds than it is for human beings: "Physical entities too can influence and be influenced by their environment in ways that go beyond the mechanistic picture. Quantum entanglement points to the ecstatic character of constant creation and re-creation at the level of physical existence."[62]

What characterizes reality in this view is change: Existence (and time) is only the constant (and instantaneous, at the atomic and subatomic levels) process of actualizing and perishing.[63] Because all reality is understood to be interrelated, constantly interacting, characterized by stochastic change, the future is indeterminate, and reality is dependent on the transformation from possibility into actuality. What is real, then, is related to creative and dynamic freedom; it is not the work of a cosmic clockmaker who created the universe, set it in motion, and intervenes only when necessary. Rather, in a view informed by quantum process, "what was a possibility one moment becomes actual through the exercise of creative freedom, the free decision of a momentary experience as to how it constitutes itself" in the next moment.[64]

Order out of Chaos

Chaos theory in quantum mechanics has demonstrated that entities that seem concrete (e.g., a rock, a bird, a person, or an organization)—all of which are comprised mostly of space—exist because energy and matter self-organized.[65] Particles of energy organize themselves depending on the information they are receiving from the world around them. Thus, chaotic systems of all kinds find stability after a disruption, and despite entropy, systems—from the universe to ecosystems and to atoms and subatomic particles—all organize and reorganize themselves into changing patterns that fit the flux of information they are receiving from their environments.

Systems are self-organizing around certain values, and any information that disturbs a system changes its organizational pattern. The new information that a system encounters need not be significant; just a slight variation from the norm will create a shift. This is how systems create new patterns: Whenever new information is added to a system, that system chooses how to respond to it. Nothing happens in the quantum world without something encountering something else and new information being added. The world is a world of process—of creativity in relationship—that constantly responds to the information coming both from within itself and from the world around it. Nothing exists independent of its relationships or independent of the information it is constantly receiving. Because everything participates in fields of energy and potential, the world (and everything in it) is constantly being created and recreated, evoking its existence from the almost infinite possibilities that exist.[66] If a system pays attention to that new information and incorporates the information into itself, the information grows and changes as the system grows and changes.[67] When a response to new information is significant enough to disturb the system's organization and functioning, then real change occurs. When there is an overwhelming amount of new information and the system is too disturbed, it becomes chaotic, and the whole system may come apart permanently. But this is not the only possible outcome. It is also possible that as the system takes in new information and responds to it, it becomes a new organization, a new system. If a system uses the information it receives and incorporates it into its existing identity as it reorganizes, a new form of the organization will emerge. A system (including an organization) that incorporates new information and changes in response to it organizes organically into higher levels of complexity, becoming a new form of itself that can deal more effectively with the new present. In this way, disruption and disorder can be a source of new order, and growth is understood to develop from disequilibrium, not stability. There are dynamic paradoxes of freedom and order, being and becoming, order and chaos, balance and imbalance in all the corners of the universe, and they are always in play.

Because of the uncertainty principle, however, it is impossible to predict what new form a system will take.[68] Because every part is entangled with every other part, each is playing its role given the information it has about its place in the system and the relationship it creates with other parts; in this way, parts adapt to environmental shifts as a whole undergoes a change in shape or organization. When scientists shift their perspective from parts to whole, then they see that rather than chaos, there is order and that systems are organized around what are called *strange attractors*.

Organizing Around Strange Attractors

Systems are organized around what scientists call *strange attractors*. These may be understood as mathematical values that can (with today's computational capacities) be plotted by formulae, creating points, lines, curves, and even more complex formulae.[69] Strange attractors help one form of organization emerge out of the chaos to create systems that organize around a new attractor: Strange attractors are the lure toward organization that creates forms.[70]

Ecological and biological sciences have confirmed the quantum theory that all living beings are entangled, emerging from an intricate web.[71] The concrete structures of life are in some ways "ephemeral," and "transient,"[72] whose fundamental nature is change and flux, taking different forms at different times. Systems evolve and change as new information changes the relationship of energy fields and as the other systems they are related to also shift.[73] As systems respond to changes around and within them, they release themselves from the old and find new structures that fit the new situation.[74] Those forms respond to the strange attractors that they organize around, and they respond to the changes in their environment to reshape and reform themselves.[75] These scientific principles have also led to philosophies and theologies that are consistent with this view of reality, understanding strange attractors as a set of values important to an entity (person or organization).[76] These scientific theories and the theological understandings that are resonant with them implicate how leaders lead: Life-giving leadership that contributes to human flourishing will work *with* and not against the ways life is organized. The metaphor of strange attractors (understood here as values) operates on personal and organizational levels. Values can be understood as the strange attractors that bring people together as they organize in groups and congregations. The values that bring people together can be a rich resource for reorganization and revitalization for organizations, and leveraging them is important for transformational leaders.

Understanding Entanglement

Scholars and mystics in disciplines outside of science have been speaking about a fundamental interdependence and unity within the universe for millennia.[77] Many spiritual traditions, for example, propose there is a fundamental unity to all existence, understanding reality as a unified whole rather than a collection of separate, isolated entities. Early mystics such as the thirteenth-century Persian mystic Rumi and more contemporary theologians including Teilhard de Chardin understood a radically interconnected universe. Mathematician and philosopher Alfred North Whitehead and process theologians, including Charles Hartshorne, John Cobb, and Catherine Keller, have asserted from philosophical and theological perspectives that reality is inherently interconnected and that the relationships between everything that exists are dynamic, fundamentally characterized by processes, and change rather than being fixed or static entities. For process thinkers, as for quantum theorists, creativity is a central concept in which everything that exists emerges out of constant possibility or potential.[78]

Philosophies of Entanglement

As was the case with science, many classical philosophies and theologies were developed out of a dualistic understanding of God and God's relationship to the world. Classical theologians especially made several claims that more contemporary process thinkers have found incompatible with the new understanding of reality. These include the beliefs that God is an unchanging entity, that God has ultimate control over all that is, that God sanctions the status quo, and that God is a being, akin to a clockmaker living in the heavens.[79]

Process philosophers understand human experience as a "high-level exemplification of reality in general."[80] While not everything is in flux (there are basic principles that are unchanging, such as the commitment to love as the highest value), reality as the result of concrescence, or actualization, is the emergence of infinite possibility in a particular moment.[81] Alfred North Whitehead, a mathematician and philosopher, understood human beings to be in a constant "transition" from one actual state to another. In Whitehead's language, reality includes "entities," which are "momentary events" that perish immediately on coming into being. The perishing and reforming are what comprise reality: Entities such as humans or the organizations they create are better understood as "becomings" rather than "beings." Reality is always becoming. Change and flux characterize its identity, and material reality is constantly being formed and reformed.

Whitehead's notion of time relates to this constant change, even as the material world seems stable. In his schema, time is not a single smooth flow but comes into being in little droplets.[82] Time, in Whitehead's formulation, is integral to everything that is: Experience unfolds in a temporal process of becoming, in which past events influence the present as well as future possibilities.

In process thought, then, "all things flow," and reality is relational "through and through."[83] Everything must create itself out of what has been before. For process theologians, God is the source of all freedom and does not—indeed, *cannot*—coerce or control the world. Rather than understanding God as the "unmoved mover," the God of process theology is understood to be the creative aspect of the universe, the foundation of every process of becoming.[84]

Theologies of Entanglement

Process theologians seek to understand God in ways that are consistent with what is scientifically known about the world. Some have adopted entanglement as a metaphor for the nature of God and God's relation to the created order.[85] Because theology needs to make sense of a world increasingly explained by quantum science, Christian theology (and, I would argue, all theologies) is ideally based on a respectful and constructive engagement with modern science.[86] As one scientist/theologian explains, "The discovery of quantum entanglement is an invitation to consider how previous generations of Christian theological speech about the identity of God, the character of the world, and the nature of the God–world relationship might be informed and even transformed by developments in the sciences."[87] Both quantum physics and process thought assert the "ultimacy of relationality."[88] To challenge the theologies that were heavily informed by classical worldviews, process thought/theology can be helpful in imagining a God entangled with all of creation.[89] In this view, process theologians understand God as that which "enables life, its development, its increased complexity and capacity for intensity, harmony, contrast, and richness of experience through the lure of novel possibilities to be actualized and the abiding acceptance of all experience, preserved everlastingly with no loss of immediacy."[90] In this understanding, God is the life force, the energy, the invitation, the lure of creativity, and the impetus for movement toward truth, increasing creativity and growth, love, beauty, and harmony in all things always.

God is the force of creative freedom that invites all that is to join in that life-giving momentum.[91]

Christians have often claimed an omnipotent, omniscient God who creates "time" but stands outside it, who created the world and stands outside it, intervening when necessary.[92] However, in process thought, which is more consistent with extant science, God is not an exception to scientific or metaphysical categories but their highest exemplification.[93] God, too, is understood to be characterized by change, by dynamic interaction, and by process rather than being.[94]

For Whitehead—often credited with being the founder of process thought and the progenitor of process theology—creativity is ultimate; it is a force more fundamental than any other. Whitehead calls creativity the "universal of universals," which characterizes all matter. He writes, "Creativity . . . is the principle of novelty in the universe; it is what all entities embody as their very emergent process."[95] Whitehead goes on to propose that "creativity is not something that can be 'created'—even for God—since it is a presupposition of any and all creative activity, be it finite or divine."[96]

Like all else in the cosmos, God is the creative energy and has an active creative quality and a receptive creative quality. In the active quality, God "knows" all possibilities and invites those possibilities to become actualities.[97] Two of the primary traditional attributes of God, omnipotence and omniscience, are reinterpreted in process thought. While God is the foundational power of life, the creative energy that gives life, above which "none greater can be conceived," God is not the only power, and that divine power always acts persuasively rather than intervening or coercing. As far as omniscience, God "knows" possibility as possibility and actuality as actuality but cannot foresee the details or force what will actually happen.[98] God is the ground of novelty, of creativity, of change, of becoming. From Whitehead's understanding, God *is* the relational process. Not only does everything that is experience God, but God also experiences everything that is and everything that happens. God is in everything, and everything is in God.[99] God does not (indeed, *cannot*) actualize the world through divine activity alone; rather, the world actualizes God through its own self-creativity. The world requires God for its very possibility, and God requires the world for the actualization of divine value.[100] God is the "primordial exemplification of self-creative value. God is a creature of God's own self-creativity."[101] God is not the unilateral creator of all that is but the "repository of the essential conditions," allowing the world and what is in it to make itself.[102]

Quantum entanglement, understood through the lens of what is often referred to as *relational holism*, can broaden and deepen the awareness of the world's relationality by helping us more deeply appreciate the unfathomable interdependence, ubiquitous relationality, and immeasurable reciprocity of the universe.[103]

Understanding God as ontologically entangled with the world through mutual creativity suggests that God and the world are freely and mutually constituting, and God cannot intervene in the world outside of its scientifically established principles; God can only invite participation in what is good through the spark of creaturely imagination. If the very act of creation is itself an entangling act, then the fact that an entangled God and an entangled world are in relation to one another becomes theologically basic to God's nature as well as the world's existence. The entangled nature of this relation preserves both the freedom of God in the creative act and the freedom of creation in its own activity.[104]

Process thinkers understand that God is not a distant, unchanging being outside of history and time but, rather, is fundamentally entangled in the world, implicated in but not wholly responsible for what is, through a creative process.[105] An entangled God does not (cannot) visibly intervene in the world's processes because "visible intervention" implies an ontological separation between God and the world that does not exist.[106] God's entangled relationship with the world is a relationship that grants it full freedom: God, as ontological relationality, is the basis of relationship "and nothing more—creation is truly free to be itself."[107] Humans instantiate their freedom insofar as they can choose to respond (or not) to God's invitation; they make decisions and act on them. They also instantiate creative freedom insofar as they know themselves to be the product of an unguided creative evolutionary process.[108]

One way to understand human beings is that each person is part of a web that is pure relationship, sustained by energy that is available to everything that exists. It is the energy, or life force, that has been around since the universe was born. God is understood as the web, the energy, the space, the light, the "invitation" or "urging" of the world to come into being, to form itself, to organize from energy into matter.[109] God is revealed as the singular, vast net of relationship that animates all that is.[110] In this line of thinking, all that is—not just living creatures—possesses a form of experience, or subjectivity. This does not imply that everything has consciousness but rather that even inanimate objects participate in the ongoing process—unfolding creativity of the universe—and thus they participate in God.[111] As Buddhist monk Thich Nhat Hanh put it, "The source of one thing is all things."[112]

Human Beings and Entanglement

A nonreligious example of this line of thinking comes from developmental theorists and psychologists.[113] This perspective points to an integrative theory that encompasses individual and collective development, psychology, spirituality, science, philosophy, and culture and emphasizes a holistic understanding of reality that transcends that material and connects all that is. In a view of the self that is consistent with understanding the universe as one system, the distinction between self and other is "an artificial one," just one way to make the world intelligible.[114] Human beings, in a process understanding, are fundamentally characterized by relationship. People are inherently interconnected to others, and their identities and experiences are shaped by their relationships to others.[115] People and groups are constantly evolving, changing, and growing (if they are open to it) in response to experiences and dynamics both internal to themselves and in dynamic relation to what is happening around them.[116] Consistent with the model that developed out of quantum mechanics, people change when they allow new information about themselves and their surroundings to enter their awareness. People change, organizations change, and when both are intentional about the transformations they make, they can shift their perspective and their behaviors to increase their own flourishing and that of others. Understanding reality in these ways will necessarily inform a view of human flourishing and the vision for what is possible that religious leaders are called to hold. Generative leaders who value growth and change understand that life phases have an impact on individuals' values, beliefs, emotions, and behaviors, and they can draw on this knowledge to help people emerge in their most mature form.

The possibility that everything is entangled in some way and interdependent has profound implications for how individuals perceive themselves and their relationships to others, to their place in the world, and to the understanding of what flourishing looks like and how it happens. It also has profound implications for the ultimate goals of transformational religious leadership. This worldview emphasizes the importance of relationality, empathy, and cooperation. If all reality is interconnected, there must be a strong sense of responsibility toward other beings and their environments, including the natural one. Leaders who can marshal the power of entanglement and help systems form and reform themselves out of chaos will be transformative indeed.

The Flourishing of All

The consequences of the possibility that the universe and everything in it are entangled and interdependent invite an understanding of flourishing that involves every part. Humans are essentially social creatures who depend on each other for individual and collective survival, progress, and success. When one person in a group becomes more focused on their own needs than others' or the group's, it leads to conflict and dysfunction; the group will never be able to achieve its full potential under these conditions.[117] A more comprehensive and congruent view of flourishing must account for the flourishing of both individual parts and the whole, as individual parts are connected to the whole. Studies on happiness that relate flourishing and justice help transformative religious leaders attend to flourishing at the personal level but only as it is related to flourishing at the communal, state, and even global levels. Flourishing requires some freedom of choice for people, some basic material resources, satisfying and life-giving intimate relationships with friends and family, and time to reflect on what matters most.[118] Flourishing includes opportunities to pursue forms of engagement that express one's most compelling values—or strange attractors—at a particular moment and across one's lifespan.[119] It implies being treated with dignity and respect by oneself and others, being valued by oneself and others, maximizing one's capacities, and having a sense of satisfaction, even pride, in one's accomplishments. Flourishing also requires a *polis*, or society, whose organizations and institutions encourage and support the good for all its members and the natural environment on which it depends. Flourishing has many components that support faring well, living well, and being well. In addition, flourishing adds the element of joy or zest to the features of well-being.[120] Flourishing can be recognized when it is seen in others and when it is experienced subjectively; the descriptors that come to mind include creative fullness, liveliness, responsiveness, passion, compassion, zest, awe in the wonder and mystery of life itself (all life), some measure of freedom, and participation in systems that support the good of the whole. In other words, when people are flourishing, they are more able to live with dynamic faith; with hope; with a sense of deep connection to themselves, others, and the earth; with profound love and even joy.[121]

Scientists sometimes use the term *evolution* to describe the cosmic allurement into flourishing, but the concept of love may be a better word, especially for transformative religious leaders, and it is one employed to describe both cosmologists and theologians.[122] Yearning for wholeness through love is at the heart of all creation for some cosmologies and from a religious perspective.[123] The experience of wholeness is the awareness, at some level, of belonging to another, the awareness of being part of a whole, in participating with all things in the mysteries of the universe. Love is the means to and the result of this awareness. The degree to which people and societies are (and are aware of being) part of this whole is fundamental to flourishing. The sacred can be materialized only when love, justice, and care are. In theological language, God is the "insistence that strains to exist" as flourishing, but because everything on earth is interdependent, none can fully thrive until all are well.[124] These convictions are anathema to the economic and political systems that currently dominate in the West.

A person's motivating values—their strange attractors—must be affirmed by objective criteria grounded in history and by the best of what societies have achieved thus far; they must be worthy and sustaining values. The virtues that early philosophers extolled, which contemporary psychological scientific research demonstrates supports flourishing, can provide guidance for a vision of God's longing for the world.

Those who would nurture flourishing in their role as religious leaders must seek to know what is right, moment to moment, in their context and circumstance; that is, they must cultivate their own attention to what matters. Sometimes that will mean being primarily motivated by love for another, sometimes by love for oneself (but never only for oneself), sometimes by respect or principle, and sometimes by likely consequence or outcome. These discernments require wisdom, defined as knowing what is best when joined with motivation to act on it. In other words, wisdom and virtuous action require at least an intuitive understanding of what lies behind each situation, insight into how things hang together and what makes individuals and societal systems tick, and the practical knowhow to apply this to concrete situations and determine how best to proceed.[125]

A life of well-being—or better, flourishing—is a collective endeavor that also has unique, local, contextual, and deeply personal aspects. Flourishing necessitates the development of one's strengths and the possibilities for living out one's deepest values, as affirmed by wise others. Flourishing requires being clear and realistic about one's gifts and limitations and having opportunities for ongoing growth and development. As Aristotle suggested, flourishing depends on both opportunities and capacities for self-definition and self-expression through imagination, reflection, and creativity. To flourish, one must be able both to experience and to develop one's exquisite uniqueness even as one develops moral capacities for generous participation in what is good for others. Flourishing is enlivened by and enlivens one's sense of being a being animated by the Sacred in a world invited into existence by that life force—and loved by it. Experiences of flourishing increase as individual and group capacities for helping create and nurture such a world increase. Flourishing is active and perspectival, immediate and personal, and also whole thinking and future-directed. A sense of flourishing holds together the now and the future. It attends to both the individual and the deeply personal while always keeping an eye on the world. More than just self-actualization or loving and working better, the highest value in flourishing is the cultivation of what is required for the flourishing of all—and the meaning of life is found in this pursuit. Those who would cultivate flourishing must be able to account for the many paradoxes of human existence, including care and accountability, giving and receiving non-possessive love, and committing deeply while holding loosely. Flourishing includes awareness and acknowledgment of finitude, faults, and brokenness—one's own and others'. It requires taking responsibility for and being accountable to the wounds each, in finite humanness, inevitably inflicts on others. Because of this, an understanding of flourishing must integrate the losses and the inevitable griefs of life, rather than their escape, and finding God amid them. The fullness of one's humanity—which necessarily includes finitude, pain, and grief—must be included in an understanding of flourishing. For this reason, flourishing will require that people are resilient, courageous, resolute, responsive, relational, dynamic, and responsible to one another as well as to themselves.

With a view of all that exists as potentially radically entangled and emergent, a flourishing world is one in which individuals, communities, and ecosystems thrive continuously grow and change and where attention is paid to both the material and nonmaterial worlds, creating harmony between them. Flourishing prioritizes environmental sustainability, as this is the first requirement for the survival of the human and the more-than-human world. By promoting social justice and inclusion, ensuring that all people have access to basic resources, opportunities, and rights, even those most vulnerable and marginalized have the chance to pursue their own flourishing. Making sure each person and community have some measure of economic stability and shared prosperity through sustainable growth and increased income equality through education, training, and skills development; supporting innovation; and ensuring fair wages along with safe and reasonable working conditions must be parts of flourishing. Prioritizing the physical health of individuals and communities, which includes access to clean water, nutritious food, and safe living conditions, is instrumental. A world that celebrates cultural diversity and creativity, as well as ensures peace and security, is fundamental to flourishing. A world governed by democratic principles, open and transparent communication with accountability for the flourishing of one and all, and cooperative relationships is elemental to flourishing, as is harnessing technical advancements that are guided by ethical principles and advance public interests.

None of these values, these commitments, these strange attractors around which an organization can form will have much meaning without the understanding of a world radically entangled, without compassion and respect for all that is, without the sense of solidarity that must develop when a worldview shifts from a dualistic one to a quantum mechanics one. If flourishing and happiness are related by joy, this emerges from the transcendence of self to the perspective of the whole. Thus, while the arc of justice is long, often sputters, and even loses ground at times, the full inclusion of all in the activities toward flourishing is crucial for the fulfillment of a religious vision of flourishing. Working to achieve flourishing for all people is a creative and meaningful endeavor worth pursuing, for by the definition being proposed here, if some are excluded from pursuing flourishing, none can fully achieve it.

This view of the world from quantum mechanics and a theology informed by similar perspectives informs transformative religious leaders' practice: "Whatever 'God' means, it must mean more life."[126] If religious leaders are responding to a call to their work, it must mean more life for all they seek to serve. Flourishing is a journey; the path is rarely a straight line, and it requires a prophetic critique of the current global situation.

* * *

Quantum science has demonstrated, and process philosophies and theologies have developed, the idea that all of reality emerges through complex interactions among entities, or energies, or particles, each of which is responding to information coming from both within itself and its environment. What is received and incorporated is integrated from moment to moment as entities respond. Individual responses together create patterns of behavior, of organization, of the world as it is known. New science tells of a world of interconnected networks, at least at the quantum level, where even slight disturbances in one part of the system can create changes in other parts of the system. It is a world that emerges out of infinite possibility, in which new information organizes patterns out of chaos around strange attractors such as values. Chaos disintegrates existing structures and creates conditions for new orders to emerge. This is the context of religious leadership that seeks to be transformational.

Because of the ways the universe functions in dynamic and constantly changing patterns, collections of people—corporations and churches, for example—are not independent, separate entities but rather part of a "complex, never still, always weaving tapestry."[127] Flourishing has to do with each part and the whole becoming the best expression of itself (as an entangled element of an entangled world) to the fullest extent possible.[128] While each concrete expression of life—each person and each thing that exists—will be different because it is a unique expression of the potential in all the universe, there are attractors (values) that have helped individuals and communities create meaning in life through the pursuit of what is worthy.

When the dominant paradigm for understanding of the world shifts from a mechanized world that is predictable and inherently stable to one that is dynamic, constantly changing, creative, and responding to new information to form and reform itself, then religious leadership that seeks to be transformative will do well to follow. The understanding of flourishing being proposed here, which is based on the understanding of life and the universe being entangled, changes how leadership is understood. No longer will control and coercion be fruitful or sustainable (if they ever really were). Despite Darwin's belief in the value of competition for survival, collaboration and participation are now understood to be most essential in life's flourishing.

To help people and organizations flourish, genuinely transformational religious leaders help cultivate awareness of the ways all of life is a response to the invitation of the Sacred toward love and justice. At their best, world religions recognize that individuals' and communities' ability to respond to the Sacred has something to do with capacities that must be cultivated; Aristotle was right that no person is born wise.

The Sacred Strange Attractor, the principle of the most life-giving values, urges creation into being—indeed, it invites the world into existence in every moment. The cosmic allurement of love is at the heart of all creation in some cosmologies and many religious perspectives. The experience of wholeness is the awareness, at some level, of belonging to another, the awareness of being part of a whole. Love is the means to and the result of this awareness. The degree to which people and societies are (and are aware of being) part of this whole is fundamental to flourishing.

Flourishing—both for oneself and for all else—depends on resisting what is destructive of the good; it also requires saying no to oppressive systems and actively dismantling them. In other words, the world's flourishing is part and parcel of becoming more complexly human, and it includes a profound solidarity with all of creation and the ability to care for selves, others, the environment, and institutions.[129] However, this is not the way the world currently works. Because leadership is always contextual, religious leaders need to better understand the impediments to individuals' and communities' flourishing.

CHAPTER 4

Constraints on Human Flourishing

UNDERSTANDING RELIGIOUS LEADERSHIP as a call and a privilege challenges the dominant value systems in which people currently live. Whereas managers are primarily concerned with the function and preservation of the organization or group they are tasked with leading, transformational religious leaders are called to more. Organizational preservation and management, while critical, cannot be the only function of a leader. In fact, when a religious leader is more interested in preserving the congregation as it is than responding to what God is calling for, then that community has belied its mission.[1]

The twenty-first century is a time of great upheaval, both in religious contexts and outside of them. Destructive storms of all kinds rage with greater frequency and intensity. The problems of the world are overwhelming, and religious leaders are often asked to step into the breach and attend to suffering, alleviate pain, and help people and communities make meaning of what is happening around them and in their own lives. Religious leaders themselves often feel unsure about how to make a difference and can develop compassion fatigue. Religious leaders' personal challenges exist alongside challenges in their professional roles: Decreasing congregations, the decline of religious adherence and practice in most traditions, and the lessening power of religious institutions around the globe have posed significant difficulties for religious leaders.[2] Religious leaders, who have often spent many years and significant investment being trained to lead congregations, are finding themselves alone behind a pulpit, speaking words that ring hollow to a world in crisis. There are many explanations for why this is, but one is that the dominant values in the West are no longer the virtues that so captured earlier philosophical and religious imaginations.

The subjective side of happiness—or good feelings and positive emotions—is emphasized more in contemporary life than in Aristotle's or Augustine's understanding of happiness. Nevertheless, Aristotle's formulation of the *eudaimonic* life—a well-lived life—has been seminal since he developed it. Still, identifying the elements of flourishing is difficult, given the complexity of human experience and the context-specific nature of flourishing. It is also true that flourishing can only be achieved if it is cultivated by and nurtured in both individuals and collectives. At the individual level, flourishing requires positive, meaningful relationships; engagement in meaningful activities and the accomplishment of goals; and a subjective experience of joy. Flourishing is an achievement that is gained, at least to some degree, by having basic needs met, living into one's deepest values, and developing capacities that include both self- and other interest and can be used to build life-giving societies.[3] Flourishing is the by-product of living virtuously.

Believers are encouraged in sacred texts to choose life, not death.[4] But one might ask how since no one lives an unconstrained life.[5] No one makes choices as freely as they might wish; opportunities for loving intimate relationships, chances to choose meaningful work, the privilege of relative safety, and opportunities to realize some measure of individual freedom and other signs of self-actualization are always constrained by the "givenness" of the worlds in which all people live.[6] Some of these constraints are to be expected, given the finitude of humanness. Some are the results of decisions people (individually and together) make, moment to moment, in their own lives, and some limits on flourishing are the result of both personal and collective choices and behaviors. For example, all people participate in hierarchies that divide, rank, and exclude certain people and particular groups. Oppressive hierarchies are built into the structures of legal systems, encoded in global economic strategies, and included in environmental policies.[7] These destructive hierarchies are the results of members of advantaged groups working together to define, target, oppress, and exclude others based on race, age, gender expression, class, physical ability, sexuality, or religious belief. These destructive systems are often unconscious and usually well hidden, yet they significantly shape people's life chances and sense of possibility. Limits on flourishing are embedded in societies and enacted in interpersonal and intergroup relations. The decision to pursue a flourishing life is not only a personal one.

The new science's entangled view of the physical universe suggests what theologians claim about the human realm: The force that pulls planets together is the same force that pulls everything that exists toward increasing wholeness and completeness.[8] This understanding suggests that every atom, every cell, each plant and animal, every planet and star, and each person—*everything* is pulled by the same primal force, the allurement toward the larger whole within which it is a part, growing in interconnected and interdependent complexity.[9] Everything within the universe is evolving into ever-deepening patterns of interdependence.[10] Cosmic and biological scientists, psychologists, and theologians have known this and argued for deeper understandings of this entanglement and its implications for life together.[11]

This perspective lends itself to an understanding of flourishing that always simultaneously attends to individual, interpersonal, and group/institutional/organizational well-being, and although one may necessarily be emphasized over the other in a particular moment or when viewed with a particular lens, flourishing cannot, by definition, ignore any of these aspects of human experience in the long term. The flourishing life values *all* life as having more than instrumental value and cultivates the wisdom of the virtues and moral living to achieve flourishing for all. This is a significant challenge, especially given the dominant forces in the world today.

Empire's Effects on Human Flourishing

The introduction to history can be told in terms of domination. Since the dawn of time, mightier empires have dominated and colonized smaller and weaker ones. Some societies have survived, and others have died. Those who dominated imposed their religious beliefs and practices, worldviews, and cultural practices (such as patriarchy) on those they dominated, and colonizers routinely enslaved (physically, spiritually, and psychologically) those who were not like them.[12] That long history of colonization has developed into contemporary economic systems, white supremacy, misogyny, environmental exploitation, consumerism, and oppression—to disastrous effects on all people; however, it most profoundly affects those on the underside of these machinations of power.

One of the most dominant forms of empire in the first quarter of the twenty-first century is neoliberal capitalism, in which money is the most important—or even the only—value, and everything else, such as forming meaningful relationship in community, justice, mutual care, and hope, is devalued or dismissed in favor of economic gain. Political systems, economic systems, societies, organizations, groups, and individuals collude with, participate in, and promote this oppressive use of power and the marginalization, exclusion, and violent abuse it depends on and generates. Such is the context in which religious leaders are called to lead; it is a world ruled by money that is destroying the very collectives that religious leaders are called to cultivate.

Neoliberalism's Path to Destruction

Neoliberalism developed historically out of the noble commitment to the equality of all persons, in the tradition of the Declaration of Independence, in which the belief that all people are created equal is to be "self-evident."[13] In the process of neoliberalism's development, however, the value of each person has been warped and twisted to the needs of the market. Neoliberalism has come to view people first and foremost as individuals "constituted atomistically, apart from their families, countries, faith communities, classes, ethnicities, sexes, vocations, or places in the flow of history."[14] Humans' primary desire, proponents of neoliberalism hold, is for freedom (defined as *autonomy*), a liberation that releases them from anything that would constrain them in any way. It is freedom from the "interference of or dependence on others."[15] It is a false freedom that insists each person is responsible for themselves.

Neoliberalism has emerged since the late twentieth century as the dominant philosophical, political, and economic model worldwide. The economic model this perspective has engendered, neoliberal capitalism (also referred to as *finance capitalism*, *extractive capitalism*, *disaster capitalism*, *cannibal capitalism*, and *cutthroat capitalism*) is the financial system that has ruled almost all of life—most clearly in the western world—since the1980s.[16] This form of capitalism has become an overarching metasystem consisting of three primary dimensions: economics, politics, and culture. It puts the production and exchange of material goods and the value of profit over all else "at the heart of human experience."[17] Neoliberal capitalism, the dominant global financial philosophy, applies neoliberal assumptions about human beings and systems to the marketplace. The word *capital* simply means *money* or *wealth*, and the suffix *ism* identifies capitalism as a system—or, more accurately, "a system composed of subsystems"—that strives to give money the highest value and place it at the center of all human life.[18] *Neoliberal capitalism* is an umbrella term that covers a range of political and economic values, philosophies, and practices that are rooted in promoting the "free market" without constraint and the deregulation of all industries. Neoliberal capitalists argue for smaller governments and promote the privatization and specialization of key resources that have historically been government-owned and publicly accessible. Neoliberalism champions unlimited "free" trade, and, for some, fiscal austerity, including the reduction of spending for the public good and social welfare programs, thus reducing the public safety net that has historically ensured "the least of these" have support.[19]

Neoliberal capitalism has come to subordinate everything else to itself, including church, government, education, health care, and social networks provided by the state. This extractive, cutthroat capitalism is an all-encompassing and extraordinarily powerful network, in which the flow and control of money and power, along with elite interests, are at the center. Neoliberal, extractive capitalism gained traction and momentum in the United States under President Ronald Reagan and Prime Minister Margaret Thatcher; it has since spread to the rest of the developed and developing world as dominant economies and superpowers such as the United States, Russia, and China have sought new sources of revenue. This model of economic and political systems also now dominates global markets and the policies of global banks, including the International Monetary Fund and World Bank.

Extractive capitalism, or disaster capitalism, prioritizes a "free" market as the most effective way to allocate resources. In a free market, it is claimed, the government should refrain from supporting or limiting the exchange of goods and money, instead of allowing every individual to fight for their own private wealth, property, and prosperity. The stated fear of neoliberal principals is that excessive regulation of private wealth hinders efficiency and innovation, and industry regulations increase barriers to trade, entrepreneurship, and wealth generation. Proponents of neoliberal capitalism argue that deregulation fosters competition, lowers costs, and promotes economic growth. Likewise, they assert that transferring public assets and services such as health care and education to private ownership will create a market for the best goods and services and increase competition, allowing the consumer to benefit from the increased quality of those goods and services. In such a political and economic climate, individuals become responsible for their own success or failure, and no person or community can rely on government assistance, public education, or any program aimed at social welfare, which inevitably costs other citizens by way of tax revenue (historically seen as the way to share the responsibility of a humane network of services but its value dismissed under neoliberal capitalism).

Neoliberal capitalism has put money at the center of all human life and interactions; it has made (or tried to make) money—and the power to get and control money—the most important thing in people's lives. Whereas capitalism has always been about money, neoliberal capitalism is capitalism *empowered* so that money has "taken over every area of life and is 'driving the bus'" of all of life, including religion and spirituality.[20] It is now the case that "neoliberalism is the water we're all swimming in—and too many are drowning in."[21]

Cutthroat capitalism is a hegemony that has created enormous global monopolies run by a handful of extraordinarily wealthy "rentiers" who maintain and extend their power through hidden systems of law and market.[22] These owners/rentiers charge all others to access what the owners control. Rentiers do not live off any of their own labor but rather make their wealth from charging for access to basic goods including water, food, information, the internet, health care, education, and affordable housing. Rentiers make their money from passive income, controlling access to the goods that the rest of the world needs. In this way, neoliberalism is in fact completely opposed to free market capitalism, even though neoliberal proponents claim to support it. Instead, those in the rentier class have colluded to create a world in which a very small number of monopolies and their owners control all the systems and access to resources, wealth, and power in the world. The number of owners/rentiers of these monopolies is "small enough that they become not competitors, but co-conspirators," effectively killing the free market and locking all others out of the means to create stability.[23]

Extractive capitalism is profit-maximization without limits. There is no ceiling to what some can make and little accountability for sharing, paying it forward, or using the profits to make others' lives better. Part of cutthroat capitalism's sinister dynamic is that it does not just profit off basic human need; it sets the norm of what is good and desirable and sells to those who have money rather than providing basic goods to those who need them.[24] Under extractive capitalism, the income gap increases and is even seen as a good thing.[25] Extractive capitalism thrives on the oppression and suffering it creates—the very human experiences that religious leaders are called to address.

In a neoliberal capitalist society, the dominant values are competition, entrepreneurship, and personal responsibility. Individuals are on their own to support themselves, often working multiple jobs and driving a gig economy in which there is little security, agency, or support. However, there is no competition among the big monopolies; they have effectively rendered competition impossible and futile for anyone but themselves. Not surprisingly, the necessary outcome of "unrelenting competition" is inequality.[26] The competition people feel is toward other people in their own socioeconomic sphere: People are forced to compete for the limited goods available to them in a zero-sum game. As pastoral theologian Bruce Rogers-Vaughn puts it, "We are nurtured to think of ourselves as our own little businesses, cornering our individual brands and increasing our personal capital as best we can."[27] Neoliberalism has "transformed us, heart, body, and soul . . . the market [has] swallowed us whole."[28]

Extractive capitalism has terrible environmental and economic consequences. It creates a sense that the world is hostile, competitive, and harsh. Competition for the scarce resources among those not in the owner/rentier class makes people and communities lonely, alienated, and prone to sin understood as the "negation of relation."[29] It is not a situation that supports flourishing. Indeed, neoliberal capitalism and the financial systems it controls exploit the weaknesses of all but the owners/rentiers. Neoliberal capitalism renders helpless everyone but those at the very top.[30] It is essentially a predatory system benefiting a very small number at the expense of the rest. It is a system that overburdens individuals, leaving them on their own—alone and helpless. Cutthroat capitalism convinces each person that they are nothing but a resource to be maximized, that they alone are responsible to achieve certain accomplishments or a particular status, that each person is their own capital to be leveraged by the neoliberal system.[31] It sets up a structure in which individuals alone are responsible for their own flourishing, which, as has already been argued, is untenable.

Neoliberal capitalism permeates our entire personhoods, from our work to our family life to our communities and even our spiritual and religious practices. It has become a religion in and of itself.[32] Extractive capitalism completely subordinates the whole person to the market with the goal of making a profit. In so doing, neoliberal capitalism reduces the meaning of people's lives, erodes the state's function of protecting the most vulnerable, deteriorates civil society, and reduces people to nothing but consumers. Cutthroat capitalism insists that all individuals be entrepreneurs and demands that they compete against one another yet deprives them of the resources that would be necessary to succeed.[33] "We are living out 'the Hunger Games' in real time," says Rogers-Vaughn.[34]

Life in a Neoliberal Capitalist System

While social theorists, economists, and historians trace neoliberalism's permeation into all spheres of life, its roots are in colonization, a thoroughly capitalist project. Black scholar Cedric Johnson writes that "racial capitalism" is a world system utterly dependent on slavery, violence, imperialism, and genocide and calls neoliberalism a trauma built on Black lives.[35] As another scholar notes, "Capital—accrued by the wealthiest over generations—was built on the lacerated backs of Black people."[36] Indeed, capitalism and class struggle have always been deeply entangled with racism. Malcolm X summed it up when he flatly declared, "You can't have capitalism without racism."[37] This is exemplified in bell hooks's persistent use of "transnational white supremacist capitalist patriarchy" (always without commas) to denote this global system.[38] In fact, the wealthy classes historically wanted to find a way to "bring a world brimming with the liberation of colonized masses back under their control, so that the accumulation of wealth and power to themselves would not be disturbed. In the new order, it was clear, this would have to be accomplished without actually annexing any territories."[39] Using a global banking and finance system that subjugates and exploits people is extraordinarily effective. It is a new kind of violence; it is "finance as warfare."[40] Not surprisingly, the neoliberal capitalist system has been very effective in subjugating those on the underside of the system to do its bidding. Those in the Global South, people of color, and women and children are suffering disproportionally in the current neoliberal capitalist world.[41] It is today's form of colonialism, as neoliberal capitalism is just as white supremacist and patriarchal as previous versions of capitalism that depended on enslaved humans to do the hard labor for the masters.

Growing economic inequality, and the suffering it engenders, is the result of the owner/rentier class of elites who are able and willing to impose their will through legislation, the courts, and penal systems.[42] The outcome of all this is that the working class and even those in the middle class have virtually no political influence.[43] Neoliberalism was antidemocratic from its roots in the early twentieth century, and it remains so to this day. It "inevitably replaces democracy with oligarchy" so that those who are not powerful politically and economically—which is to say the vast majority of people around the world—become masochists.[44] People simply do not have the resources to be all they can be and blame themselves for failing. No wonder people are becoming lonelier, more depressed, anxious, and addicted. They "hardly have a chance."[45]

Neoliberal Systems and the Collapse of Societies

Historians of cultures and anthropologists have documented the collapse of societies over millennia, and it has been argued that neoliberal, extractive capitalism is leading to the collapse of the world in its current form.[46] Indeed, the patterns of societal decline are quite consistent, predictable, and clear.[47] Collapse is a recurrent feature of human societies, and it is this fact that makes it worthwhile to explore its recurrent history, which is global in its distribution.[48]

The process of moral decay ends in collapse after about ten generations or roughly 250 years. As one historian writes, "The life-expectation of a great nation, it appears, commences with a violent and usually unforeseen outburst of energy and ends in a lowering of moral standards, cynicism, pessimism, and frivolity."[49] The pattern observed in studying thirteen empires from Assyria in 859 BCE to modern Britain in 1950 is consistent. These societies all declined in the same stages: Each generation experiences better socioeconomic circumstances than the generation before it, creating a march toward increasing materialism. Better conditions create the expectation of even more wealth, which then results in the erosion of morality and the subsequent decline of the social fabric. A society that values only wealth and the ability to generate wealth over everything else implodes on itself. This pattern accurately describes the consequences of neoliberal capitalist systems.

By multiple accounts, there are six stages to a society's collapse. The first is the age of pioneers, in which invaders, driven by a sense of honor and purpose and a willingness to sacrifice their own comforts, colonize a village or country, leading, second, to an age of conquest, in which the invaders take control. There is often a strong religious imperative to this conquest: They understand themselves to be doing their God's bidding. Third is the age of commerce, in which a strong military protects the new territories and explorers move out, seeking wealth through new enterprises. Visions of mission give way to the values of profit and personal wealth, and an infrastructure of roads, communications networks, and militant protection develops to increase wealth and protect it. The fourth predictable stage is the age of affluence, when the ethics and expectations of service disappear, and selfishness takes over. Education shifts from the goal of learning to obtaining the qualifications needed for high-paying jobs. Younger generations seek to make money rather than to serve others. Fifth is the age of intellect, where experts become prevalent, and talking, consulting, and writing are substituted for action as well as changes in behaviors and the ways systems function. Scientific research advances theories, but its insights are not leveraged to prevent suffering. Competition and conflict increase as the empire starts to crumble from within. The center cannot hold under these conditions. Instead of cooperating with one another to solve the wicked problems around the globe, villages, states, and nations compete for limited resources and try to destroy one another.[50] The sixth and final stage is the age of decadence, in which wealth and power lead to antisocial behaviors such as competitive materialism, consumerism, selfishness, and greed. A celebrity culture arises in which the heroes are athletes, actors, and singers. The masses are distracted from the realities of what is happening by entertainment and sporting events, which only heighten the norm of competition and help create a sense of entitlement to win while others lose. Mutual responsibility, mutual care, and the value of service are replaced by the desire to keep up with the Joneses (or destroy them in the competition for limited resources). In the age of decadence, wealthy leaders (owners/rentiers) appear generous as they build universities and hospitals or give to charities and the arts. However, when the limited supply of resources (natural and otherwise) begins to dwindle and wealth starts to dry up, these owners stop giving, and these institutions fall apart, creating larger and larger inequities and fewer and fewer opportunities for those in the drowning classes to catch up. Disorder, violence, and eventually chaos ensues, and the system collapses. This happens when money replaces care and service as primary motivators, when those in power focus on maintaining the extractive system at all costs, when there is no vision of a better future to guide decision-making, and when those who benefit from the status quo are protected from its consequences. As things continue to deteriorate, relationships disintegrate into distrust, self-protection, and oppression. Conflicts increase, and no one even notices the threats to the whole as they fight for their tiny piece of the pie. Politicians and other leaders use fear to control and manipulate people, and everyone moves into self-protection mode. Distractions, entertainment, and entitlement become "primary instruments of allaying people's fears and for controlling them."[51] As one scholar puts it, "No matter the geography, ethnicity, or spiritual traditions, humans most often develop high culture, hierarchy, civic institutions, religion, infrastructures, courts, arts, roles, and class distinctions. And then, when in decline, negative destructive behaviors, both personal and political are also identical. . . . This is the true DNA of our species, how we organize and behave through generations of creation and decline, no matter who we are culturally, where we are geographically, or when we lived in human history."[52]

The neoliberal capitalist system clearly has disastrous results for human beings and for the planet on which we depend. For the first time in history, for example, humans are changing the environment rather than adapting to it, destroying ecological systems on which we and all other creatures depend, and this is just one of the ways that human beings and the societies we create engender our own demise through divisiveness, narcissism, arrogance, and greed.

Suffering in a Cutthroat-Capitalist World

Critiques of extractive capitalism have been levied from scholars in various domains, including politics, economics, environmental studies, and social theory. Some of the dominant critiques include arguments that extractive capitalism increases income inequality, exacerbating poverty and social inequity; that it weakens social safety nets including health care and education; and that it emboldens environmental degradation by exploiting natural resources and increasing pollution and climate change, all of which disproportionately impact already oppressed groups. Cannibal capitalism has global effects as well: Rich countries exploit the natural resources and labor in developing countries, creating job displacement and income inequality, and corporate greed undermines democratic decision-making in weaker and colonized nations. In addition, critics argue that neoliberal capitalism results in cultural homogenization by eroding local cultures in favor of consumer culture, media, and the control of multinational corporations.[53] Critics also point to instances when neoliberal policies have led to financial crises, increased poverty, and exploited workers and natural resources. People are left on their own to fight for their dignity, rights, and flourishing without social safety nets to support them.

Exacerbating the problem is that large corporations and the owners/rentiers control the media and manipulate information for their own economic and political gain.[54] Being in a post-truth world means that dissembling and lying no longer surprise or disturb. Evidence does not matter, and when people try to hold the owners/rentiers responsible for their falsehoods, they are gaslighted, silenced, and dismissed. In a post-truth world, information is not a tool for organization and a source of order as it should be; rather, it is intentionally manipulated to create disorder—even chaos—to benefit those in charge. It becomes very difficult to separate what is real from disinformation, to distinguish who is trustworthy and who is not, and to put a finger on the real problem because under the current world order, so much is hidden, the ground is constantly shifting, and people have lost touch with themselves, one another, and what is true.[55]

In the stages of societal collapse, the twenty-first century would be considered the age of decadence. People are so distracted, anxious, and confused as they try to navigate their own troubled lives that it is difficult to notice what is happening with others. Neoliberal, extractive capitalism has so numbed people with its practices that it is difficult to notice what impact it is having on everyone, including those in the owner/rentier class.[56] The ways of life where communities of caring relationships create nurturing contexts in which to live and be known are under siege in the neoliberal capitalist system. Communities that will hold people accountable and promote values beyond wealth, the values that that are diminished in the age of decadence, are under threat. People's primary forms of interaction under the influence of neoliberal capitalist systems are through dominating organizations with complex hierarchies, hidden systems of power and privilege, and dehumanizing expectations. The loss of authentic communities where people can belong and grow forces individuals to rely on their own capacities and focus on their own needs, and they become increasingly likely to relate primarily to their own people, like-minded individuals who see the world in the same ways. Violence against those who are different increases as divisions become reified and competition is reinforced.

While this may sound like a problem for economists and politicians, it is also a challenge for religious leaders. It is the task of religious leaders to cultivate flourishing, which requires them to call out what is real, to name what is happening, and to help people respond in meaningful and transformative ways. The present realm, not just the next life, is religious leaders' purview, and they must attend to it if they seek to be transformative. Religious organizations are themselves often embedded within larger systems of power and privilege, and their leaders, if they are called to address human suffering and cultivate flourishing, will need to name the systems and practices that produce and reproduce suffering, including in faith-based organizations. The current situation requires that religious leaders commit to understanding the ways the world works under the global neoliberal capitalist system and pay attention to the social ills and subsequent suffering it engenders. Until religious leaders understand the ways extractive capitalism functions, its ongoing relationship to racism and colonialism, and the suffering these powers and principalities create, it will be difficult for them to nurture the flourishing of all those they wish to serve and to whom they are responsible.

Neoliberalism has "muted and mutated" the suffering caused by oppressive systems such as racism, homophobia, and sexism, such that they are now entangled with what one scholar calls "third order suffering."[57] Because neoliberalism as an ideology controls the media and the flow of information, it has "stripped away the narratives needed to see the situation clearly, much less understand precisely how the owners/rentiers do their dirty work."[58] As long as people believe that various forms of oppression and exclusion such as racism, patriarchy, classism, and so forth are only personal attitudes, unconscious bias, and personal prejudice that are not related to established economic practices, public policies, and legal strategies, institutions will continue to produce and maintain individual prejudice, not the other way around.[59] Systems of oppression and exclusion such as racism and sexism are largely motivated by economics and the attendant "will to power" they afford whites and men.[60] While everyone (including those in the owner/rentier class) suffers from this system in material, relational, and emotional ways, the suffering is not equally distributed; it is much worse for those who are in the working class or working poor, the Global South, women, children, and people of color.[61] Change, however, is difficult to effect because of the power that neoliberalism has had "in suppressing opposing voices" since the 1980s.[62] Unless the current neoliberal economic system is overturned wholesale and new regulations require the owner/rentier class to pay their share in taxes, fair and living wages, and worker protections, and unless independent media are resourced, the veneer of progress will make individuals feel better, while the neoliberal system "remains firmly in power and therefore that money continues to roll uphill, making inequality worse with every passing day."[63]

Extractive capitalism has been criticized as a reigning ideology precisely for its potential to exploit labor and natural resources for the benefit of a few. Cannibal capitalism, it appears, is contributing to the collapse of societies, as they have existed, for as long as human beings have been organizing into collectives. The forms of suffering created in an extractive capitalist world demand religious attention. In third-order suffering, the origins of suffering are hidden and difficult to name.[64] In this schema, "third-order suffering" differs from "first-order suffering." First-order suffering is natural to the human condition and includes death, grief, illness, disability, pain, and natural (not human-exacerbated) calamities. "Second-order suffering" is produced by human evil, whether individual or collective, and is both direct and indirect. Examples of second-order suffering include violence, enslavement, oppressive working conditions, and discrimination based on age, gender, race, or sexual identity. As common as first- and second-order suffering is in contemporary life, third-order suffering is the "new normal" form of suffering under neoliberal capitalism. It is different from the first two as it is almost impossible to identify and name, creates/generates deep shame and distress among people who do not have adequate narrative resources to understand or make sense of their suffering, and leaves individuals stranded with only market-generated narratives of "personal recovery" and the pursuit of happiness and well-being.

Conditions such as diffuse depression, amorphous anxiety, and addictions, and the intense shame that accompanies these are some of the symptoms of suffering under neoliberal capitalism. "The people I now see," one clinician writes about his clinical practice, "tend to manifest a far more diffuse or fragmented sense of self, are frequently more overwhelmed, experience powerful forms of anxiety and depression too vague to be named, display less self-awareness, have often loosened or dropped affiliations with conventional human collectives, and are increasingly haunted by shame rooted in a nebulous sense of personal failure."[65] Because the self under neoliberalism is atomistic, individualistic, fragmented, and insecure, the problems people present with in counseling practices reflect that. Yet people seeking relief are not able to identify any root cause of their dis-ease.

Under this regime, people struggle to figure out what flourishing might look like for them and how to pursue it—in part because they cannot identify the sources of their confusion, frustration, and spiritual distress. If they cannot identify what is affecting them, much less address it, people have no way to make meaning of what they are experiencing, and traditional systems of meaning such as telling and hearing the stories of what is happening can become less effective unless they are processes by which to name what is really going on. Indeed, the effects of third-order suffering are easy to see. Suicide is on the rise globally, especially among youths, who can see no future for themselves in the "system" and despair about not being seen, heard, and understood for who they are as human beings.[66] Under the empire of extractive capitalism that values people only as producers and consumers and creates competition between them, suicide is understandable, even though it is tragic. Systemic inequities and injustices, the fragmentation of communities, and the dissolution of shared meaning are primary causes of the suffering religious leaders seek to address. Individuals and communities need transformative religious leaders to name what their congregants may not be able to see and help them find a way forward into more meaningful ways of being.

Neoliberalization as the Context of Religious Leadership

It is not hard to see the parallels between the research on the decline of earlier societies and what is happening in the twenty-first century. The evidence of collapse is everywhere—on a global scale and in religious communities. But there is hope because of the lessons from quantum mechanics that have provided the metaphor for understanding that all living systems are characterized by entanglement, change, and adaptation. Unlike machines in Newton's understanding, living systems—from human beings to communities and organizations, states and nations—can learn and change. The decline of a system's functioning is a form of information that those paying attention can see and feel. Those who stay alert to their internal and external environments can learn to respond intelligently, shift values, alter practices, and engage in systems' transformation.

The suffering caused by the oppressive systems, including racism, classism, heterosexism, and sexism, is only exacerbated by the extractive capitalist system, and religious leaders, as they are called to nurture thriving, are also called to adopt a decolonialist approach in their ministry that both names the global realities that people are living in and seeks to transform their communities. Through just and caring practices that restore people to their humanity, to one another, and to their God, acts of resistance and subversion can reclaim the value and dignity of those most harmed.

Humans need something meaningful to hold on to, and they need an identity that is richer and more complex than extractive capitalism allows. As the research on human flourishing shows, people need to be able to engage in meaningful activity, mutual relationship, and real community where they can be themselves. These deep needs cannot be satisfied virtually. The internet cannot supply them in any meaningful way in the long term. When people lose touch with themselves and each other, they quickly close in on themselves, seeing the outer world and those in it as threats. Factions form, divisions solidify, and alienation and violence ensue. When values systems close in around one thing (e.g., money, influence, power, control of resources), systems become rigid and lose their diversity, creativity, and sense of meaning and purpose. Having only one set of values (e.g., money and the power that comes with it) forecloses cooperation and heightens competition.[67] None of this is consistent with human flourishing, nor is it in line with what the Creative Divine longs for.

Newton's laws of mechanics suggest that systems inevitably wear down and collapse in the process of entropy, but the new quantum understanding invokes more openness and possibility. Transformative religious leaders lean into the sense of possibility generated by open systems that are learning and adapting along the way. Transformational religious leaders resist the fear and despair brought on by the natural death of one form of community and lead congregations into finding new forms of community. Rather than giving in to the grief that the suffering of so many brings, religious leaders who wish to transform are invited to shift their perspective and find the ground of hope and possibility that understanding quantum science invokes. To do this, they can also lean into the resources of their own traditions as embodied in their own communities and help those communities and the people within them find life. As one leadership expert notes, ideally, "The Chaos Cycle doesn't end in chaos. It ends with heightened clarity and intensified meaning for how we can use our power and influence to serve this time. We can trust this path—it leads us out of the dark woods into a bright clearing where we realize what is truly meaningful in our lives and work."[68]

Sacred texts such as those in the Judeo-Christian tradition provide resources for resisting the hegemony of extractive capitalism. For example, the biblical focus on the value of each person; the emphasis on stewardship (meaning that everything belongs to God, and humans are caretakers rather than owners of the world's resources); the caution against love of money; the ways religious traditions speak to the importance of generosity, compassion, and hospitality; and the promotion of a covenantal and communal ethic all provide resources for resisting the dominant neoliberal narrative.[69]

Since neoliberal capitalism is an utterly fragmenting and atomizing economic system that metes out third-order suffering on all people—especially those treading- or under-water in the current economic and cultural systems—an adequate theology of thriving will give an account of personal and communal resistance toward the global economic model that currently dominates and will offer theological underpinnings of such responses. Sociocultural and economic-political factors deeply and directly affect the thriving of individuals and communities.[70] Despair is born of thinking that things will never change, that they cannot change. The essence of hope is the belief that things do not have to be as they are, that things have been different and can be different again. Ideally, religious leaders understand the challenges of the human condition and what it is like to live as constrained creatures and yet can lean into the hope—the conviction—that this is not all there is. Although neoliberalism and its financial model, cutthroat capitalism, have extracted humans from their communities and the stories that historically have bound them together, the work of religious leaders includes retelling the stories that invoke a flourishing life.[71]

Religious leaders have the benefit of traditions that tell a different story. They are traditions that have witnessed human folly and developed wisdom for addressing it. They are traditions that know, at least intuitively, what people need to thrive and offer hope for such an outcome. Religious traditions can be sources of hope as their followers begin to trust that something, someone, outside the life-limiting systems that human beings have created is with them, resisting what is death dealing and urging people and communities into thriving. Although transformational religious leaders cannot be certain what the future will look like, they can speak to the hope of a future and help shape a new (or return to a previous, more communally focused) way of being together.

Transformative religious leaders can cultivate virtues that are the opposite of consumerism and materialism, the opposite of competition and oppression of others, the opposite of despair and fear and reactivity and self-protection. Religious leaders can choose to be awake and aware, to name what is and speak to the suffering, to practice compassion, to care, and to serve. Awareness, learning, naming, and responding are the antidotes to the decline that is all around. Even in the direst circumstances, transformational religious leaders hold faith in people's capacities to be generous, caring, creative, and kind. Even in the most chaotic circumstances, religious leaders cultivate the conditions for these capacities to grow and develop so that those who are suffering—that is, all of us—can find the way forward together.

For any person or community to move out of the mess that human beings have created, transformational religious leaders will need to attend to the quality of the relationships in their organizations and their communities.[72] They will need to help those in their community know one another as human beings, not just consumers or bosses or workers. They will want to pay attention to the level of trust that members have for each other, asking how well and how often they communicate with each other, how well they understand and care, and how far they are willing to go for one another when the chips are down. Transformative religious leaders attend to the levels of fear in their communities and nurture people's capacities to love. They ask themselves about the nature and quality of the thinking and behaving among members.[73] Effective leaders observe whether people are willing to lean in, engage, and contribute to improving the situation or whether they get reactive or shut down. All of these are symptoms of whether the individuals and the system are healthy, and which interventions might be recommended in the moment.

By staying calm themselves, transformational religious leaders ensure they do not feed the anxiety when there are high levels of reactivity. When people are self-protective, transformative religious leaders encourage mutual vulnerability and care. When fear is a primary motivator in the system, transformational religious leaders tap into the values of community members and help them find what it is important to them—what they want to link arms to protect.

Transformative religious leaders examine the values that shape the identity of the organization they lead. They ask whether money is the primary motivator and whether success is determined by size or growth of membership. Effective transformational religious leaders are honest about what motivates them and their staff and what values shape their leadership. They continuously investigate whether it is only financial gain, prestige, or ego inflation that drives their work and whether selfishness ever replaces a commitment to service. The most transformative religious leaders explore the proposal that religious organizations are called not to be successful in financial or growth terms but instead to be faithful to the vision of God for the kindom.[74] As one observer notes, the church's distinctiveness is not what it possesses, but what it is possessed by.[75]

If religious leaders are called to cultivate communities in which people have their needs met, where cooperation and mutual compassion and care are the coin of the realm, and where there is joy, the people in their care can be returned to themselves and to each other, and the community can get on with the business of its mission of cultivating redemption. The invitation may sound strange in the contemporary culture, when so much has been lost. But the sacred texts teach that wherever two or more are gathered, the Sacred can be there also.[76] As one pastoral theologian teaches us, joy comes from self-transcendence.[77] It emerges when human beings transcend their own fears and find ways to come together. Joy happens when people transcend the limits of self and of systemic machinations to discover new (old) ways of being human together.

Part II

Implications

CHAPTER 5

Creating a Thriving Organization

ALL LIVING SYSTEMS continuously create themselves or die, and they "always and only" organize around their strange attractors, or values, around an identity, a membrane, or a boundary that distinguishes them from others.[1] Without identity, there would be no means to differentiate one thing from another. There would be no possibility to organize into greater complexity and order. Without identities, life would be a "never-ending mess of primordial soup devoid of form and possibility."[2] The membrane of identity, however, is semipermeable, letting in new information from the organization's environment. If the membrane is too rigid, the system shuts down. However, if the membrane is too porous and the organization's identity too undefined, it has nothing to organize around.

When an organization knows itself, when it has a sense of its purpose, it is freed to be creative in finding its way forward, organizing itself in new ways that meet the current challenges. Quantum science suggests that living systems organize around an identity; the relationships that are woven together into complex networks and the shared meaning of its members create coherent and ideally "unpoliced" collectives.[3] However, if a living system closes itself off from its desired identity (presumably in religious organizations, the identity that the divine is calling it into) and separates itself from the wisdom in its relationships and if it resists responding creatively to new information, there is no possibility for change and growth. Closed systems that do not respond creatively to the changes in their environment have no potential to access life's adaptive capacities.[4] An organization's identity is its firmest ground, and the relationships within it are the pathways to the intelligence of the system.[5] Through relationships, information is created and transformed, the organization's identity expands to include more stakeholders and their perspectives, and the whole becomes wiser. The more access people have to one another, the more possibilities there are. Without connections, nothing happens: "Organizations held at equilibrium by well-designed organization charts die. In self-organizing systems, people need access to everyone; they need to be free to reach anywhere in the organization to accomplish their work."[6] Opening up the organization to clarify its identity, to know itself, to include its stakeholders, and to distribute its leadership is the best path toward fresh possibilities.

Attend to Meaningful Information

Living systems self-organize around the information they receive from their environment, and they use that information to adapt to changing conditions. Organizations filter information through their identity, deciding what is relevant and what is not. All systems possess the freedom to decide what to pay attention to and how to respond to what is noticed.[7] For this reason, knowledge management is a survival issue. Handled well, meaningful information gives organizations (i.e., their leaders and members) what they need most: the capacity to act with intelligence and intentionality rather than being reactive, rushing into the future like lemmings without using the organization's inherent intelligence to develop longer-term organizational capacities.[8]

Being willing to notice and take account of new information and challenges is not easy; the habits developed over years ("the ways things have always been done around here") save time, making it easier to get through a day or a week using familiar tools. However, being able to respond to new information and situations is key to an organization's survival: Information is that which changes organizations and helps them stay alive.[9] Religious leaders can help their organizations maintain the core of their identity while also responding in fresh ways to information about what is happening within them and in the world around them.[10]

New information and possibilities will lead to increased options because new information invites change. If leaders and members alike want to focus on their own security, withdrawing and becoming more self-serving and defensive, this is a good way to kill an organization.[11] Fearful people will focus on small details and what they can control, losing sight of the possibilities that are opening for them.[12] However, greater openness is the path to greater order, and everyone who cares and is invested in the organization's healthy sustainability must be provided the information they need to collaborate with others in the emergence of the new, thriving organization that can support the life of its members and community.[13] Meaningful information about the context in which the organization finds itself and the challenges it faces is the lifeblood of a thriving and sustainable organization, if it can meaningfully and creatively respond to it.

Nurture Relationships

Organizations are collections of people who come together to do something meaningful that they could not do as well alone. People naturally create organizations, from families to book groups, from governments to communities of faith. The recognition that individuals need each other lies at the heart of every system. From that realization, individuals reach out to others, and seemingly divergent self-interests develop into a system of interdependency. All organizations form through collaboration, born of the recognition that human beings need one another to survive.[14] When leaders can strengthen the connections between people in their organization, new possibilities emerge, especially when members share values and a sense of purpose.

Communities form when people who share some core values make a commitment to be available to each other, to offer support, to share learning, and to consciously develop new knowledge together. Ideally, they are there not only for their own needs but for the needs of others too. Authentic communities succeed best when they start with some type of community formation process.[15] People need to clarify their personal intent and commitment, and as a group, they need to agree on how they will work together, how they will support one another, and what their work will be.[16] For authentic communities to develop, they must encourage sharing meaningful information as transparently and as quickly as possible so that other members can act on that knowledge. The speed at which knowledge develops and is exchanged is crucial for organizations to mature into creative, dynamic, and sustainable living systems.

Share Responsibilities

The world desperately needs leaders who can bring people together in authentic communities to address the most significant needs human beings have: to belong, create meaning together, serve others, to have a sense of purpose, and grow as people of God.[17] For religious leaders, this work is explicitly spiritual. It involves leaning into the trust in human goodness and understanding that everything good is cocreated with God.[18] It depends on hearing a new sacred call about what an organization and its members are to be about in the world. It requires humility, willingness, and courage to do the work at hand.[19] Part of the spiritual potential of religious leadership includes trusting oneself, others, and God to move forward together in creative and meaningful ways. It means leading with humility and vulnerability and humanness, sharing what is most important, and hearing from others at a deep level. Furthermore, religious leadership is spiritual because it depends on faithful hope. As Czech statesman and poet Václav Havel writes, "Hope is a dimension of the soul . . . an orientation of the spirit, an orientation of the heart. It transcends the world that is immediately experienced and is anchored somewhere beyond its horizons. It is not the conviction that something will turn out well, but the certainty that something makes sense regardless of how it turns out."[20] This may mean walking in confusion and darkness for some time, enacting faith in seeking understanding.[21]

Religious traditions have long histories of exploring and being with people in the dark nights of the soul when people have felt hopeless, abandoned by their God, alone, and afraid. Religious leaders can model trust in God and in the processes that are known to work: creating meaningful communities of people who share values and a sense of purpose, who have all the information they need (or the capacities to find it) to figure out what to do next, and who have developed processes to work through challenges together, pooling the wisdom present in the system. When circumstances feel chaotic and threaten the identity of the organization, transformative religious leaders lean into their spiritual wisdom rather than trying to escape the discomfort or save others and/or the organization. Transformative religious leaders help people stay present to challenges, one another, and the processes they have developed and to allow new insights and capacities to emerge—because "they always do."[22]

This transformational work requires clearly seeing the system(s) one is participating in and becoming more systemic thinkers.[23] It has other implications for religious leaders, too, including the need to help the organization clarify and articulate its values, sense of purpose, and identity, ensuring that meaningful information is shared openly and widely and that everyone who has a stake in the outcome is invited into the processes of change and renewal. This is a central idea in transformational leadership: One can be appointed to a position, but only that person can choose to lead, and only would-be followers can choose to follow, join the effort, and lead themselves. When a person cares and is concerned about the need for something to change and influences others to voluntarily join that effort, they are leading, whether they have a position of authority or not. A leader is anyone who wants to help. And if one wants to lead change, it begins with seeing the system as a whole and observing its functioning and dynamics.

See the Whole

Genuinely transformational leaders study their organization as a whole to see the dynamics that contribute to individual behaviors and to assess why the organization is where it is in its life course.[24] To better see and understand the whole, leaders involve as many other perspectives as possible to collaborate, together painting a picture of the system and how it operates. Once a picture of the whole system has emerged, leaders, in collaboration with the members of their organization, can be about creating processes for addressing the challenges the organization is facing.

Once processes are in place for conversing, listening, and deepening understanding, new possibilities will emerge.[25] In one model, this includes understanding which information each person or subgroup is operating with, making sure everyone has the same data, that they have as much data as others have, and that everyone has complete information.[26] It also includes understanding the various interpretations being made of that information and identifying where interpretations differ and which interpretations are shared. Transformative forms of communication require understanding how the data and its interpretations are affecting individuals and subgroups, noticing which feelings emerge in people and the group, and understanding what people need.[27]

Understand Change

Given that all organizations are fallible, one might wonder how an organization gets from here to there—from being an organization that is dying and thus failing its members to one that is healthy, providing the kind of life-giving opportunities and support those members imagined when they joined together in the first place. Leading change in organizations is inherently difficult due to the many factors involved, including difficult personalities of members, challenging group dynamics, and entrenched organizational culture, and yet change is necessary for an organization to remain healthy and viable. Beyond understanding the existing organizational culture, a religious leader can begin to change negative perspectives and processes, rewriting policies and procedures as well as inscribing more positive, inclusive, open, and life-enhancing perspectives, attitudes, and processes.[28]

If organizations are to contribute to human flourishing, they must change in response to the challenges they experience, both internally and externally. It is a "paradox of evolution or development that the more we learn how to do things and to stabilize what we have learned, the more unwilling or unable we become to adapt, change, and grow into new patterns, even when our changing environment demands such new patterns."[29] It is indeed a paradox to suggest that one of an organization's greatest strengths is its ability to remain constant (or at least true to its identity) while also arguing that this same organization must change to remain effective, yet this paradox is at the heart of organizational resilience and sustainability. To this end, it is the "inevitable dilemma" for any group to "avoid becoming so stable in its approach to its environment that it loses its ability to adapt, innovate, and grow."[30] Religious leaders might wonder how they can hold to tradition while also being open to the movement and invitations of a consistent and dependable yet surprising and reforming God.

Organizations exist in the paradoxes of change, stability, and renewal. The question is how a particular organization can remain both stable and open to change. Creating an organizational culture centered on a mindset of constant learning that is inherently adaptive and flexible is the best resource for an organization to thrive.[31] This kind of organization lives in the paradox of the constant need to perpetually learn and change, even as it maintains its most important values.

Clarify Values

While not easy to do, it is the responsibility of leaders, with the help of others in the organization, to foster cultural change while keeping an eye on the explicit values of the body gathered. Formal organizational leaders need others within the organization to provide a variety of viewpoints while leveraging relationships with other stakeholders to diagnose problems, develop solutions, and support organizational change. Formal and informal leaders together can explore the existing culture, direction, and policies in the organization, speaking up about their own experiences about what is working and what is not. This can be challenging, but it is necessary to ensure the continuing health of the organization. For this to happen, transformative religious leaders help create relationships and environments of trust and safety—brave spaces for people to speak honestly. This work also requires seeing chaos and dissolution as potent and generative forces for the changes necessary for sustainability. It means trusting the system itself to find its own solutions, understanding that the chaos cycle is triggered by changes in the environment and that everything that once held the organization together (its beliefs, meanings, and structures) may no longer work in the new environment. An organization has two choices at this point: Either it can reorganize using new beliefs and structures that work well in the changed environment, or it can insist on the old ways, fail to reorganize itself, and die.[32] Both death and rebirth (universal religious themes) are possible as an outcome of the passage through chaos. Working *with* the forces of change is required: attempts to keep chaos at bay, maintain the status quo, or hold tight to the way it has always been done will likely lead to the death of an organization.[33] In fact, it is when everything is falling apart that real change is possible. One question religious leaders might pose to those collaborating in the process of change is what it might mean for their organization to be faithful to their God rather than try to be successful by others' standards.[34]

Responsibility for organizational faithfulness includes improving an organization's culture. Leaders (both formal and not) in organizations will want to ask one another questions such as what kind of organization they want to have, what impact they want to make, what matters most about their organization to its members, which values they hold dearest, what it means to be faithful, how their organization might participate in that work, who their God is calling them to be, and what their God is calling them to do in this moment.

While some organizations may answer these questions solely in relation to financial considerations, this is a shortsighted perspective, even for nonreligiously oriented organizations. No organization that achieves "success" from the exploitation of others, for example, would be considered a success—even if it was financially viable—when understood ethically, morally, or religiously. Financial gains do not outweigh injustice against the most vulnerable in any organization. To properly answer the fundamental question regarding success, successful and transformative religious leaders involve multiple parties within the organization to consult on these questions.

Yet in most organizations, there is little understanding of these important considerations, especially among those involved in formal leadership.[35] In most cases, this is not the fault of the leaders themselves; business and leadership trainings as well as theological education usually have very little in the way of curriculum on moral leadership or organizational ethics.[36] Given the importance of ethical and just decision-making for the well-being and success of one's organization, however, more attention needs to be paid to these questions. It is crucial that an organization increase its learning agility, creativity, and flexibility while also maintaining its identity and sense of God-given purpose.

Clarify Values

One of the first things organizations do once they have some structure is to create an identity. Created from the values, a sense of purpose, and commitments that brought people together in the first place, an organization's identity can provide a guide amid the confusion and fear that chaos and change can generate. It can be frightening to face one's own powerlessness amid change and even the possibility of dissolution. Leaders do well to name and embrace the confusion and fear as old ways disintegrate. However, even amid the grief work in relation to what is being lost, when an organization is clear about its identity and shares it widely, its members can figure out what to do next in times of crisis.[37] A transformational leader continually asks about the larger sense of purpose among members and whether those members are following the processes they set out for working together, solving problems, communicating, and making decisions. A transformational leader also models being less anxious, remaining patient for the solutions to emerge.[38] New insights can be used to determine which actions, measures, and strategies make the most sense for the organization as it undergoes change and figures out next steps. Clarity of direction and the commitment to pursue it will occur naturally, as people proceed to change and discard existing processes and methods that are dysfunctional or no longer make sense.[39]

When people who have a stake in the outcome of decisions and are invested in the thriving of the organization are included in the processes toward finding solutions, they begin to care more about what is happening. They find themselves leaning in, bringing their best to the task at hand. When people begin to understand the situation that a community they care about is facing and are clear on what is at stake and when they are reconnected to their values and sense of purpose in joining the organization in the first place, they become motivated.[40] Most people want something meaningful to be engaged in and are motivated by the desire to serve.[41]

Organizations are the forms that come together as people come together seeking life. They naturally form and reform over time. They come together, and they come apart. The strength of a group, community, or organization is maintained when its members and leaders are clear about the identity and purpose of their joining together. This clarity helps the organization and its members stay the course even during significant change. Formal religious leaders' role in this is to support the system as it reforms itself into a more sustainable and life-giving organization. Religious leaders can keep pointing to the values, the North Star, that gives the organization its sense of purpose. They can gather people for important conversations and facilitate their work together to find solutions. Formal leaders are in a strong position to pose the more significant and relevant questions of the moment and help people come together to engage the challenges, but they are not responsible to come up with the path forward on their own.

To engage in the real work of leadership, leaders need to have their finger on the pulse of what is happening both systemically and with individual people. They also need to be able to facilitate grief processes as members let go of important parts of the organization's history and traditions they have valued.[42] Formal leaders can remind their members that ends are beginnings in the cycles of death and renewal, especially from religious perspectives.[43] Religious leaders can facilitate the transition from one state of the organization to another, even as they lament what is inevitably being lost as things change.

Address Abuses of Power

Religious leaders need to explore the uses and abuses of power that are operative in their organization. Power, understood as the ability to influence others or events, is operative in every organization, no matter its structure. Some organizations are very hierarchical with a top-heavy model of leadership. In these kinds of structured organizations, those at the top (president, senior pastor, bishop, rabbi, imam) are expected to have and wield the most power, and they do, at least formally. In organizations with intentionally flat hierarchies, leadership is spread among all members, with the expectation that each member and group of members within that organization will equally exercise certain amounts and forms of power. However, there are formal structures of power, and there are informal structures of power, just as there are formal leaders and informal leaders. Formal leaders are those whom the organization has explicitly chosen to lead it (say, the senior pastor or the board of directors). Informal leaders are members of a group whom others choose to follow for a variety of reasons (e.g., because they seem to have a clarity of vision, they are emotionally mature, they have courage to engage the challenges that the organization is facing, or they are trusted by other members of the organization). Analyzing power and how it operates in one's organization is critical if a leader wants to engage in positive transformational leadership. Unfortunately, those who are powerful usually defend the status quo because it is the source of their power and privilege. Any change that benefits others would destroy their position, and they usually want to hold on to that.[44] Truly transformational leaders are willing to share power and to use the power they have for the benefit of others.[45] These leaders are the ones who access the wisdom in the organization and bring their organization into new life.

Prioritize Action

Sharing power and information is the lifeblood of a self-creating, adapting, and sustainable organization. However, in a world that is saturated with opinions and fake news rather than contextualized, accurate, and meaningful knowledge, effective transformational leaders will put a premium on action, on trying new things, on taking risks and learning from them to gather meaningful information. And leaders will orient their members to do the same. Transformational leaders understand that systems are self-organizing, and they value initiative, experimentation, creativity, and responsiveness as a way of practicing learning agility. The most effective leaders build cultures and expectations of learning and growth, and they encourage innovation through trial and error. Transformational leaders provide information, connect people, clarify the values that connect people together, and help create a sense of purpose and meaningful work. Effective leaders provide resources, trust others, model being trustworthy, and practice patience. There are no quick fixes in open, living, adapting, and changing systems. For most organizations, meaningful change takes at least three to five years.[46] Trying new things and engaging the information that comes from experimentation are the best ways to gain meaningful information, and transformative, generative leaders constantly review what worked and what did not—and why—with others who were involved.

Perform After-Action Reviews

While transformational leaders prioritize action, risk-taking, and trial and error, it is very helpful for leaders to adopt a regular practice of after-action review, sometimes called a *postmortem reflection*.[47] Any experience or event can be a rich learning experience, but only if those involved or affected reflect on a few key questions, including how well they communicated, where trust and distrust emerged, and whether their most important values were evident in their behaviors. The practice of an after-action review, in which the focus is learning how to do things better, can be very helpful in finding ways forward. The more perspectives on the questions, the better.

No matter what, transformational leaders gather all who were part of the action or touched by the crisis and ask these questions in this order: *What happened when we tried X?*[48] In the process of answering this question, everyone involved offers a personal description; no one is challenged on whether their description is accurate. Different viewpoints are valued, as widely divergent descriptions give the most information. There is no blame cast if an intentional trial fails; it is viewed as a rich learning opportunity. Second, leaders ask, *why do you think it happened?* In answering this question, people offer their interpretations, again without being challenged. Then these interpretations are explored for their diversity and commonality. This exploration usually reveals a great deal of information beyond the incident. The culture around the event becomes visible, especially around hierarchy, communications, and trust. Third, leaders ask, *what can we learn from this?* Here is where the richness of diverse perceptions can be shaped into learning outcomes that build on the complexity of the situation rather than overly simplified analyses. Finally, leaders invite those gathered to consider *how will we apply these learnings?* Specific actions, defined outcomes, specified work, and a motivated team are all possible because of this process.

Using the after-action review process, leaders can involve members in creating the structure, plans, and forms of measurement that the team, community, or organization will follow going forward. An after-action review is a kind of feedback loop that enriches a learning-agile organization and its leaders to integrate more and more information that is meaningful to its life. This form of feedback is the most useful kind because it is generated by those trying new things and seeing what happens. Because people only genuinely support and engage what they have a hand in creating, trial and error and after-action reviews are the best ways to continue to learn and find what works and what does not.

By involving everyone who cares about the outcome of an action in this process and taking the decisions of the group seriously, leaders will find that people gain confidence and trust, improve their relationships with one another, and lean into the invitation to be creative and try new things without fear of reprisal. Other questions that members of an organization engaged in action reflection might include conversation about who else needs to be included, whether members can talk about what really matters or what is really going on without fear of reprisal, what the organization has become, and what it aspires to be.[49] Obviously, answering these questions as a group, listening to others' perspectives, implementing new initiatives, and waiting to see how it goes will take time and effort, but this is the best way to help people become invested in the organization and be willing to try out their ideas to help it succeed.[50] Agreeing on how to measure success or attend to the outcomes of experimentation is also crucial, as this will provide the feedback (i.e., the ongoing meaningful information) the system needs to adjust, learn, and grow.

Welcome, Include, and Diversify

Genuinely transformational leaders know they cannot force anyone to change, they cannot force an organization to change, and they cannot save an organization by themselves. Bringing whole-systems thinking to the leadership roles and processing new information as a community are the only ways to ensure that the change that happens is fruitful, sustainable, and life-giving. When people believe a change is positive and meaningful, and it makes sense to them, they will embrace it. For this reason, transformational leaders will include others as cocreators in the process.

Because the systems that people live through are complex and because each person is unique in their experiences and perspectives, no two people will see things the same or identically interpret the data they have. For this reason, transformational leaders invite everyone who cares or has been touched by an event or experience to take part in the after-action review. Transformative leaders reject the idea that some people's experiences count, while others' do not, and they reject inequality as the norm.[51] Transformational leaders tap into the wisdom, insights, and creative perspectives of those around them to develop together a more complete picture of what happened and what needs to happen next. However, this must be done without judgment, blame, or scapegoating. In establishing these kinds of processes, transformational leaders identify and challenge the injustices in many organizational systems, encouraging them to be more life-giving for all their members and for the communities in which they find themselves.[52] The work of any team or organization begins with a clear sense of what it wants to accomplish and how its members want to work together. Once this is established, they can continue to remind one another of their goals, values, and identity to get back on track.

In this kind of work, diversity is a desirable norm. Diversity is not about meeting an arbitrary mandate for inclusion but rather comes from the awareness that no one can ever see the wholeness of a situation and that everyone needs others' perspectives to see the whole.[53] Diversity values difference because difference of life experience, information, opinions, feelings, beliefs, interpretations, and behaviors helps organizations gain clarity about what is working and what is not. When the going gets rough, the fact that processes have been established that support trust, openness, respectful challenge, and shared purpose helps people find their way through difficulties to gain consensus about the next steps. Transformative leaders cannot accomplish anything well without the input of those whom the changes will affect most. Other questions transformational leaders might ask include who is missing; who else needs to be included to do the work; whether the meaning of the work is still clear and if it is changing; whether they are becoming more truthful with each other; whether information is becoming more open and easier to access; where power is being used for the good of all; and what is being learned about the organization, one another, and themselves in this process.[54] The more people are engaged in this discernment, the better because the system will have more viewpoints, experiences, perspectives, and interpretations to use toward its thriving.

Furthermore, organizations that want to be sustainable will seek surprises, trusting the Creating God who continues to surprise. This might mean looking for what is uncomfortable, even startling. Those involved need to reflect on the unsettling information together and be encouraged to look for variances, to travel far afield and bring in newness.[55] Where there is diversity in an organization, innovative solutions are continuously created because different people see and do things differently, providing a rich source of options and fresh perspectives. They are encouraged to think together about what the new information and situation mean for their organization and for them. In so doing, members and leaders become intentional disturbers of the equilibrium, embracing the chaos so that the system can take in new information and reform itself in response.[56]

Nurture

One of the most important aspects of any organization is its capacity for healthy relationships in which people listen well to one another, seek to understand rather than to be right, and trust one another to have good intentions and the good of the whole at heart. There is mutual respect, openness and curiosity, compassion, and willingness to honestly and openly share experiences and information. By being intimately involved in the processes of change, people will be more willing to do the work required to accomplish what needs to happen and to own responsibility for it. In this way, intelligence about the organization and its leadership becomes a distributed capacity, not dependent solely on the vision, energy, passion, values, and commitments of one person or small group. Following these procedures invites all members to become leaders in various aspects of organizational life, and everyone will be better able to deal with the challenges that arise in their area.

People without authority are more likely to step up and lead if and when those in authority step back and create the space for them to engage. Thus, one of the primary functions of those with formal authority is to nurture a life-giving organizational culture—to create the structures, help develop the processes, and craft the strategies that can allow and encourage those without formal authority to step up and lead. Effective leaders foster good conversation between people and teams, facilitate the flow of information, and encourage collaboration and collective action. It is the formal leaders who are primarily responsible to create conditions for others to contribute their ideas, talents, energy, and experience to a problem, understanding challenges as problems to be solved rather than impediments.

* * *

Organizations are necessary because they structure the world, expand opportunities and resources, create meaningful work, and meet people's and communities' needs. Organizations also mediate good and ill through the culture, laws, and social structures they embody; in short, organizations can be life-giving to greater and lesser degrees. At their best, religious organizations can be mediators of justice, diversity, equality, inclusion, belonging, meaning making and purpose that many will not experience in their homes or other organizations. They can be contexts in which people learn, grow, and change for the better. However, unless organizations are intentional about it, they import racist, sexist, and homophobic tropes that create suffering and lead to anxiety, low self-esteem, a sense of alienation, depression, and despair among their members.

Neoliberal, extractive capitalism, especially in its most insidious and prevalent form, which currently drives many Western systems and organizations, is anathema to religious faith and practice and has created an urgent need for genuinely transformational religious leaders. Because capitalism strives to place money at the center of all that is, the logics of neoliberal capitalism are something religious leaders must guide their communities in resisting. For example, because neoliberalism has been the dominant ideology for almost fifty years, many people know little else. They do not know how to create genuine communities. Leaders who can create communities where humility, love and mutual care, hope, justice, and equity are the dominant values can help "empower people to *resist* the system (instead of adapt to it), to embrace *communion* and *wholeness* in relation to others and the earth (instead of functioning in accord with the values of production and consumption) and to pursue *interdependent* reliance within the web of human relationships (instead of accepting shame-based personal responsibility narratives)."[57] Religious leaders and the communities of faith they guide can be sources of defiance, as they are communities motivated by the most significant religious values of love and care for all.

Although neoliberal values have insidiously insinuated themselves into every domain of contemporary life, they are not all that is there. Religious leaders are called to see, identify, name, and celebrate the places where resistance is happening, to help community members see them and build on them, and in so doing, embolden their communities of faith. Flourishing is an activity in which people are engaged in meaningful and virtuous work, creating more goodness where and when they can, growing and learning individually and together.

The good news is that organizations are malleable, always in flux, and can be reformed. Even as they maintain the core elements of their identity, organizations are constantly changing and ideally can adapt to the changes in their environment. A core purpose of religious organizations is to promote the flourishing of their members and communities, an activity that cannot be accomplished alone.

Genuine community among teams and in not-for-profit, mission- and values-driven organizations can serve as an antidote to the dominant system of neoliberal capitalism, first by encouraging the organization to be clear on the life-giving values embedded in its identity, purpose, and mission. Transformative religious leaders encourage thinking and speaking globally ("for all creation") but acting locally in their own contexts.[58] People need visionary leaders whom they can trust to embody the values and purpose that the group or community is founded on. Religious leaders do not have to be perfect, and in fact, being vulnerable with one's own challenges and limitations with humility can build trust, but people need someone to help them name the sources of their despair and imagine what else is possible—that human beings can still live lives of integrity, care, compassion, honesty, courage, and love. Effective leaders who understand how living systems such as religious organizations work can trust others' humanness, are curious about differences, delight in surprise and inventiveness, and nurture and connect people. They trust that people can create wisely and well, seeking the best interests of their communities and organizations and wanting to bring more goodness into the world, and they give people the freedom to experiment.[59]

This model of leadership is not a quick fix. In fact, it takes time, patience, and intentionality. It takes being willing to calm down, even amid crisis; to think about both the big and small pictures; to pose deep questions; to listen deeply for understanding; to settle into the work; and to articulate what one is trying to accomplish, focusing on process rather than any known outcome. The world needs leaders who are committed to serving others; who are calm and steady through failures and chaotic crises; who can attend to others' experiences, thoughts, and feelings as well as their own; and who can bring people in to engage in the creative work the organization needs.

CHAPTER 6

Leading Organizations

THE WORLD AS described by new science is one of relational networks—entities—entangled by fields of energy, where small changes can make big differences, where creation and dissolution are part of the same processes and are dependent on one another for (re)organization, in which change is a fundamental principle, order is something that emerges from systems that are clear on their identity and values, and leaders are not the ones who have all the answers but rather understand something about the systems and processes that strengthen organizations.[1] Every organization wrestles with a similar challenge: how to maintain its integrity, direction, and effectiveness as it copes with relentless turbulence and change. For organizations to thrive in the world today, a new model of leadership is required.[2] Transformational leadership, a model that draws on the wisdom in the community itself, is the way forward toward meaningful and sustainable organizations.[3]

In the current world of fragmentation, chaos, and despair, leaders of faith- and values-based organizations are more important than ever; the organizations they lead hold great potential for good, for creating and sustaining opportunities for people and communities to thrive, and for finding meaning in a morass of data and information, both credible and fake.[4] Organizations should exist for the well-being of their members and communities.[5] At a basic level, the goal of religious leadership is to promote flourishing (in theological language, to participate in God's processes of salvation, redemption, sanctification, or *geulah*).[6] How religious leaders understand what flourishing is and how they can strive to achieve it is the necessary starting point of transformational leadership.

Flourishing is understood in expansive and active ways. The religious vocation is twofold: "the care of persons and the care of worlds."[7] Yet critics have noted that for much of the twentieth century, religious leadership has primarily been practiced in a personalistic mode and has not recognized the centrality of institutions in the ordering of human lives.[8] Attending to the wellness, wholeness, and flourishing of God's world in an expansive mode will mean critically engaging with the social order and working in and among organizational life to help humanize the organizations that give life in the twenty-first-century structure and hold them accountable to imagine and enact in a different way. Transformative religious leadership is meaningful, even sacred, work.[9] Indeed, communities of faith could be one of the best resources to help people live balanced and meaningful lives by offering theological, ethical, and practical resources to help transform corporate life and its impact on society; however, they remain "largely silent."[10] Critically engaging organizations, and their functioning and processes, is indeed the responsibility of theologically trained transformational leaders, as they recognize the patterns of organizations that constitute the basic fabric of their society. One of the tasks of transformative religious leaders is to analyze and critically evaluate the perceptions of needs, requirements, or desires, on the one hand, and the definitions of what is right or good, on the other, to see whether that which is institutionalized is morally valid.[11]

Religious leaders are called to be engaged in this effort and bring not just the ability to critically evaluate and analyze organizational life against a vision of flourishing but also to develop and leverage the skills to help change organizations considering that vision as well. In this way, religious organizations can be understood as communities of life, where members can practice flourishing in unique ways. Religious leadership as a form of public theology constructs theories and practices of personal and corporate care, contributing to the "constructive theological task and the common good by identifying, evaluating, and modifying the technical practices, core meaning systems, and normative value structures operating within and between all the efforts of care brought to bear upon individuals and groups within the organized common life."[12] And this work is needed now more than ever.[13]

Because for-profit organizations (and many not-for-profits as well, including misled houses of worship) are driven by neoliberal capitalism that prioritizes the financial bottom line, fierce competition, and goals of productivity, they can crush the heart and soul of their members, killing the life spirit and limiting the definition of flourishing to monetary terms as the neoliberal capitalist system they seek to emulate tries to transmute human souls into human resources for financial gain. However, organizations are not necessarily always a threat to members' well-being. Organizations can support people, and well-led organizations are essential to people's well-being. Religious leaders are called to promote flourishing, which requires critical and productive engagement with the social order even as they resist its oppressions. In fact, by avoiding the arenas of work and organizational life and focusing primarily on the realms of familial relationships and individual experience, religious leaders have avoided key social contexts that are significant sources of psychic and spiritual distress, thereby losing opportunities to address some of the common roots of contemporary dis-ease among those they seek to serve. People experience some of their greatest distress (and also for some, a sense of fulfillment and even joy) in the organizations of which they are a part. A robust theology of organizations is important both to critique current practices and to provide both members and leaders with a realistic and practical vision of the purposes and meaning of good organizations. Religious leaders can help people understand what a good organization looks like, why they are theologically important, and how they function when they are at their best. They can help develop a healthy organization in their role as a leader. By modeling new practices, transformational leaders offer imaginative possibilities and provide an example of what effective leadership toward healthy and life-giving organizations can look like. Genuinely transformational religious leaders also create opportunities for people to experience genuine, authentic, and life-giving community.

Religious leaders need more than a critique of the alienating and exploitative dimensions of organizations, however; they also need to think of ways to redeem them to make them more conducive to human flourishing. Transformative religious leaders can be an important part of imagining organizations that are life-giving rather than life-denying. Institutions and the organizations that mediate them are the *necessary* contexts within which people live; they are fallen and can and must be redeemed if they are to support human well-being. When they fail to do so, religious leaders might also fail to recognize the ways *isms* (ethnocentrism, sexism, ageism, racism, trans- and homophobia, and classism, to name common forms of oppression in the United States) are mediated through organizational policies and structure, and the fact that organizational life is an appropriate context for pastoral (and prophetic) engagement.[14] Transformational leaders transform the expectations, *telos*, culture, people's experience of and the vision for their organization, creating a model of creative, adaptable, and sustainable organizations for others to learn from.[15] Unless they are recognized and addressed, organizational life can hide, normalize, and mystify the ways certain people are advantaged by the oppression of others.[16]

The most effective leaders enliven and direct the energy and sense of meaning, purpose, and values of those willing to follow them to undertake the good work that must be done. Transformational leaders do not have all the answers, but they do raise the important, insightful, courageous questions and help create formal and informal opportunities for the organization's members to engage those questions. This helps members understand what is important to the organization and its membership and how that relates to the mission of the organization. It helps them understand where challenges lie. Leaders are the most effective when they hold information-sharing meetings that help members understand each other's perspectives. Good leaders, leaders for the good—transformational leaders—help others see and diagnose what is happening at multiple levels, ask incisive questions, and frame conversations in ways that help others understand what is working and not working. They empower members to brainstorm ideas about how to move through challenges. Transformational leaders frame situations and events in helpful ways, a skill that takes insight, wisdom, and experience. They are clear about what they want to transform their organization and its membership into. Transformative leaders seek to change situations from what they are to something better; a transformational leader can be anyone who wants to help the organization become more just, inclusive, caring, sustainable, faithful, and sustainable.

Transformative leaders understand that change is inevitable, a constant, and they intentionally manage and direct the changes underway, guiding members to learn new positive and life-giving practices.[17] They understand that organizations are always changing even if they maintain some stable elements. This work requires continuous learning, however.[18]

Understand Organizations for Human Flourishing

Because humans (and, in fact, all creatures) naturally organize, organizations possess the potential to support flourishing and serve critical functions in societies.[19] Organizations help preserve cultural memory and enable positive collaborative efforts.[20] Each organization "enacts its vision of the 'good life,' if not for an entire society, at least for its members."[21]

The question of the purpose of organizations has been asked for millennia. In philosopher Aristotle's thought, the purpose of human beings is inextricably linked to humans' communal nature, wherein people come together in organized societies to seek mutual flourishing. Here, the *telos* (goal or purpose) of the sociopolitical establishment is to facilitate development "for the sake of the good life [*eudaimonia,* or thriving/well-being]."[22] Aristotle viewed organizations of various kinds—from family units to political bodies, businesses, and faith-based organizations—as vital to individual and communal human flourishing. Organizations provide social support and community, opportunities for meaningful engagement, employment and economic opportunities, opportunities to learn and grow, and the chance to create something meaningful with others. Simply put, people can achieve more together than they can alone, and organizations of all kinds are vital to human flourishing. However, not all organizations cultivate the thriving of their members. Organizations can also support exclusion, oppression, and suffering.[23] They often are systems that create suffering through unjust practices, hoarding of power, and the use of corporate resources for the good of just a select few.

Telos

Religious leadership ought to contribute to the common good by critically analyzing the norms and practices that structure common life and developing strategic practices to intervene, with an eye toward the well-being of both individuals and the social order, including the natural environment and the basic structures of life together.[24] Indeed, the values and biases carried by institutional policies and practices often operate to enforce and reinforce injustices and create contexts in which individual employees suffer.

Organizations are in place, at least ideally, to serve the common good and support the flourishing of all. Consequently, the institutions and systems that order people's lives are not inherently evil—not even financial institutions so caught in the neoliberal paradigm. Rather, they are good, have fallen, and can be redeemed.[25] The powers that organizations mediate do not simply destroy; they also make good possible. The challenge, of course, is that they often do good and evil at the same time.

An organization's *purpose and goals* (its mission, whether explicit or implicit) give it its moral value. The good, including human flourishing, is the goal, but how flourishing is understood in a particular organization, how the organization seeks to achieve it, and whether it accomplishes that are open questions worth considering. The point is that an organization's vision of "the good" and its goals in relation to this vision are moral considerations. Yet these purposes and actions may be interpreted as possessing different moral values. Religious leaders are responsible to create opportunities for those in their organization to define the good and develop the practices to achieve it. In other words, they need to attend to the culture of their organization.[26]

Culture

Organizational culture describes the internal world and "personality" of an organization, including its moral orientation, goals, and purpose.[27] An organization's values or culture does not only *describe* the organization; it also *prescribes*: Organizational culture sets the expectations for and fosters growth toward what an organization believes is necessary for its ongoing success and well-being. "That's the way we do things around here," some like to say, which is another means of describing an aspect of organizational culture.[28]

Implicit organizational culture is so powerful that it is difficult to shift. Organizations try to protect the values they have held over time by being slow and difficult to change (often because "this is the way it has always been"). Organizational culture can influence members of an organization to act in ways they would normally not act (either for good or for ill), both inside and outside the organizational context. Organizational values and culture support organizational preservation (or degradation) and even its resilience, which allow it to return to a stable state after a challenge.[29] However, although individuals often take on the culture of an organization (and live it out by engaging in well-established practices), it is also true that organizations often take on the moral codes of the people who lead and influence them. Thus, religious leaders can be active in positively shaping the moral cultures of the organizations to which they belong. Nonetheless, many pressures from within and outside an organization can complicate this effort. "'Organizational fallibility' is real," writes one scholar, "which is to say that all organizations are flawed, just like the individuals who comprise them."[30]

Fallibility

Organizations are necessary, though fallible, constructions of human culture and society. Human beings cannot live meaningfully without them, and so it behooves religious leaders to see how they might best influence organizations, not only supporting their survival but also seeking the flourishing of their members and the people and communities they serve, as well as the betterment of the organizations themselves.[31] Given the optimism that Aristotle and other thinkers had for the possibility of organizations to benefit humankind, a critical question is whether current organizations—including not-for-profits, houses of worship, and other values-driven organizations—can participate in improving the world and seeking the good for all. If so, it is important to explore what would need to happen for this to occur, given that so many of these organizations are driven by values and goals that are limited in their focus and are distracted by their own survival.

Unfortunately, despite Aristotle's optimism that organizations can serve as a vital part of human and societal flourishing, too often, organizations maintain control over a *status quo* of injustice and discrimination, promoting values of isolationism and capitalism rather than love, inclusion, and justice. Not only do organizations often improve the lives of people, especially their members; they are often a source of perpetuating evils such as racist, classist, ableist, homophobic, and misogynist perspectives and practices. These realities present a dual challenge and opportunity regarding the nature of organizations themselves.

Fundamentally, organizations consist of and are controlled by human beings. The same fallibilities that are present in individual people—selfishness, abuses of power, self-deception—are also present in organizations and their cultures and are amplified through the organization's structures and processes. A person who holds racist views, for instance, may enact (unknowingly, even) organizational policies and procedures that affect many individuals beyond the leader's personal sphere of influence, and this influence may then inform the organization's culture.[32] Change, however, is possible not only through the influence of a single leader (formal or not) but also through the activities of many of the organization's members.[33] Organizations can misuse their power to create structures that themselves become sinful when they reinforce and perpetuate systems of abuse, neglect, and exclusion. Even so, organizations have the potential to use their implicit power for great benefits. While there is always the potential for evil, systems can also aid in preserving and maintaining freedom, justice, and morality. An organization's resilience and openness to creative *re*organization can become a site where flourishing is promoted, influencing individuals away from negative patterns toward those that promote the flourishing of all.

Understand Organizations as Living Systems

Even though organizations often perpetuate evil, they do not *necessarily* do so. In addition, even failures can become points of growth—opportunities for organizational learning and reforming. Although an organization's resistance to change can too often perpetuate the negative aspects of cultures in organizations, it can also be understood positively in terms of organizational resilience. Resilience can be illustrated by a tree sapling: The wind may blow against it, but it bends with the wind rather than breaks under its power.[34] That is, eventually the tree will rebound from the stressor, at least somewhat changed by it but not destroyed.[35] This capacity is itself a type of strength—not a rigid and brittle strength but a strength displayed in its flexibility. If an organization is to be successful in the long term, it will have to weather any number of storms, many of which will be new and unanticipated. Because of this, if they wish to survive, organizations must be resilient, embodying an almost paradoxical mix of openness to change and commitment to already established, successful organizational values, a sense of purpose, and vision. There are continuity and stability even as things change. It is the values an organization holds, promotes, and embodies/models that can make the difference whether that organization is resilient or not. An organization interested only in its own survival is less likely to be strong enough to weather, for example, cultural changes than is an organization that values other virtues such as courage, care, integrity, service, and community and aims to form itself around those.

Because organizations can change—and, in fact, *necessarily* must change over time—the question that remains is *what type of change* will occur. Transformative leaders ask whether the organization will adapt in positive ways or become further entrenched in dysfunctional and life-limiting patterns. The fact that an organization *will* change is a necessary factor in its resilience. In one sense, organizations do change over time (they flourish or flounder as their context shifts, and their innovation or lack of innovation makes all the difference in their survival). However, organizations retain a particular identity: A fast-food chain does not suddenly become a motorcycle manufacturer, nor does a bank come to identify as a church.[36] These two aspects of organizational life (change and constancy) are related to each other in a mutually interdependent relationship often called a *dialectic*.[37] Neither aspect can be divorced from the other, but when speaking of organizational identity, constancy often wins out over change due to the strength of organizational culture and its resistance to change. This is not always to the benefit of the organization.[38] However, understanding that organizations are part of the ever-changing, flexible, and creative processes and that they can be self-renewing, resilient, and intelligent can help their leaders find new footing in shifting sands.

Organizations are almost always in flux, incorporating new members, responding to new challenges, trying new practices to meet the current situation. Nevertheless, one of the most significant characteristics of organizations is their resistance to change, which, in practice, gives them a lot of power. An organization's lifespan may go well beyond that of any one person. Indeed, by definition, an organization is a conglomerate of individuals, all working together for a purpose that suits them and the values they share, and it is also larger than any one or even a small group of them. Each organization develops unique practices, traditions, and values: a culture that transcends any one member. Each individual organizational culture has its own center of gravity, or fundamental purpose, that enables the organization to achieve its mission—whether that is to make money (as in a bank), protect a nation (as in the military), or create a community of faithful members who seek together to participate in the life of God.[39] Each organization creates its own set of rules, regulations, and policies that enable its members to fulfill its mission. These (which, collectively, comprise the organizational culture) may be consciously shaped, but more often, they are implicitly felt, learned, and carried on by members of the organization. Hence, one hears talk of toxic work environments or, conversely, of an organizational team so unified that the members feel like family. Both descriptions are naming the felt culture, embodying the values, goals, and practices of that specific organization.

As leaders better understand how living systems operate, they develop the skills they need: They become resilient, adaptive, aware, and creative—and they learn to cultivate the same in others, thereby distributing leadership responsibilities and capacities throughout the organization. These are skills transformative religious leaders need to transform stagnant and dying organizations.

Far from the mechanistic model of leadership influenced by a Newtonian cosmology, new science provides contemporary leaders with new possibilities. Rather than being responsible for having all the answers; providing the mission and values that others will adopt; and building the organization's structure, culture, and plans for its future, transformative leaders draw on the strengths and inherent wisdom of the members of their organization, the concerns and needs that brought them together in the first place, to find the best way forward. The fact that life is self-organizing allows leaders to create the conditions for creativity and reformation, drawing on those invested in the organization. As quantum science suggests and process theologies affirm, ours is a participative universe where nothing lives alone, and everything comes into being because of relationship. Leaders are working with webs of relations, not machines.[40] Given the fundamental relatedness of all systems, if one wants to make a system stronger, one must create stronger relationships and have faith in the processes of the system.

Effective leaders trust that the system can solve its own problems, and the solution the system needs are usually already present in it.[41] If an organization is struggling, this indicates that it lacks sufficient access to itself, its core identity, and the wisdom within it.[42] It may be lacking information, it might have lost clarity about who it is, it might have troubled relationships, it might be ignoring those who have important insights. To bring health to a system, leaders should connect it to more of itself.[43] Once an organization can do that, the primary change strategy becomes quite straightforward. To change and have a life-giving future, the system needs to learn more about its own values and sense of purpose. With strong and positive relationships, a clear identity, open communication and an abundance of knowledge about what is happening, and a procedure that members can process together, the system can heal itself.[44] Once the organization is "more connected to the truth of who it is, the more connected to its environment and [its members], more connected to people everywhere in the system," the members of the organization will begin to imagine new possibilities and develop greater capacities.[45] With leaders' help, members can explore and clarify the fundamental identity of the organization or community, examining who they are, who they aspire to become, and how they want to be together. Members need to be connected to new information, asking what else they need to know and where the new information is to be found. Finally, members need to reach out to those they may have not connected to before and develop relationships with people across the system, asking who else needs to be present to do the work at hand.[46]

Understand Organizational Dynamics

As people form organizations for various purposes, a world of shared meaning develops; relationships are established; information is noticed, shared, interpreted, and changed; and a culture or identity is formed.[47] The core of the organization emerges. As one leadership scholar writes, "All organizing efforts begin with an intent, a belief that something more is possible now that the group is together. Organizing occurs around an identity—there is a 'self' that gets organized. Once this identity is set in motion, it becomes the sense-making process of the organization."[48] In deciding what to do, a system's members refer to its sense of self, interpreting all events and data according to who they think they are together and who they aspire to be.[49]

Because identity is the sense-making lens of the organization, every organizing effort needs to begin by exploring and clarifying the intention and desires of its members. They must ask themselves why they are doing, what they are doing, what is possible now that they have agreed to try this thing together, and how this commitment connects to individuals' and the larger organizations' sense of values and purposes.[50]

When organizations are struggling or in crisis, as many religious institutions currently are, the most common response of both leaders and members is to hold more tightly to what has been done in the past. People are afraid and want to insist that an old system must work because it used to work. However, resisting change is not a productive way forward: "People come to resent the organization they created, because now it is a major impediment to their creativity, to their hope, to their dreams."[51] Leaning *into* crises can be a way forward if transformative religious leaders encourage all involved to let go of certainty and explore what is happening with curiosity and humility. If they can do this, religious leaders will be better able to create the conditions for the system to reorganize itself.[52] The human needs and desires that led them to organize in the first place—"to find more meaning in life, to bring more good into the world, to serve others—emerge with a new story."[53] By including members who are genuinely invested, the system will find its most workable structure, possibly a new identity, and even a new imagination for the future because an organization is a process, not a structure.[54] As one organizational expert writes,

> Self-organizing systems have what all leaders crave: the capacity to respond continuously to change. In these systems, change is the organizing force, not a problematic intrusion. Structures and solutions are temporary. Resources and people come together to create new initiatives, to respond to new regulations, to shift the organization's processes. Leaders emerge from the needs of the moment. . . . Experimentation is the norm. Local solutions predominate but are kept local, not elevated to models for the whole organization. Involvement and participation constantly deepen. These organizations are experts at the process of change. They understand their organization as a process of continuous organizing. Self-organization offers hope for a simpler and more effective way to accomplish work.[55]

The path to self-(re)organization is never known ahead of time, but the domains of identity, information, and relationships operate in a dynamic cycle: New relationships connect more and more to the system, creating information pathways that affect the organization's identity. As information freely circulates, it creates new awareness and propels people into new relationships. As the organization responds to new information and relationships, its identity becomes clearer even as the organization changes.[56]

The work that faith-based leaders must undertake if they wish to contribute to a sustainable organization and human flourishing will require educating those in charge of corporate mission and culture about the responsibilities of organizations, helping them imagine the possibilities of contributing to the common good while attending to the survival of the organization. One way to do this is by developing leaders' (both formal and not) values, commitments, insights, identities, and purposes and asking how their values are being expressed by organizational policy and culture.[57]

CHAPTER 7

Leading Others

NO LONGER CAN formal religious leaders be expected to have all the answers, to alone know what is best, or to carry all the responsibilities of creating healthy, sustainable, and successful organizations. For one thing, the challenges leaders face are increasingly complex; for another, people in contemporary organizations are more assertive about how they want to be led than they might have previously been. A new vision of leadership resists the controlling, bureaucratic, untrusting, demanding, exhausting, and exhausted models of the past. They never were effective in the long term, and they will not help organizations find their footing in chaotic and uncertain times. Leaders who bring out the best in others, help create opportunities for others to do good work, enjoy healthy relationships, find and give support, and participate in what matters deeply to them create participative processes that produce stronger and more visionary organizations and resist the social ills of a fragmenting neoliberal society. Transformational religious leaders bring people together in meaningful ways—they listen, use conflict for good, and bring both clarity of vision for the kind of organization they want to help create and humility to know and practice that they are not able to do it alone. The most effective leaders resist the isolation, despair, and loneliness that plague people in organizations everywhere and even, perhaps, in themselves.

The model of leadership being advocated here requires slowing down, even in (especially in) the midst of chaos—to be still and calm, to listen quietly, to be responsive and not reactive, to stay grounded in one's own values and commitments to the greater good. Religious leaders across traditions and in a variety of organizational contexts find themselves in situations where their cultural capital is waning, their leadership is questioned, and their communities are faltering. This is the time to return to the basics—to lean into the deepest religious values of inclusion, belonging, justice, and care and to lead from those. Religious leaders' best ways forward include grounding in history while also imagining innovative ways of being faithful. Transformative religious leaders focus on service rather than authority and practice the future to which their God is calling them.

Today's most effective leaders know that people want to be a part of and contribute to something good that will leave a positive legacy for their children, neighbors, communities and the life of God. They know that work is meaningful when it contributes to this legacy. Today's most effective leaders learn how to facilitate processes that strengthen people, relationships, organizations, and communities. This is the work of truly transformational leaders: to attend to the invisible dynamics that will strengthen the fabric of all, for the flourishing of all. Attending to those dynamics requires recognizing and trusting the ways the universe and everything in it self-organize. It requires understanding how relational dynamics influence behaviors and the ways a shared sense of purpose that forms the basis of an organizational identity creates excitement and commitment among its members for the good work ahead. Understanding what motivates people, knowing how to work productively with conflict, and seeking to develop wisdom as their organization and its members learn together are basic practices of transformational leaders. In addition, continuously incorporating new information and engaging after-action reviews are ways to keep leaders, members, and organizations agile, innovative, and alive. Nurturing organizations where people make meaning together; learn how true community works; and teach skills for grieving, communicating, disagreeing, working together, and caring about others are the fundamental work of religious leadership.

Religious leaders are called to resist the evils of destructive social systems, both economic and relational, and to build genuine community in thriving organizations. This work is a good way to resist the ways neoliberal, extractive, divisive capitalism is destroying people's lives and to bring back hope to people and communities as they respond to God's longing for them to thrive. Religious leadership is a calling and a privileged responsibility that can upend the dominant social value systems in which people live, demonstrating a form of transformational leadership that genuinely transforms people and organizations.[1] The new model of leadership valorizes the soft, or people, skills that are necessary to form authentic connections with others.[2] Leading others well depends on leaders being able to understand both others and themselves, the capacity to understand what is going on in people and in their organization, communication of those dynamics, and facilitation of processes for how these areas might be improved. These skills are what leaders use to unite people around their highest-order values and a common goal. This is spiritual work. It builds the sense of being held in trustworthy relational webs.[3]

Lead Positive Change

Being a transformational leader—one who can change people's minds and hearts, help them lean into their aspirational values and goals rather than their basest desires, and improve the processes by which things get done in an organization—requires the capacities to build strong relationships based on trust, empathy, and respect.[4] Getting to know others, including their values, strengths, and opportunities for growth, is the first and most important skill to bring to the leadership role. To be able to communicate the shared goals that emerge once a leader begins to really listen is the second most important skill to develop. That is followed by the capacity to lead by example, especially when things are difficult, and to share a compelling vision and purpose that resonates with members' (and leaders') values and aspirations.[5] The most effective leaders demonstrate integrity, honesty, and professionalism in their actions, decisions, and relationships. The ability to admit mistakes and learn from failures and from others, and the willingness and capacity to show vulnerability and humanness when appropriate, will go far in bringing others along. By constantly sharing and referring to the compelling vision that is emerging as people begin to talk openly and honestly with one another will motivate others to be challenged and to learn.

Effective transformational leaders set high standards and expectations, give lots of productive and developmental feedback, and celebrate people's and the organization's successes along the way. Helping members of organizations develop clarity about what they want to achieve and why, giving them decision-making power, allowing them to make mistakes, and trusting they are making good-faith efforts all increase participants' willingness to take ownership and lean into the work that needs doing. By delegating to others, matching responsibilities with individual strengths and interests, and providing encouragement and resources along the way, effective leaders present opportunities for people to grow and learn, one of the most highly prized capacities of any organization.[6]

Holding after-action review sessions in which members and leaders can weigh in without judgment about what is working and what might not be working provides opportunities for coaching, skill development, higher levels of success, and increasing confidence. Effective leaders can foster collaborative environments by being supportive and inclusive; modeling effective behaviors; and fostering a culture of mutual trust, cooperation, and shared accountability where everyone feels empowered to contribute. Transformative leaders model adaptability and resilience in the face of challenges and approach change as an opportunity for growth and innovation. By recognizing the diversity of talents, experiences, perspectives, and passions, effective leaders help create opportunities for everyone to contribute their unique strengths and insights and generate an environment where everyone feels included and respected. By showing compassion toward all and by understanding their feelings, concerns, and needs, effective leaders can demonstrate kindness and patience and cultivate an organization where all members feel welcomed and valued.[7] These capacities engender inspiration, passion, innovation, and hard work. A transformational religious leader's primary responsibility is to create an organizational culture that creates a place where people want to be and bring people together to decide what the most important work is and how best to accomplish it.[8] Previously dominant models of leadership that have prized individualism and competition will eventually lead twenty-first-century organizations off the cliff they are currently teetering on.[9]

Rather than taking control, transformational leaders are the disrupters of the status quo, gentle disturbers of the old ways.[10] By attending to what is not working, by inviting new and perhaps surprising information, transformative leaders help harness the inevitable processes of chaos and change to help the organization and its members find their way forward into new forms of the collective. By attending to what is already falling apart, transformational leaders need not create new chaos but work better with what is already at hand.

Part of the crucial information transformational leaders incorporate is the nature of the real organization, not the idealized one. Genuinely transformational leaders lead conversations in which members of the organization name the hard truths about what is happening, what is not working, and the threats the organization is facing. They acknowledge what is working well with appreciation and manage the grief about what is falling apart while still knowing that the new version cannot form until the old is dismantled.[11] Transformational leaders work with instability, change, chaos, and surprises, helping create vibrant and sustainable organizations. Genuinely transformational leaders understand that every relationship, every person, allows for new possibilities, new visions, new directions and should be valued, in part, for that.

Truly transformative leaders know that positive emotions are contagious, and that genuinely positive leadership energizes others and motivates people better than any other form.[12] Transformational leaders trust that people self-organize around the values, the attractors, that matter to them. Transformative leaders hold things more loosely even as they are deeply committed, and they trust in others' capacities and motivations; in fact, sometimes the formal leader's best decision is to get out of the way and let others lead.

Lead with Values

To hold steady to what matters most to them, as well as to the organization and its members, religious leaders must be able to explicitly articulate the values that orient their purpose. All leadership (and, indeed, all human action) is based on values.[13] However, most leaders do not know how to investigate *which values* are being embodied in their organization, nor do they know how to critically analyze whether those values are the most important—in fact, generative—values.[14] Religious leaders gain significant resources when they examine and clarify which values drive their leadership, which values are embedded in their organization, and whether those are the most life-giving values possible.

All organizations are structured around and led by implicit values. Those that are intentionally led using positive values "are the most successful organizations on the planet."[15] People are increasingly choosing to be a part of organizations where they feel they are treated with respect, openness, transparency, and fairness and are valued as people.[16] They want to be free to take responsibility and accountability for their own lives, to exercise their own agency in community, and to be able to trust and be trusted. They also want to be part of an organization that is doing good for itself and for the community, and they will join something they feel resonates with their values and that they can take pride in. Most people in the industrialized West have their basic needs met and are looking to satisfy their growth needs.[17] Organizations that recognize people's "evolution in consciousness," the fulfillment that transitions from meeting people's basic needs such as food and security to nurturing their psychological development and capacities for wisdom and justice, for example, are desperately needed and wanted.[18]

Transformative leaders dispense with leadership models that depend on control, hierarchy, status, and fear and instead promote freedom, inclusion, equality, accountability, fairness, openness, transparency, and trust. By helping others build their skills, nurture their talents, and find their passion and sense of meaning and purpose, transformational leaders help meet members' growth needs, thus increasing members' capacities as well as their commitment and engagement. As one leadership scholar puts it,

> In the face of turbulence and change, culture and values become the major source of continuity and coherence, of renewal and sustainability. Leaders must be institution-builders who imbue the organization with meaning that inspires today and endures tomorrow. They must find an underlying purpose and a strong set of values that serve as a basis for longer-term decisions even in the midst of volatility. They must find the common purpose and universal values that unite highly diverse people while still permitting individual identities to be expressed and enhanced. Indeed, emphasizing purpose and values helps leaders support and facilitate self-organizing networks that can respond quickly to change because they share an understanding of the right thing to do.[19]

Values are the *sine qua non* of effective leadership: Who a leader is and what they stand for are more important than anything else they do.[20] Nurturing the growth of the members of an organization and creating identity cohesion and goodwill by clarifying values help leaders lead, especially in uncertainty. People and organizations need to be able to use their deepest held values to guide their decisions. What is done and how it is done must be guided by the most widely held values in the organization as well as the aspirational values that only a few can clearly imagine. An organization's most life-giving values must be embedded in every policy, system, and process of the organization and govern how members behave. They must be held up as the guiding centers of the organization and its leadership.[21]

Defined as a priority that people and organizations enact, values are the "ideals that give significance to our lives, that are reflected through the priorities that we choose, and that we act on consistently and repeatedly."[22] Values are universal and arise from the experience of being human.[23] They both express and change people's consciousness.[24] Values help determine human behavior by informing what meaning people make and which goals they have. Values enable people to understand the meaning of their feelings and behaviors, and they guide people toward their goals.[25]

People process information from two sources: the internal world of consciousness and their unconscious and the external world, "from the psyche and from the external world of sensory perception."[26] Values mediate this reflective processing by bringing the images of a person's consciousness into language and narrative form, or stories.[27] A person's values disclose important information about what they are experiencing and what meaning they are making of it. For this reason, values unveil people's inner dynamics as they are expressed in their everyday lives, making sense of their priorities, feelings, behaviors, and meaning-making processes. If a leader wants to better understand the members of their organization and why they think, feel, and do what they do, they will want to better understand their values.[28]

Values are embodied in organizational structures, expressed by organizational leaders, and captured in the cultures and policies of an organization. They shape commitments and goals and help determine the behavior of members through socialization. Organizations embodying high-level values contribute to a better world where justice, equality, creativity, health, balance, and ecological sustainability are built into the organizational life. These have enormous impact, not just on their members and the people those members interact with; they affect in enormous ways their local and global communities as well. However, nothing in the organization can change until the leaders' values and consequent assumptions about leadership and the organization become a "shared reality" of the system and its members.[29]

What is often required is a values shift at both the personal and organizational levels. Embodying values that are directed toward personal and social flourishing, as those at the higher developmental stages do, will increase the possibility of thriving for all. Holding and acting on values that are complex enough to enliven transformation at the social level requires a certain developmental achievement at both the individual and the organizational levels.

Both individuals and organizations develop more complex perspectives and understandings as they mature, and these perspectives help determine what is important and thus attended to in their lives. For example, a child whose highest-priority values are safety and security might actualize family/belonging over self-worth and hide the secret of abuse to preserve a relationship with the family member who is hurting them.[30] Values can change and have been shown to develop from self-interests such as self-preservation to other-interested and globally interested values such as world harmony as people mature.[31]

Research has shown that each person is motivated by values at three levels. First are those values that provide the basis of security (called *foundation values*). Then there are those that are actively being integrated in day-to-day life, which describe a person's present worldview, their criteria for decision-making, and the focus of most of their energy at their current state of development (one's *focus values*, such as education/certification). Finally, *vision values* such as global harmony and human rights are aspirational values and part of who a person wants to be.[32] Though values are mostly unconscious, they deeply shape people's and organizations' priorities and consistently influence actions and commitments. Identifying the operative values accelerates growth and the likelihood that higher-order values will be more consistently acted on. Helping individuals and organizations clarify and more intentionally live out their highest-order values is an important task for transformative religious leaders.

Certain values take precedence at certain stages of maturity, but change at the individual level is "intricately connected to organizational transformation."[33] This is true because "people are able to change when they get positive reinforcement from the institutions in their lives—their families, their schools and their work environments" and also because individuals and organizations are mutually constitutive.[34] Individual change requires organizational and systemic change and vice versa.[35] Individuals develop when the organizations of which they are a part embody high-order values toward which they can aspire and grow—values that raise their consciousness and enliven their moral imaginations. This raised consciousness then lures people further into the ongoing process of maturation.

Values are closely related to human needs.[36] In fact, they help individuals meet their needs, both individually and collectively. Foundation values can be considered a reflection of what people consider to be their needs, and positive values create benefits because they enable people to meet their most fundamental needs.[37] Foundation values "support our individual and collective survival, and they help people and organizations improve the social conditions in which they live. Positive values build connectedness and help create the future people want to experience."[38]

This values model assumes that human beings desire to grow in maturity, and its founders argue that when people can meet their growth needs, they feel a feeling deeper than happiness; it is more akin to contentment, deep satisfaction, and joy.[39] When people feel deep satisfaction, they are more motivated to continue to meet their growth needs because they are discovering themselves and realizing their deepest values in the process, making meaning of their own lives in ways that resonate.[40] The key to finding joy and contentment is for people to create meaning in their lives, and this is best done together by living into shared values.[41] Thus, the key to getting people involved and engaged in an organization is to meet their basic needs and help them create a sense of meaning for their lives. Once people (including leaders) have examined and understood their own values, they can then align those with the organization's values by taking on responsibilities that express their passions.[42]

Values are significant components in the active construction of meaning making and are often understood across the phases of human development.[43] They develop and unfold in a person's life along a stage-like progression, from simple values that operate in the earliest years to complex values that do not develop until one has reached psychological maturity. The stage-like development of values is accompanied by stage-like shifts in a person's consciousness—that is, in their way of knowing and making meaning of their experiences.[44]

As predicted by various developmental theories, lower-stage values (foundation values such as safety and survival) continue to operate as priorities in people's lives regardless of the higher-stage values (vision values such as global justice, interdependence, and prophet/vision) they hold or the end goals they hope to achieve. The lower-stage priorities reflect the requirements of human existence imposed by people's basic biological, social, and psychological needs and dynamics. For example, difficult or traumatic experiences that affect such foundational needs as self-preservation and self-worth can quickly elevate those needs to a level of priority in one's life.[45] If these basic needs are not met, they can stunt one's development.[46] When basic needs are not met, they can act like rip currents, holding a person down, under the chaos of the storm, and limiting their developmental progress.[47]

Higher-stage values exercise a powerful effect on human development, operating as lures or strange attractors that pull people forward in their development as they seek to more fully embody their highest ideals.[48] As people mature out of adolescence, these higher-stage values exert an ever greater pull on their development.[49] Vision, or future, values are the more complex, higher-stage values toward which humans aspire. In general, developmental progress toward the higher-stage values is characterized by the increasing differentiation and complex integration of individuals and their environment.[50] Cognitively, the higher-stage values cannot be fully comprehended or appreciated without complex and highly differentiated conceptual understanding. For example, a person will find it difficult to understand how to sustain the global environment or develop deep wisdom without understanding biological, physical, economic, and social-political systems and their complex interactions.[51] The higher-order priorities—for example, the capacity to care about and serve others—require a great deal of maturity and differentiation to identify, accept, and regulate one's beliefs, feelings, and behaviors. Thus, personal development is necessary if a leader wishes to be positively transformative.

Human beings must choose and act in the present moment even as they consider an imagined future and are informed by memories of the outcomes of previous choices. A person's values are those images, past and future, that inform their choices and actions. Positive memories of past choices and actions, together with positive images of imagined future realities, set up a virtuous cycle of growth that enables one to make oneself vulnerable in risking new behaviors that expand one's capacities and achieve more adequate outcomes. As one values theorist argues, "When we can remember successful action in the past, we have confidence and can imagine creative alternatives for the future; this in turn generates possible new choices."[52] This virtuous cycle sets up a pattern of hope that fuels human growth and flourishing within the limiting conditions of existence.

Unfortunately, the contrary also holds true. A vicious dynamic can be established when the person has negative, painful memories of past choices and actions, together with negative images of the anticipated future. Guilt from past experiences of failure in trying to achieve one's priorities or goals, and anxiety about one's ability to achieve them in the future, create frustration and fear in the present and cause the person to act in ways that protect them from the anticipated negative consequences.[53] Prolonged or severe negative cycles create despondency. When the experience is traumatic and long term, as in the case of severe grief, the symptoms can be anger turned into depression, boredom, and apathy. Eventually, a person can feel that life is meaningless and begin to despair.[54]

A person's growth continues as their capacity to choose and act in ways that enable them to embody their vision values grows.[55] When people choose and act on their vision, or highest-level, values, they create a dynamic that generates hope.[56] Choices become meaningful as people learn that they enhance connection to and cooperation with, rather than alienation from, other people. This is the source of creativity and intimacy in people's lives. Human beings create when they have the freedom to choose, and they gain perspective on reality only as they can relate to others with care and authenticity. Usually this means confronting and working through the anxiety and fear people have about their foundation needs rather than denying them and helping people lean into their vision values even as they consolidate the skills at their focus level, such as the common focus values of Communication, Efficiency/Planning, or Authority/Honesty.

Lead to Serve

Devout Quaker and famed leadership expert Robert Greenleaf defined servant leadership, a model influenced by one's higher-level values, as flowing from the intention of serving others.[57] The difference between the leader-first approach and the servant-first approach manifests in the care taken by the servant to make sure that other people's highest-priority needs are being served first. Greenleaf argued that the best test is to ask whether those served grow as people and, while being served, become healthier, wiser, freer, more autonomous, and more likely themselves to become servants. In addition, serving leaders consider the effect of their work on those least privileged in society, asking whether they benefit or, at least, not be further deprived.[58]

Greenleaf argued that servant leadership is a form of leadership that emerges from a desire to serve the highest-priority needs of those least served in society.[59] It seeks to meet the foundational needs of those who have been under-resourced and strives to help them grow into their own capacities. Contrary to many recent and popular views, however, serving leadership, a form of transformational leadership, is always a distributed capacity.[60] In other words, leadership at this level of human development is not the possession of any one person in the system but, paradoxically, is a characteristic of the system itself, refracted and embodied in individual members. Serving leadership is different than all the earlier forms in that it not only moves beyond any form of autocracy but also transforms the value of independence into interdependence. It recognizes that when people build relationships with high levels of trust and appropriate intimacy, there is a synergistic creativity that cannot be obtained by any one individual. In other words, leadership at and beyond this cycle is always plural in form.[61] Serving, or transformational, leadership requires deep, personal engagement characteristic of intentional communities. Without such engagement, the skills required of leaders trying to operate at this level cannot be maintained.

Listen

Whether or not people have their foundation values met influences whether they will move into their future hope or despair. The same holds true for whether people can articulate their vision values. Hope is the activation of one's future values; despair is their negation.[62] Values, embedded in the stories and images of people's past and imagined future, give rise to their experience of hope or despair by informing their choices and shaping their actions.[63] Using stories to share values is one of the most significant acts a religious leader can engage in to spark others' growth as well as their own.[64]

Once a transformational leader has helped build the organizational culture around a set of shared values and a shared sense of purpose and identity, people will want to contribute, make positive changes, and adapt to the new information they are being provided. This depends on creating opportunities for people to get to know one another and what they care most about. Hearing one another's stories is the best way to begin to care about one another. Hearing one another's stories is a good reminder that human beings and experiences are messy and complex, but that people often care more and try harder than they are trusted to do.

Deep listening, sometimes called *active listening*, is a skill too few people, including religious leaders, have learned, even though it is one of the most, if not the most, important skills there is in transformational leadership. Good listeners are created as people feel listened to. Deep listening is a mutual and reciprocal process and hearing one another into speech is a gift. As one scholar states, "Being deeply listened to is so close to being loved that most people can't tell the difference."[65]

Coming to understand one another through deep listening to stories helps people make meaning of their experiences and identify what matters most to them, their values. Because meaningmaking is a fundamental quality and need of being human (some might say it is the fundamental spiritual need), hearing people speaking their own stories opens space within people and between people. By sharing and listening deeply to stories, people come to know and understand themselves better, where their feelings come from, what led them to behave the way they did, and what matters most to them and why. They often begin to reconstruct new interpretations of their experience as their stories are heard and told. This helps them reclaim a sense of agency and identity as they reframe and reconstruct the meanings of their experiences.[66]

All people long to be seen, understood, accepted, and cared about. They want someone to see their pain and understand something about who they are. They want their values to be understood and appreciated. Transformative religious leaders can hear and understand the significance of people's stories, facilitate processes of meaningmaking, and help people interpret situations and experiences considering spiritual and religious traditions. They bring a different angle of vision when they engage questions of meaning and purpose. The different angle of vision includes a religious perspective that sees people's experience in light of God's love and grace and cultivates the ability to discern the meaning people are creating in their lives through the lens of their values. This work is best accomplished by the practices of deep, or reflective, listening. This form of listening is active because it goes beyond passive hearing to attentive engagement. Deep, active listening involves a profound level of awareness and achieves a significant level of understanding, not just of the other but of oneself and God as well.[67]

Deep listening requires the full attention and concentration of the listener, not just to the words the speaker is saying but also to what they are communicating through their body language, tone of voice, facial expressions, and the emotional tenor of what they are communicating and how. Active listening begins with empathy, a desire to understand, and a nonjudging and less-anxious attitude.[68]

The reflective and engaged practice of deep listening has several components that are useful skills to develop.[69] To be an effective story companion, it is helpful to meet in a place that allows the story to unfold without interruption or distractions.[70] Giving one's full attention to the speaker includes using nonverbal cues such as nodding, maintaining eye contact, and even taking notes (with permission and a conversation about why one is taking notes and what will be done with them). Invite the storyteller to begin. When they have shared a coherent piece of their story, paraphrase what has been said, restating it in one's own words to show attention and understanding. It can be helpful to reflect, too, the emotional or experiential undertones of what is being shared. Ask whether the paraphrase is accurate. If the storyteller says yes, encourage them to continue. If they say no (perhaps an important detail has been missed or misunderstood), invite them to try again. Next, a good listener invites further sharing by saying something like "I noticed you mentioned grief. I wonder if you want to say more about that?" or summarizing/paraphrasing, as in "What I hear is that the sadness about losing your partner is affecting your life. Is that what you mean to say?" If the storyteller affirms that the listener has understood, invite them to go on. Again, if the storyteller indicates that the listener missed something important in the paraphrase or summary, allow them to correct the understanding and then encourage them to go on. Again, paraphrase and restate what has been said and check for understanding. Continue this practice until the speaker reaches what feels to them like the end of the story. Once the back-and-forth of telling and summarizing has come to a natural end, summarize the core message that has been communicated and affirm the emotions being conveyed.[71] Acknowledge and validate the person's feelings about what has been shared.[72] The summary and affirmation might be something like "You lost your partner three years ago, but you still miss them terribly and find it hard to experience joy in your life. I can see why getting out of bed some mornings would be difficult."

Along the way, when appropriate, the listener might ask clarifying questions to make sure they are understanding, but clarifying questions should not be used when they interrupt or derail the storyteller. Once the storyteller has shared what is important to them and has acknowledged that the listener has clearly heard not only the details of the story but also its meaning and significance, the story companion might explore the meaning of the story for resonance with what is happening in the present. Ask which elements are affecting the storyteller's feelings about a present situation. Inquire whether and how elements of the story might be used to encourage or guide the storyteller in new situations.

Transformative religious leaders genuinely care about others and their stories and understand deep listening as a sacred act. Being a story companion is a way to help others uncover root causes of their struggle and the values that are at play in how they make meaning of it.[73] As story companions, religious leaders pay attention to how God's story is woven into people's life stories. But serving and transformational leaders, who can come alongside others to transform pain into possibility and despair into hope, must pay attention to the environments of the storyteller as well. Religious story companions listen with four ears: two for the storyteller and their context, one for themselves, and one for God. They listen to the person's story while monitoring their own reactions. They listen for what matters most to the storyteller and attend to the story to deepen their appreciation for the other. They also listen for the ways God is speaking.

Sometimes stories change over time, and good story companions are open to the changes and curious about them; these changes are often a sign of developmental growth, of shifts in values, and of the new interpretations of life experiences this expansion of consciousness allows. As story companions, religious leaders use their imagination, empathy, and analytical skills to help provide a different angle on someone's story that the teller may not see.[74] Transformative religious leaders are aware of their own thoughts and feelings and can sit with others as they share theirs without needing to try to change them. They can sit in quiet reflection or prayer to reflect on the opportunities for learning and transformation that are in the story being told and heard.

Deep listening conveys a person's value not just to the listener but to the community and to their God as well. Deep listening can generate in storytellers a sense of being connected to themselves, to others, and to the Sacred. When people are in touch with their own values, hear others speak about what matters most to them, and connect to their desire to make even a small difference, people find new energy for the work and for relationships with each other. Values have enormous power for motivating people. As religious leaders guide those around them to find the *why* of what they are doing, people come together in powerful ways.[75]

By connecting people to their unique values, deep listening is a spiritual act.[76] Transformational and serving religious leaders develop the skills they need to ask good questions, to hear beneath and behind words being used to understand the real meaning of what is being said. They can listen with openness and curiosity, paraphrasing and mirroring and asking questions that help the storyteller better understand themselves and their experience. Effective deep listeners can clarify a storyteller's unspoken assumptions, beliefs, feelings, and values. Effective listeners are also able to help storytellers construct a preferred narrative that includes their spiritual self and life that will help them thrive, enabling them to more consistently live into their vision values.[77] Finally, transformative religious leaders can create space for the storyteller in their organization, helping them find a role that suits their capacities and values. Deep listening helps people examine their experiences, values, and beliefs to hear whether they are life-giving. Helping people identify their needs and values is a way to provide a way forward from despair to hope and love.

Story companions empower others by hearing into speech the meaning of the experiences in others' lives. The benefits of being able to deeply hear others (and, for that matter, oneself) include enhanced relationships and deeper connections, increased empathy, conflict resolution, and trustbuilding.[78] These outcomes benefit leaders as they seek to deepen relationships, build authentic communities, and collaborate on a vision and path forward. By helping people tell their stories, explore those stories' meanings, and relate them to what is happening currently, leaders help others find their way forward. They increase trust and clarify the values and passions others have for important work, enhancing the motivation to engage in it.

Transformative leaders understand that the values of those gathered give rise to the values, mission, and identity of the organization. Being clear on members' values as well as the operative values of the organization is vital. It can be equally important to discern which values are shared, which are not, and whether the values of current members are reflected in the mission, structure, policies, and processes of the organization.

Motivate

Community members' level of commitment and engagement in the organization is directly related to the level of emotional and intellectual attachment that members have with an organization. This has a direct impact on the amount of enthusiasm and commitment they bring to their work.[79] The three factors at the heart of engagement in any organization are autonomy, mastery, and purpose.[80] Autonomy is the freedom to make choices about how, where, when, and with whom people choose to relate to and work alongside. Mastery is the desire to get better at something that matters to them and others, and purpose is when people "hitch their desires to a cause larger than themselves."[81] When people feel aligned with the mission, vision, and values of an organization, they commit to the work that organization requires to sustain itself.

For Aristotle, acquiring the virtues that create *eudaimonia*, well-being or flourishing, requires more than studying or habituation; it requires a kind of practical wisdom or mastery that comes only with autonomy and a sense of purpose. Aristotle understood the good life to require that people both live up to their fullest potential and find happiness, but he also argued that *eudaimonia* requires that each person contribute to a just and well-functioning community and society. Thus, the good life for Aristotle had everything to do with people's character development and meaningful participation in the state, or *polis*, to support the well-being of others. Both relate directly to the continuing development of values as individual members of a community and as an organization.

Certain external conditions must be present for the cultivation of higher-order values, though these conditions are often out of the full control of individuals. People must live in a community and state (*polis*) and in organizations that allow them to live well, grow, and thrive. The role of the *polis*, Aristotle argued, is to help individuals progress from a vicious, primitive state to a virtuous, mature one. Laws help citizens choose the right actions, and as people habituate to what is right, they develop an affinity for what is good and right, and they will choose the good in the future.[82] Communities and the organizations that structure them can be part of this work as well.

People need to part of something that matters to them, and most want to participate in cocreating the common good. They also need to feel heard and understood. Life is often cruel, and the current fragmentation and dissolution of authentic communities in which people can be cared for make the needs for genuine engagement even more acute. Religious leaders are on the front lines of spiritual care in their organizations and the wider community, and this care is the foundation of their transforming, serving leadership. When difficult things happen, people need to be able to make meaning of them, reflect on their experience, and explore how it will inform their lives going forward. When a religious leader helps in that work, people become especially attached to them. People care about those who care about them; when people are attended to, they attend to others. Purpose is related to meaning-making, which is also related to motivation, and these processes help people become more human together.[83] When people become more human together, they are more willing to take risks together, to make sacrifices for one another, and to bind together as they sense themselves connected to something that transcends their own lives.

Hearing people's stories helps others get to know them, care about them, and better understand them. Having a sense of people's values gives leaders a point of connection and shared purpose. People who are deeply connected to a cause do not need directives, rewards, or leaders to tell them what to do. When people work with informed, passionate, and like-minded others, they find creative pathways to accomplish their goals. When leaders understand that values are what motivate people, they can tap into them to empower and transform the ways people work together and what they are working toward. The power of creativity and passion and the sense of purpose that all people carry are lost when leaders insist on hierarchies and control-and-command leadership. The best way to release the capacities in people to accomplish meaningful work is to help them identify and then tap into what matters most to them with creativity, freedom, and mastery.

Motivating others, then, does not come from the outside but rather from helping them trust their own passion, values, and sense of direction.[84] A combination of shared purpose and the freedom to determine one's own actions is how systems grow to be increasingly effective and energized. Transformational, serving leaders help define the shared purpose by listening deeply to the stories and the meaning-making efforts people engage in and the values of those around them, helping them find a common cause that is always related to the identity of the organization and its mission.[85] Keeping the identity and shared values and mission of the organization in front of people as they are making decisions is one of the most important things a transformational leader can do. This is high-level and challenging work. Getting distracted by the day-to-day management of the organization can allow leaders to lose sight of the core purpose and identity of the organization, and when that happens, people lose the North Star, the attractors, the values that can best guide their actions. Bringing people together to share their guiding values and to discuss with one another what that star means to them is a way to both honor the diversity among them as a desirable norm and unite a diverse group of people in meaningful ways.[86]

People will come together around those who really see and understand them, and they are willing to make sacrifices for others when they feel valued, cared for, understood, and respected. When transformational leaders help people listen to themselves and others, they strengthen the relationships between them, which always increase the possibilities for the good work that can be done. Transformational leadership is not a competitive endeavor; it is a collaborative, relational, and distributed one. When people agree on what is a worthy pursuit, they will come together to accomplish it. Transformational leaders need to personally know those around them: their emotions, values, sense of purpose, strengths and growth edges, hopes, and dreams. When people feel seen and understood, they are much more willing to step into the breach and give their best to the work at hand.

Communicate

One of the most important skills for transformational leaders is to listen. A second skill leaders must cultivate if they want to transform the ways the organization functions, change the ways people engage, and build a sustainable community is the capacity to communicate well. Good, clear, frequent, thorough, and honest communication to remind stakeholders of the urgency for change, the costs of not changing, the shared values directing them, the vision they hold, and mission and purposes people want to accomplish can develop a common commitment to move forward. Clarity about what is working and what is not working is the best way to help others understand what is happening in the organization, giving members opportunities to think creatively about ways to address the challenges, nurture the possibilities, and begin to take steps toward change. Clearly and frequently communicating the vision of the future that is emerging helps give people something to aspire and work toward.

Effective communicators know their audience and tailor their messages accordingly. This means that communicating and listening are two sides of the same coin. When leaders truly listen to another to understand their perspectives, values, experiences, and sense of purpose, leaders can communicate with them in ways that will connect. The importance of quality communication holds true no matter the form: Speaking, emailing, and writing are all forms of communication that need to be clear, frequent, and honest.[87] Effective communication gives people the information they need to decide how to take the next step.

Mentor

Creating an organizational culture in which people (including leaders) are expected to change, grow, and be challenged is an important factor in transformational and serving leadership. Best practices in developmental, or growth-oriented, feedback are relatively simple, but they are not easy. Effective practices include being specific about the behavior being observed, focusing on the impact on oneself or the group, using "I" statements, and welcoming discussion.[88] Feedback providers must always leave the recipient free to decide whether, how, and when to change their behavior; this is part of leaving people free to be autonomous, to decide whether a change would help them more closely align with their intent and sense of purpose, and to develop mastery on their own terms.

Building a feedback-rich environment, which is required if people are going to grow and change, also requires that all parties need to expect to both give and receive feedback. When one is receiving feedback, it is important to remain open-minded, seek clarification when the feedback provider is saying something that is not clear, reflect on what has been said and how it can be applied to enhance one's skills and capacities, and ask for ongoing feedback on the changes one has made.

Solve Complex Problems

Conflict is one sign that communication and understanding has broken down and people are not open to others or feeling free to be themselves.[89] Each person (including the leader) brings to an organization their own experiences, interpretations of experiences, values, needs, and emotions. Conflict often arises when goals, responsibilities, and roles—and perspectives on those—differ. It can occur when people have different information, when their interpretation of that information varies, when the information has different effects on people, and when their needs and values are not being met. Transformational leaders transform conflict from something that creates distance and dissonance to something that brings people to deeper levels of understanding and cooperation by helping others (and themselves) listen carefully for the roots of conflict.[90] Understanding where people differ in five elements of relationship and communication and *why* they think differently about them can help deepen connections between people and bring them together to collaborate more effectively, creating win-win solutions that accomplish the shared goals. These elements include the data each party is working with, their beliefs/assumptions about that data, the impact (usually feelings but could be more than feelings) they have about the data and their beliefs about it, their needs, and any solutions they hope to achieve.[91]

Systems thinking, rather than individualistic thinking, is the key to achieving sustainable, breakthrough change.[92] Following a well-established process can be a way to change conflict into something productive. Challenges and conflict, if led well, can be the source of great growth and creative endeavors, bringing the best out of people, groups, and organizations. Transformational leaders can help shift the negative, angry energy in the room and among people by following a carefully prescribed process by seeking to understand.[93] Transformational leaders gather all the key stakeholders on an issue and follow the process in the order of these five steps.

Transformative leaders first cool the heat in the room so that people can get quiet and begin listening to themselves and one another. Sitting in a circle, a form of equality and listening, can help reduce the drama in the room.[94] Circles can foster collaboration and more participation as the transformational leader invites people to respectfully speak about their position, experience, and feelings while others listen. Once people can speak honestly and hear one another to the point of understanding and accepting another's perspective, they can collaborate. A transformational, serving leader can begin by asking simple questions that focus on people's personal, values-oriented experiences of the issue, such as why this issue is important to them, how it affects their work or life, and what their experience has been in trying to resolve this challenge.[95] The desired orientation of this first step is patience and curiosity. Allowing everyone to speak in the same amount of time reduces anxiety. This is not a time for debates, though others may ask clarifying questions. Hearing people speak from their own perspectives increases awareness of the complexity of the problem and people's sense of connection with each other, even if they have different perspectives.[96] In this first step, the group members build the foundation for change and establish their readiness for it. They begin to see the benefits of change and the potential costs of not changing.[97] They start to shift from trying to optimize their own part of the system to understanding the relationships among its constituent parts.[98] This begins the process of change because it establishes the discrepancy between what people want and where they are.[99] At this stage, establishing a sense of urgency is crucial to gaining needed cooperation. This sense of urgency must be repeatedly communicated by the stakeholders of the organization.[100]

The next step is enriching through fruitful opposition. After the initial step of quieting and hearing, the group must return to the source of conflict, which is usually differences among the five elements described above: data, interpretation/meaning, impact, needs, and assumed solutions. In this step, the differences are clarified and amplified so that participants can gain more clarity on the complexity of the situation since no one person or position has the full picture. This step is best engaged around a square table, "where people are literally taking sides."[101] Each side is responsible for developing its position in depth to explore the rationale and logic of each position. At this point, compromise is not sought, but clear thinking and nonjudgmental respect for difference are needed. Toward the end of this step, the boundaries of the different positions will begin to soften, and people unite, wanting to solve the problem together.

The third step is magnetizing resources. Magnetized objects repel each other if the same poles are in proximity, yet when opposite poles are aligned, they snap together. After the first two steps of cooling down and enriching understanding, people more fully grasp the complexity of the issue and often feel good about working together to solve it. People will be "both tired and motivated, confused yet confident."[102] They will want to jump to solutions. However, if solutions are rushed, they will likely be the wrong ones. The shape of the group in stage three is a half-circle, where people are staring out at the empty side of the circle; this position is "inviting yet humbling."[103] Because they have gotten through the first two steps, participants feel more confident to engage in the third. Generosity should be the posture of this step: On flip charts in the incomplete side of the circle, fill one side with the summary of the understanding that the group has generated. Leave the other side blank to be filled in during this process. To help fill in the blank side, ask who else needs to be involved in the discussion, what the group's blind spots are, what is not yet known, and which further information or perspectives are needed. Those identified as needing to be included are invited. Whatever data are missing is researched and presented for discussion. There must be sufficient time allotted for this stage, though a realistic but efficient timeline needs to be set.

The penultimate step is precise destroying, often the first response of leaders and members of an organization when things are not going well, but if this step is engaged prior to the other three, "weapons of mass destruction rather than smart bombs" are typically used.[104] Destruction is part of the cycle of life (creation, destruction, recreation). Everything has a season, and all organizational structures, processes, values, commitments, and habits eventually lose their effectiveness. As much harm can be done in holding on to ineffective elements of the organization as introducing new ones.[105] However, destruction must come only after careful clarifying and identifying of what is working and what is not. At this stage, "precision destroying is necessary to create more capacity for the work going forward."[106] After the first three steps, participants can now see what is impeding the sustainability, creativity, and (re)formation of the organization. They ask what has been tried and what the effects were of those actions.[107] The shape the group takes in this fourth step is the triangle with a white board or flip chart at its narrow apex. The triangle is a stable shape allowing for "naturally compassionate" precision destroying.[108] Because the group members have coalesced around clarity of the problem(s) and are joined in their commitment to solve them, the energy in the room is kindness and focus. No longer are people acting from self-defensive postures. Because of the narrow apex in the triangle, only a few things can be destroyed. In this step, many things must be considered for destruction: outmoded beliefs, regressive values, traditions that no longer meet needs, dysfunctional behaviors, aspects of the culture that inhibit growth and change, programs that are no longer useful, policies that do not work as intended, and individuals who refuse to change or who block forward movement.[109] This careful and disciplined discernment allows for real clarity about what must be destroyed first, and how.

The fifth and final step is figuring out together how to take intelligent action.[110] This step harvests the work of the first four steps. The smart and collaborative group can now see the complexity of the challenges and the multiple elements at play. Members have become better listeners to one another and more open to and curious about others' perspectives. The group has become more intelligent, diverse, inclusive, confident, and collaborative. The core behaviors in stage five are commitment and teamwork. The form for this stage is the existing organization and its familiar processes of prioritizing, action planning, strategy setting, budgeting, employing trial and error, and performing after-action reviews. Newly developed insights can be used to intelligently determine together which next steps make sense. This is an opportunity for the group to assess who is responsible for what and what people are willing to do to support the mission of the organization. At this stage, it is important to remember that change takes time, "sometimes lots of time."[111] Ensuring that people design short-term wins is crucial so that they don't lose hope.[112]

After engaging these five steps, group members need to be prepared for significant changes in the organization. Once any group has developed this level of insight and relationship, they cannot be pushed back into small boxes or compliant behavior: "With their intelligence awakened, people want to contribute, want to change things, want to make things happen. They will work with existing structures and processes, but they will be altering and adapting them as needed."[113] Leaders who fear a loss of control will attempt to rein in such groups. Their own fear sends them back to the familiar patterns of command and control.[114] However, an effective, transformational, serving leader allows what the group has accomplished to guide the organization's change processes and can celebrate how much the group has done for the common good.

Following this process can help leaders transform conflict into productivity; failing organizations into thriving ones; and stuck people into growing, creative, and engaged members of the community the leader is trying to lead.

* * *

Transformational religious leaders support the psychological, relational, and spiritual development of the people they serve by creating structures, policies, systems, processes, and a culture that allows them to care for one another; form relationships with others in the community; excel at what they do best; nurture and encourage autonomy, freedom, and creativity; generate meaning and a sense of common purpose; have opportunities to make a difference; and, if possible, leave a positive legacy.[115]

Genuinely transforming leaders create a culture of individual and organizational growth and ongoing values-driven collaboration. Thriving organizations are those in which the expectations of listening and collaborating to define what is working, what is not, and ways forward are understood to be key to organizations' creative sustainability. The five-step process of cooling down, enriching opposition, finding magnetic resonance, employing precision destroying, and intelligently moving forward is an effective tool for building community, strengthening an organization, and finding ways to evolve. After-action reviews, as described in chapter 5, can be effective tools for ongoing learning and directing change, especially after the five-step process. When groups gather and ask themselves what just happened, why it happened, what can be learned from it, and how to apply the lessons, people begin to trust one another to experiment in good faith, learn from their failures and successes, and try again.

This is the work of generative, transformative, serving leadership, and it is also the hard work of building authentic community around shared values. It is a way effective religious leaders can help people have an experience of inclusion, justice, and care, which they crave. Doing this work in religious or values- and mission-based organizations can be a way to resist the despair-inducing realities of the contemporary world and promote life-giving organizations and processes.

People are motivated and engaged when they believe in what they are doing; when they feel included, respected, and valued; when they are given the opportunity to be creative and bring their best, try something, and learn from failures and successes; and when they are learning how to do the deeply human and restoring work that authentic community requires. Caring about the needs of members (their basic, foundational, needs and their growth/vision needs) is significantly correlated to an organization's success, and there are three primary reasons that transforming, serving religious leaders are well suited for this work. First, they often have experience with their own growth processes and can offer appropriately complex explanations that account for the ways past personal experiences shape and intersect with present contexts to inhibit growth and well-being. Second, at the individual level, they often already participate in the personal development and self-actualization of other individuals, guiding and supporting them as they develop increasingly deep and spiritual awareness of themselves and increasingly complex understandings of the world and their relation to it. They help people devise strategic and effective interventions toward individual and organizational/systemic change. Third, transformational, serving leaders help others see the ways current structures impede human flourishing and create suffering, articulating a theological vision for the longing God has for God's creation. Religious leaders, drawing on the best of their religious and spiritual traditions, can support their efforts to change the status quo; challenge business as usual, both explicitly and subversively; and cultivate an organization that is motivated by and expresses morally adequate values more consonant with the flourishing of all.

A transformational, serving leader helps their organization find a strong narrative about itself and its identity, where it comes from and where it is going. They focus on people and give them responsibility; treat them as valued individuals; and support, stretch, and encourage them. In this way, members are given a voice to reinforce or challenge existing views.

CHAPTER 8

Leading Self

MOST RELIGIOUS LEADERS want to contribute something positive to the organization they are responsible to lead. Most religious leaders want to leave a positive legacy and be remembered as someone who made a significant difference in the lives of those they served. The most effective leaders are those who create "islands of sanity" where people are seen as fully human despite their being reduced to consumers in a destructive neoliberal environment.[1]

People want to be in organizations where they experience healthy relationships and life-giving community, even amid social and organizational chaos; life-limiting social, economic, and political systems; violence; and isolation. Religious leaders of various organizations are invited to ask who they choose to be for this time and to reflect on how they might use their power, position, and influence to create spaces where people can be human together, where they can learn how to work productively with change, conflict, and difference and find paths forward together. Even with faith, religious leadership in the twenty-first century takes courage, clarity, and stamina. Transformational religious leadership requires the capacity to see the big picture and attend to organizations as well as human beings and lean into moments of possibility. Truly transformative religious leaders make actions primary while also trying to be present to feelings, beliefs, challenges, and selves. Successful religious leadership today requires learning new perspectives and skills that allow for a fresh mode of leadership.

If genuine flourishing requires, at its most fundamental level, interdependence, creative participation, and responsiveness, then lack of awareness of the interrelatedness of the world must be a root impediment to thriving. *Not* flourishing has something to do with believing and acting as if one is disconnected from oneself, others, and the Sacred, the goodness beyond Being, or God.[2] When one inflicts pain on others intentionally or out of ignorance; when one serves only one's own interest; when individuals and systems impoverish, exploit, or deny basic rights (including recognition, dignity, and justice) to anyone; when people incite hatred or denigrate others; and when groups resort to tribalism and define their identity by the exclusions fueled by mistrust and contempt, then they deny creation's radical interrelatedness. Even though flourishing has to do with a sense of fulfillment, meaning, abundance, and joy, not all that feels pleasant or good supports flourishing. The work of flourishing includes coming to terms with one's proper place within the great nest of being, in which everything and everyone are understood to have an ontological value, and to find ways to cultivate the wholeness of other people and the systems that support them.

A life of well-being—or better, flourishing—is a collective endeavor that has unique, local, contextual, and deeply personal aspects. Flourishing necessitates the development of one's strengths and the possibilities for living out one's deepest high-level values. Flourishing requires being clear, realistic, and honest about one's gifts and limitations and having opportunities for ongoing growth and development.[3] Flourishing depends on both opportunities and capacities for self-definition and self-expression through imagination, reflection, and creativity. To flourish, one must be able both to experience and to develop one's exquisite uniqueness even as one develops moral capacities for generous participation for the good of others.[4] Flourishing is enlivened by and enlivens one's sense of being, a being animated by God's invitation to thriving in a world brought into existence by that life force—and loved by it. Experiences of flourishing increase as individual and group capacities for helping create and nurture such a world increase. Whatever *God* means to religious leaders, it must mean life—more life.[5]

Flourishing is active and perspectival, both personal and communal. It is whole thinking and future-directed. The activities of flourishing hold together the now and the future. They attend to both the individual and the deeply personal while always keeping an eye on the world.[6] Those who would cultivate flourishing must be able to account for the many paradoxes of human existence, including care and accountability, giving and receiving non-possessive love, and committing deeply while holding loosely. Flourishing includes awareness and ownership of finitude, faults, and brokenness—one's own and others'. The flourishing of all requires taking responsibility for and being accountable to the wounds each, in their finite humanness, inevitably inflict on others. Because of this, practices toward flourishing must incorporate coming to some terms with the losses and inevitable griefs of life rather than their escape. The fullness of one's humanity—which necessarily includes finitude, pain, and grief—must be included in an understanding of flourishing. For this reason, flourishing will require that people (including leaders) are resilient, courageous, resolute, responsive, relational, dynamic, and responsible to one another, themselves, God, and the earth, both in periods of intense activity and in quiet solitude.

Cultivate Wisdom

The complex task of flourishing requires the exercise, practice, or discipline of wisdom, which the Greeks considered the most important virtue.[7] Wisdom, defined as the "ability to make theoretical as well as practical distinctions that allow one to see beyond appearances, below the surface," needs to be developed so that one establishes intuitive knowing in a way appropriate to the situation.[8] Wisdom both comes from and allows the capacities to see the connections in one's life experiences, among all people, and, indeed, in all of life. It also comes from intentionally reflecting on one's experiences, values, behaviors, and goals as life is being lived. Taking care to apply what one has learned in one's moment-to-moment responses and behaviors is the "alpha and omega" of wisdom.[9]

Effective leadership requires deep reflection, self-awareness, and authenticity.[10] Values and beliefs are expressed through one's actions and behaviors, and in leadership—especially, perhaps, in religious leadership—actions have enormous consequences for the organization, for the spiritual life of a community of faith, and for the flourishing of its members. In religious leadership, those consequences are felt as being aligned or not aligned with the values of one's religious tradition and listening (or not) to the God of that community.

Shift Mindsets

Cultivating a particular mindset separates managers from leaders. Managers tend to value stability and can try to resolve problems quickly, sometimes before an issue is fully understood. Managers focus on tasks and are not typically responsible for completing more than their to-do list for each day. They stay inside the confines of a plan and are results-oriented, focused on shorter-term goals. Transformational leaders, however, think differently, envisioning the big picture and collaborating to create and improve a plan. Those with a leadership mindset tend to have a higher tolerance for ambiguity, chaos, and change. Leaders recognize the need to understand challenges as fully as possible and remain open to new information.[11] They are most effective when they surround themselves with people who understand the distributed nature of leadership and the importance of collaboration to do the work together. Leaders focus on the future, on processes, and on relationships. They can see and hold on to the big picture as well as attend to details, and they help others do the same. While leaders often manage, managers only sometimes lead, and it is not typically part of their job description. Leadership, especially religious leadership, is a unique endeavor, and the competencies for effective leadership must be developed and expanded over the course of one's career. Learning transformative leadership practices is a lifelong task requiring practice and a unique and authentic touch.[12]

Transformational religious leadership in the twenty-first century, in the context of neoliberal capitalism, invites, first and foremost, a clear understanding of the final *telos* of leadership: human thriving. It then requires certain qualities that include self-awareness, the capacities to understand others, the ability to see how systems function and affect individuals, and the capacity to remain present to oneself and to the other even amid conflict. The twelve capacities that make for the most effective leaders involve self-awareness, respect for self and others, compassion for self and others, vision, the ability to communicate well, the capacity to continuously learn and grow, the ability to collaborate, integrity, the capacity to positively influence others, courage, gratitude, and resilience/adaptability.[13] Transformative leaders have a passion for helping others succeed and for cultivating productive, engaged, and caring teams.[14] They accept responsibility even as they empower others. Transformational religious leaders nurture spiritual growth in themselves and others even as they attend to the development of capacities toward wisdom.

A transformational leader is a wise person who is skilled at analyzing what is going on, diagnosing what is not working, and clearly and correctly seeing what the processes of discernment should be.[15] But these capacities are significant achievements for those who accomplish them, and they are not guaranteed; growing into wise maturity and spiritual depth is not an inevitable outcome of life or the passage of time. To be developed most fully, these capacities require conscious effort, focused awareness, and a willingness to be vulnerable with oneself and others.

Notice

Since transformative leadership is about relationship, effective leaders become increasingly better systems thinkers, noticing the patterns of relationships between parts of organizations as well as the dynamics between people. They work to understand the systems they are operating in, and they notice the human beings who participate in those systems, remembering that interrelated systems are messy, ambiguous, uncertain, and sometimes volatile.[16]

Effective leaders can sort out the threads that connect people, decisions, and behaviors. Noticing who speaks to whom, who aligns with whom, and how things get done (or are avoided) is important. So is taking account of what is surprising or unexpected. Effective leaders can stay open to difference, to others' feelings and opinions, and are curious about both big-picture dynamics and individual dynamics. Truly effective, transformative leaders notice where the passion and energy are, both in themselves and in others, and know they are reflections of values. They learn how to understand others at a deeper and more complex level, discerning and exploring what is going on between and behind words.[17] The most effective leaders know how to listen deeply.

Listen

The German philosopher Martin Heidegger wrote that waiting and listening are the most profound ways to serve God.[18] As the biblical passage has it, "Whenever two or more are gathered in my name, I am there."[19] This suggests there is holiness in listening. By listening to one another, people can nurture wholeness in others and themselves.[20] When a leader listens, they move closer to the other and create the possibility of genuine relationship.[21]

Effective leaders create spaces in their offices and buildings that encourage informal conversations. Effective leaders also invite people to tell their stories more formally. Transformational leaders need time to reflect and listen to others, themselves, and God. But learning how to listen well, while relatively simple, is not easy and takes much practice.

If a leader has not been listened to well by parents, caregivers, friends, a partner, a therapist, a spiritual director, or a coach, it will be much more difficult for them to listen well to others.

When people listen, they are hoping to ascertain how a person defines their purpose, how they explain their current state, what their dreams and hopes are, what they see as the impediments to fulfilling them, what their deepest fears are, and which conflicts exist within their group and with other groups. Most leaders would benefit from training to be a good listener and to invite those in their midst to give ongoing feedback on their efforts to improve. Furthermore, listening can be anxiety producing. Hearing another's perspectives, feelings, needs, and visions creates a responsibility for the leader to respond, at least in some small way. Listening to others can create a burden on the listener. Listening to others gives voice to others' needs, wounds, longings, and hopes. Listening to themselves and others taps into the life force of leaders and of those they seek to serve.

Many leaders fear a loss of control and try to rein in the creativity, passion, and energy of those who would be co-leaders. Their fear leads to aggressive patterns of command and control. Wise and effective leaders, however, can notice, understand, and address their own fears and choose to respond in generative ways. The most effective leaders bring maturity, vulnerability, humility, clarity, and a sense of purpose to their role.[22] This often takes personal growth and intentional practice.[23]

Learn

Transformational leadership requires a commitment to lifelong learning and personal growth.[24] Leaders who can stay curious about themselves, others, the ever-changing organizational dynamics, and the longings of God are usually those most receptive to new ideas and experiences. When leaders seek opportunities for self-improvement, whether through formal education, professional development, coaching, or learning from evaluations and feedback from those with whom they work, they can continue to grow in their own understanding and capacities, and they can model for others what a growth-oriented organizational culture and a commitment to personal and collective development can look like. The most effective leaders are self-aware, self-disciplined, and self-motivating. Transformative leaders consider the needs and interests of others and, indeed, the common good, and they hold themselves accountable to create teams and an organizational culture that hold to the highest standards as defined by their religious traditions; this requires an ongoing growth of capacities and expansion of awareness.

By establishing specific, measurable, actionable, and time-bound goals in both the short- and long-terms, transformative leaders help shape what success looks like, both for themselves in their personal and professional lives and in the dynamics of the organization.[25] Developing habits and routines that support goals—including time management, prioritization, goal-setting, and reaching out to others—is a crucial skill for one's growth. Effective leaders prioritize and set goals by keeping the big picture in mind and putting the mission and vision of the organization, and for their own lives, front and center.[26] Goals can (and should) be broken down into smaller aims and the steps to accomplish them. Effective leaders find ways to celebrate even small wins that contribute to larger goals.[27]

The most effective leaders regularly seek feedback from others and reflect on their own performance and impact. When leaders create a feedback-rich environment, as described in chapter 7, they also invite feedback from others on their own efforts. By modeling the use of feedback in one's own growth and development, leaders help others change and grow as well.

Leaders who can take care of themselves (and invite others, such as a leadership coach, therapist, or spiritual director to care for and support them) are the most resilient leaders.[28] In other words, the capacity to cope with setbacks, failures, and challenges and even see these as opportunities for growth helps leaders maintain a positive mindset in the face of challenges.[29] Learning from mistakes and getting the support needed to be able to bounce back are critical.[30] Creating a culture of accountability for everyone, including formal leaders, is vital to building trust and genuine relationship, both of which are critical to effective leadership.[31] The most effective leaders take responsibility for their actions and mistakes, encouraging a culture of honesty and growth.[32] Transforming leaders take ownership of the consequences of their actions, working diligently toward building a positive culture and ensuring that the organization and its people are well cared for. They help keep people focused on desired outcomes and the processes by which to achieve those goals. Inviting others to provide feedback about decisions and behaviors presents an important model for others to do the same without fear of recrimination.[33]

Lead Thyself

In addition to leading organizations and other people, leaders are also responsible to lead themselves, and this may be the hardest task.[34] It may sound surprising to some, but each person has a certain relationship to different parts of themselves and is not always driven by their most mature, wisest self.

Scottish physician and psychiatrist Ronald Fairbairn argued that each person has three distinct parts:[35] One is an inner critic that is the internalization of critical and punitive voices one heard growing up. Another is the exciting self that seeks pleasure and craves excitement. This self can be irresponsible and seductive and can also bring joy and pleasure. Third is the central self, which is the core of executive functioning: the wise and responsible, mature and rational self that observes the other two parts. Leaders need to be mindful and self-reflective to know which self is leading at any moment. When the central self feels insecure or threatened, it can allow the inner self and the exciting self to take over to one's detriment. Any one of these parts can be the primary driver of people, and for leaders, prioritizing one part over the others can inform their leadership. Effective leadership requires effectively leading these three parts, ensuring that none takes control all the time.

Know Thyself

Leadership is fundamentally a task of relationship, of relating well to others and bringing them on board, getting them engaged in the processes of change. Good leadership requires a deep understanding of others and oneself, including strengths, challenges or limitations, values, beliefs, and goals. By reflecting on their passions, interests, and aspirations and identifying areas for growth, including personal and leadership development, a leader can make more conscious decisions and behave in ways that best align with their values, the organization's values, the religious tradition's values, and the goal of thriving for all. The most effective leaders have done a significant amount of their own internal work to build awareness of their own inner critics and exciting self and of how to bring their core self to the leadership role. They are aware of their biases, explore the possibility of blind spots, and work through their own life experiences, including trauma and grief, learning to set clear boundaries and practicing self-compassion.[36] They are clear about who they are and quietly confident in themselves while also being aware that they do not have all the answers, but they know what matters most to them and why.[37] Being quietly confident even in the face of challenges is a result of being differentiated.

Differentiate Thyself

People in organizations typically react to the emotions within the system.[38] Leadership requires being able to master emotional and relational processes, recognizing what one is feeling, how it differs from what others are feeling, and regulating all the emotions being experienced at once. But one must learn to manage oneself, to *lead oneself*, before trying to lead others. Effective leadership is tightly intertwined with the leader's self, and differentiation of self is crucial.[39]

Differentiation is a term from family systems theory, in which leaders are understood to have learned how to relate; manage emotions; respond to "exits" such as death, moves, and divorces and "entrances" including births and new relationships; and survive experiences of strong emotions.[40] People learn how to deal with emotions in their families of origin, and these lessons often affect how one leads.

Anxiety is a natural reaction to change, and most adults learned patterns of emotional reaction in their earliest childhoods.[41] However, repeating patterns developed in childhood rarely serves leaders well. Rather, leaders who recognize that there are systemic forces affecting their leadership are "less likely to get caught up in relational dynamics frustrating change and growth."[42] Leaders fail when they do not recognize the power of emotions in individuals and institutions because emotional processes "come before and outlast any leader" and determine all relationships and behaviors.[43]

When an organization is in flux (as they always are), it can be perceived as a threat and create anxiety among its members. The system and those within it will become anxious and begin to react in a variety of predictable ways. Some members will seek emotional distance and even leave the organization. Others will seek "deceptive emotional closeness," called *enmeshment*, and default to groupthink, where members are expected to think, act, and feel alike.[44] Some will triangulate, in which they gossip, keep secrets, and create moments of pseudo-intimacy to manufacture a sense of belonging, creating an in-group and an out-group.[45] There is also the possibility that people will become hostile and create conflict. Finally, some people (including any leader) might begin to overfunction, taking over the work and responsibilities that rightfully belong to others in an attempt to take control and bring down anxiety levels.[46]

There are several ways leaders can address these systemic patterns once they have noticed them.[47] First, try to create bridges to those who have distanced themselves; invite those who are silent to speak. Another strategy is to create distance with those who seek enmeshment with others by being clear about one's own thinking, feeling, and behaving and setting boundaries. An additional possibility is to avoid being pulled into triangles by avoiding gossip, maintaining confidentiality, and possibly bringing others into the discussion. It is advisable to learn to remain present during conflict and explore the deeper dynamics in it. Finally, it is important to learn to function for oneself, being clear about one's own goals, perspectives, and values. Emotionally differentiated leaders can "resist doing the emotional, relational, spiritual and even financial work for others," thus creating more stability in the system.[48] Effective leaders give the work back to whom it belongs, especially the emotional work.

Being a differentiated leader who can recognize the emotions in systems but does not get pulled into them lets others do the emotional work that belongs to them. Emotionally differentiated leaders can help others name what is happening. Their sense of self is strong enough to resist submitting to emotional manipulation, and they can understand what is emotionally happening in themselves, others, and the system. Well-differentiated leaders "will be much more effective than one who is easily swayed."[49] Well-differentiated leaders support others, encouraging them to do what personal and organizational work is theirs to do without trying to rescue anyone from discomfort or failure. They can recognize emotional triangles, avoid getting drawn into them, and empower others to function for themselves.[50] Well-differentiated leaders are less anxious about change and what the future holds, knowing they cannot control others or the future.[51] They are comfortable admitting when they are wrong or made a mistake and letting others take the lead, empowering them to succeed. In short, well-differentiated leaders are comfortable being human with others in their organization even while fulfilling the responsibilities of their role.

Where emotional processes are healthy and people are well-differentiated, people, relationships, and communities can flourish.[52] Ethical decisions are made for the greater good, and people learn and grow, becoming more themselves and more differentiated along the way. In poorly differentiated systems, leaders and members are chronically anxious and make poor choices; people leave, get sick or burned out, or "go to extremes to keep the illusion of power."[53] Effective, transformational leaders are differentiated people.

Well-differentiated religious leaders know themselves and their organizations, lead purposefully with the goal of thriving for all, and help lead for the common good. They lead with authenticity, humility, and the ability to be present to themselves, others, and God. They are transparent, competent, vulnerable, boundaried, and quietly confident, as they are grounded in their own values and sense of self.

Lean Into and Shift Values

Providing leadership through, to, and with organizations and the people within them means leaders need to be skilled in relationship building and understanding the culture, values, and expectations of oneself, one's organizations, and the individuals within the organization. Transformative religious leaders are open to points of view that differ from their own and are willing to compromise for the greater good. Working across differences is a fundamental skill, and religious leaders are called to balance when to be prophetic—speaking truth to power—and when to allow the group to find its own way. Religious leaders have the benefit of a moral tradition that stands outside the organization and provides guidance for it as they seek to effect change. Religious leaders are called to harness the existing strength and resilience of organizations but also to prophetically sharpen, clarify, and redirect the organization's potential.

People's experiences, beliefs, assumptions, biases, and feelings deeply inform how they perceive and understand the world, and this is not different for religious leaders. Knowing and understanding oneself is the first path to knowing and understanding others. Being able to reframe (shift the understanding) how religious leaders perceive themselves and others is an important skill. When leaders at every level of an organization lead with a sense of purpose and mission, no matter how small, they feel their lives have more purpose, which can generate a deep sense of contentment and even joy.[54] Values are the key to a sense of purpose and help one live with authenticity and integrity.

Leaders who know their own values and work toward purposeful goals for the good of the whole are more resilient, persistent, and hopeful than leaders who do not know their own values and try to move forward without them as a rudder in choppy seas. Effective and transformative leaders are clear on what they value, what their purpose is, and how these are reflected (or not) in their daily actions. Values help define people in their leadership and can be guides in turbulent waters. Transformative leaders use their highest-order values to shape the values of the organization. Being clear on one's own values and the (often unspoken) ones embedded in the organization is a critical step to becoming a transformative leader.[55] One's sense of purpose—or, in Christian language, call—defines oneself and is communicated by what one does. It is important to gain clarity about what is nonnegotiable and to create and tell the stories about one's values and where they came from, how they formed. Stories that incorporate what a leader loved as a child, what brings the most joy, what one dreams of, and how actions are expressions of values can bring others around and help them feel closer to leaders. The most effective leaders allow their values to guide their goals and the means to achieve them, and stories about significant moments in their lives can embody the values a leader holds.

Embrace Emotional Intelligence

Emotional intelligence (EQ) is related to emotional differentiation.[56] Leaders who want to be transformative must resist assuming the role of savior, even though people will expect and even ask for it. This can be increasingly difficult as people and the system become more fearful. Emotional skills are imperative, and effective leaders provide others with emotional support as well as guidance and accountability without getting drawn into the other's emotions. As the saying goes in coaching circles, everyone (especially leaders) must give the work (emotional and otherwise) back to those to whom it belongs. Leadership is about understanding people and building trust, thereby developing authentic relationships. When leaders know themselves and have meaningful stories to tell about their experiences, values, beliefs, and faith, they draw people toward them with their humility, confidence in themselves, clear boundaries, and sense of purpose, combined with their vulnerability. When people understand leaders and where they are coming from—when leaders are appropriately vulnerable—they are more willing to trust and take leaders' guidance.[57]

The most effective leaders are comfortable collaborating with others, relinquishing some authority and empowering others, and facilitating processes without determining outcomes. This means leaders must be able to help simplify the complex, be agile and flexible, and learn constantly and quickly. Effective leaders understand the need for and nature of change and are comfortable with ambiguity. By developing these skills, leaders can help inspire and develop others with the same mindset and help create self-managing teams. All change begins with changes in mindset and openness to new information.[58] Creativity and problem-solving can only emerge with a sense of curiosity, confusion, and trust that the processes of collaboration and thinking together will yield the next steps needed. When leaders admit their confusion and remain open and hopeful, others will adopt that mindset as well.[59] Effective leadership, then, requires learning to regulate one's emotions and maintain emotional balance, even in conflictual or challenging situations. It also requires being able to understand and explore others' emotions.[60] By developing their capacities for empathy, listening, differentiation, and purposeful change, leaders help transform their organization by dismantling its *isms*. Emotionally intelligent leaders understand that emotions such as hostility, bitterness, and rage are often the result of dysfunctions in an organization, and strong emotions such as these, as well as resistance to change, can be the emotional glue that holds the *isms* together in an organization.[61]

When leaders are congruent, they are more trusted. *Congruence* is understood as one's words and actions matching one's values and emotions. Congruence is important for leadership because people are often insightful: When a person is not congruent, others know it and trust the leader less. Congruent people can be less anxious and use their voice, body posture, and behaviors to bring calm to a situation even as they are present to the chaos of a situation and the anxiety in others. Less anxious leaders can bring down the anxiety in others and the intensity of a situation, even as others try to put their own unfinished business on a leader.[62] Ideally, leaders can rely on their own self-awareness and use their own experience as they work with and care for others; their own experience of grief, for example, can be used as a way to connect with and understand others' grief.[63]

Because of the complexities of emotions, the sources and meanings of people's feelings are not always clear. For this reason, careful and disciplined attention to emotions is critical to leadership and for cultivating flourishing in oneself and others.[64] This is especially true because people's avoidance or uses of emotions can be life-limiting. For example, emotions such as jealousy and hate—and the blame they often construct—are usually negative (though they may *feel* good in the moment) because they support one's personal desire to avoid humiliation, best a rival, or disassociate from someone or something one does not like. However, in the long run, these patterns do not lead to life-giving relationships, the capacity to manage conflict, or forgiveness. Although these emotions can be instructive about what matters to individuals and thus are valuable for that purpose, allowing certain emotions to perdure or acting on them is usually unwise. For this reason, the capacity to explore emotions artfully is a critical leadership skill. For example, a leader might ask why they are being affected by something that is happening, reflecting on why they are feeling a particular emotion in a certain moment, what beliefs have been or are being attached to similar situations, which values those beliefs suggest and how they shape one's behavior, which needs (foundation values) are at stake, where one learned such a response, in what ways an emotional episode is related to past experience, and in what ways it is related to the current context. It is important to ask what an emotional episode says about one's relational context, organizational context, or both; what one has learned about these feelings from parents, teachers, friends, or television; and whether there are other ways to think about or interpret their experience.[65] It can be helpful to reflect on whether there are worthier things to care about or behaviors that might need to change to shift one's emotions or the emotions of a group/system.

A deep understanding of emotions offers more avenues for exploration and engagement. Emotions, feelings, and behaviors are not automatic or given, even if they seem that way. Exploring emotions and the ways they are functioning in the current moment can allow for more life-giving engagement with oneself, others, and the world. To understand and use emotions in the cultivation of flourishing, leaders are helped when they keep in mind the origins and nature of emotions, analyzing critically the context in which emotions arise and recognizing that people often have varied and competing emotions simultaneously.[66] At the personal level, individuals ideally will become more aware of their own emotions and learn to explore, use, and, if needed, manage them. A leader might ask whether an emotion indicates the need for something to change (e.g., in a person, a relationship, or institutional or social policies). A leader might investigate whether one's own or one's group's emotions need to be changed or regulated. At the interpersonal level, flourishing requires these personal capacities as well as capacities for exploring, understanding, using, and sometimes managing others' emotions (i.e., exercising their EQ)—always toward the goals of justice, compassion, care, love, and respect. Add to these the ideals of diversity and inclusion, transparency, and a commitment for flourishing of the entire community. Using emotions in the pursuit of the flourishing of all will requires that all people concern themselves with what really matters (i.e., what God is calling them to) and develop the capacities and discipline to actualize that vision. Emotions are the tools that will enable this work at the deepest level. It takes courage to feel, but if leaders attend carefully to their own and others' emotions and let these guide them toward flourishing, such emotions will, in the end, help leaders to be successful.

If flourishing involves becoming as human as one can be and supporting the flourishing of others as fully as possible, then an important part of human flourishing is to embrace and develop each person's worth and value, uniqueness, and gifts.[67] It also requires that each person, and especially leaders, awaken to, own, accept, and address their own limitations, failures, inconsistencies, finitude, and wounds. This invites leaders to reflect on their own lives and on the world in which they live. By engaging in this work, leaders can be grounded in the realities of life, awakened to individual experiences, and emboldened to use their emotions to connect them to the truth of all humans' interdependence.

Address Power

Effective leaders can see and name the lived realities within their organization, especially in terms of who has power and who is silenced. Transformative religious leaders lean into the religious values of inclusion, justice, and care and ask whether decisions are made paternalistically or include those they will affect the most. Leaders who wish to increase justice and inclusion in their organization will need to become aware of how their own privilege and positionality obscure their ability to see how power flows and functions in their organization and the ways they are complicit in the processes and habits that create toxic stress, grief, and distress among members.[68] Well-differentiated and emotionally intelligent leaders can recognize that anger, fear, sadness, blame, guilt, hostile outbursts, denial, numbness, and disorganization can all be expressions of unprocessed grief, and they can help others name and explore those emotions. Change almost always means loss, and loss evokes grief. It is wise for leaders to remember that grieving organizations are filled with anxiety-ridden people and to do what they can to lower anxiety and attend to the unaddressed emotional undercurrents of grief and other emotions in the organization.[69] By listening to those who have been silenced and are experiencing isolation and loneliness, leaders can transform the dynamics of the organization, improve the ways meaningful information is shared, and include more members in processes of discernment and decision-making. In so doing, leaders also counteract the sociocultural trends of communal fragmentation and despair. By caring through listening and including, respecting and responding to the needs of others, religious leaders help create genuine communities in which others can find a place to belong—to be seen, understood, valued, and heard—and where they can grow in their own capacities to care and lead. This will also motivate others to take leadership responsibilities.

Efforts to transform an organization into an empathic, just, and moral entity depend on religious leaders with these values, whose identity and sense of vocation are inspired by their connection to the holy. In fact, the development of a spiritual identity is crucial because it can "disrupt the human experience of abandonment, loneliness, trauma, and grief."[70] Developing the capacity to care in the face of suffering helps people understand they are not alone and have a place among others who care about them.

Practice Hope

Hope is the bedrock motivator for religious leaders' work. Hope is understood as the desire for something to happen or to be true, accompanied with good reason to think it might.[71] Hope is sometimes understood as a problem-solving emotion. That is, it motivates people to do something to change a situation.[72] Hope is about anticipating the achievement of a meaningful good.[73] It also invites belief in someone's ability to achieve a goal, in which *someone* does not mean oneself only but also others or perhaps a societal institution or deity.[74] Some theories of hope describe it as a multidimensional concept that includes emotional, cognitive, motivational, social, and identity-related components.[75] There are distinctions between particularized hope, which is focused on a specific goal, and generalized hope, which is a more global feeling that there is some positive future a person might long for, even though they do not know what that future might hold.[76] Hope is also described as a "dynamic, cognitive and a motivational process."[77]

Understanding hope as a process rather than a state suggests that what hope means for a person or community can change over time. In addition, hope's focus and how it is experienced can vary.[78] Since hope involves a process of the ongoing appraisal of the likelihood of possible outcomes, consistent cognitive analysis for maintaining and achieving hopes, and repeated review of goals being pursued, people constantly adjust their hopes to meet the perceived chances of success.[79] For some, hope is about creating a narrative that makes sense of one's life by making a link between one's current situation and future. This creative process is motivated by an "active desiring" that allows people to envision alternative futures, set goals, and brace for possible negative outcomes.[80] Because hope is directly related to creative imagination, which is often related to a positive outcome, hope can help engender a sense of meaning and purpose in one's life, as it requires a fundamental openness to the future.[81]

Hope can be interpreted as a spiritual or theological virtue.[82] In fact, the Christian tradition includes hope in the list of religious virtues. These traditions can relate hope to faith, God's action in the world, and an ultimate meaning or end goal (telos) of life. Hope both reflects and can create the sense that people are part of something larger than themselves, instilling faith in people and even leading to spiritual experience.[83] In short, "everyone benefits from having hope."[84]

Hope can be an important activating force and help people stay focused and determined to reach their goals even in the face of obstacles.[85] Imagination is a necessary component of hope, as it allows people to explore future possibilities.[86] Because hope involves a capacity to imagine the future, even though the future cannot be known, it also involves a sense of trust.[87] In fact, people's capacities to imagine a certain future inform their expectations and aspirations. Because hope requires distinguishing realistic possibilities from fantasy, and because it requires trust and imagination, it involves creative, conscious, and rational thinking processes.[88]

Hope can be individual and also collective in the sense that it often requires a community to hold on to hope when individuals' sense of hope wanes and also in the sense that communities can share hopes and goals that nurture the good of the collective.[89] As a form of imagination, hope can allow people to transcend their situation and provide a "renewed zest for life" in difficult times, helping people and communities transcend their current situation and battle apathy.[90] Hope can entice people to invest in their future, and what is hoped for can have a large impact on how people feel and behave.[91]

People who are hopeful are usually more focused on their goals and the information that might help them achieve those goals.[92] Hope functions by inviting people to set goals, figure out pathways to achieve those goals, and focus on those pathways to maximize their ability to achieve the goals.[93] Hope serves as a motivational force that generates a drive for action, encouraging people to take action to achieve their goals.[94] In the face of obstacles and confusion about the way forward, hope can provide the persistence needed to stay the course even when the future is unclear.[95]

It is widely assumed that the opposite of hope is hopelessness; however, the opposite of hope is despair. Hopelessness can be a useful emotion, especially when the element of uncertainty in hope is forgotten and people begin to feel optimistic (or confident in an outcome, which is not hope). When people fight to hold on to cheerfulness or optimism, they often ignore what is really happening and do not attend to the emotions moving in them and their organization. There are times when accepting feeling stuck, or sad, or uncertain and staying there for a while is most productive, and leaders can help facilitate processes for attending to those emotions.[96]

Theologically, hope is understood as rooted in a dynamic relationship with an entangled, responsive God who is involved in the unfolding of the universe. God invites people and communities to co-create and participate in the processes of becoming something new. Because the future is always open, constantly changing, and always reorganizing, it is open, and new possibilities are always emerging. When religious leaders understand the nature of the quantum universe and learn to work *with* the change inherent in it, they lean into the fact that the future is not predetermined, and it invites participation into its next form. Transformative religious leaders trust that God is actively working in the world, inviting people and communities to respond to their realities with creativity and a moral vision. Because God is entangled with the world, relational and persuasive rather than coercive, religious leaders understand that hope is nurtured in relationships that value difference and new perspectives. Religious hope is founded on the trust that God yearns for love, justice, and wholeness—components of human flourishing—and is actively working toward it. As people and communities face their fears, turn toward one another, and attend to what is emerging, hope can be renewed and held by leaders and followers alike. Although the world is tragically structured, in the midst of that comes the life of God: connection, wisdom, and hope. Being human involves suffering. Human finitude invites theological reflection and the restoration of connection and meaning. Abundant life does not mean a life of material abundance but rather an abundance of the gifts of God: love, grace, mercy, forgiveness, and courage.

With hope, people lean into the virtues of compassion and wisdom, patience and courage. Religious leaders are called to be faithful, not successful. What being faithful means will look different depending on the context, the leader, the members of an organization, and the values at work therein. Practicing hope is vital for leaders and members of their organizations, especially when the outcome is unclear. It motivates people to continue the good work at hand. As Václav Havel, the former Czech leader, once offered, "Hope is not the conviction that something will turn out well, but the certainty that something is worth doing no matter how it turns out."[97] Thomas Merton, the well-known Christian mystic, further clarified the journey into hopelessness. In a letter to a friend, he suggested, "Do not depend on the hope of results. You may have to face the fact that your work will be apparently worthless and even achieve no result at all, if not perhaps results opposite to what you expect. As you get used to this idea, you start more and more to concentrate not on the results but on the value, the rightness, the truth of the work itself. You gradually struggle less and less for an idea and more and more for specific people. In the end, it is the reality of personal relationship that saves everything."[98]

People are comforted and strengthened by being together, and human thriving depends on it. Although people might wish for specific outcomes, they do not necessarily need them. They need help in being together, with authenticity and in a genuine community.

This is the work of transformative religious leadership. People can learn to live beyond hope or fear. Being together in authentic ways and engaging in meaningful effort is the antidote to the overwhelm of the chaos and violence all around. The real work is the process, not any apparent success. Flourishing is a practice, an activity, not a state. On that theme, famed Roman Catholic theologian and priest Henri Nouwen wrote,

> I stand among you as one who offers a small message of hope, that first, there are always people who dare to seek on the margin of society, who are not dependent on social acceptance, not dependent on social routine, and prefer a kind of free-floating existence under a state of risk. And among these people, if they are faithful to their own calling, to their own vocation, and to their own message from God, communication on the deepest level is possible. And the deepest level of communication is not communication, but communion. It is wordless. It is beyond words, and it is beyond speech and beyond concept.[99]

If ever there was a description of a differentiated leader, Nouwen's is one. Differentiated religious leaders who seek practices toward flourishing can do this work. They will ask themselves whether people become better versions of themselves under their leadership, whether they become more faithful to the God they worship, whether they become better at creating genuine community where people are valued as individuals and as loved creatures of God.[100] When religious leaders find themselves in a dark night of the soul, feeling hopeless, and they abandon their desire to be productive and in control, they can develop patience as they wait in hope, unsure of what the future holds but trusting nonetheless.[101] In this state, there is less anxiety. Because people often hope for the wrong thing or trust that what they hope for will come to fruition without their participation, they hope for specific outcomes (which, again, is optimism, not hope). And when people hope without participating in achieving the desired outcome, they are not practicing hope; either they are being optimistic when a particular outcome is never guaranteed, or they are leaning into despair.

Transformative religious leaders lead with hope but not optimism. They can lean into uncertainty and help others do so with less anxiety. Transformational religious leaders bring people together to face the realities of what is and join to do the work God is calling them to do. In so doing, religious leaders help resist what seems inevitable: the dissolution of communities of care and justice as they lean into love.

Nurture Self-Compassion

It is no secret that being in leadership is challenging, taxing work. It is an extremely complex and challenging role, whether that role is formal or not. The most effective leaders practice self-compassion and self-care and prioritize their physical, mental, and emotional well-being.[102] Creating boundaries is an important element of self-care, especially in the context of religious leadership, which is often not a nine-to-five, Monday-through-Friday position. Creating boundaries and carving out opportunities to attend to one's own health through regular exercise, proper nutrition, adequate sleep, stress management, positive and deep relationships outside of their leadership context, and a deep spiritual life are vital for one's own flourishing and effectiveness.[103] The same goes for ensuring there are opportunities to enjoy hobbies, time with loved ones, and activities that bring joy; being part of a community outside of the one being served is also critical.[104] Practicing self-compassion in these ways is an important model to others, sending the message that caring for oneself, leading oneself, and thriving are inextricable. If religious leaders seek to cultivate thriving in others, nurturing it in their own lives is crucial.

When leaders notice they are feeling tired most the time, withdrawing from responsibilities, losing interest in their work, and experiencing self-doubt or a sense of helplessness, it is their duty to get the support and care they need.[105] Focusing on what they can do and letting go of what they cannot control can be a helpful path. The most effective leaders practice self-compassion for their own needs and limits.

* * *

Religious leaders show up to serve. They feel a call from the Sacred to engage in good and meaningful work that will help nurture the thriving of the organization and its members they are responsible to. Transformational leaders want to express themselves fully and develop others around them so that they can express themselves fully as well. Transformative leaders understand that their leadership is not separate from who they are as human beings and that the more differentiated and deeper their spiritual lives, and the more whole they become, the stronger their capacity is to lead and serve. The most effective leaders understand that they do not have all the answers and that their job is to continue to learn and grow in the role. Leadership engages life, and each leader's path is unique.

Being a transformative religious leader invites curiosity about self, others, and God. It depends on the context within which one is leading, from the cosmological context to the global economic and political context, as well as their own organizational and psychological environments. Transformational leadership depends on being open to new possibilities and supporting the emerging form of a new organization. It brings with it a willingness to learn from mistakes and develop skills, especially soft, or people, skills so that others can help with the work of envisioning, hoping for, and working toward the future. Being a transformative leader demands the capacity to lean into uncertainty, chaos, and change with hope about what will emerge. Transformative leaders are constantly learning, taking risks with courageous intention. Transformational leadership requires having a humble and quiet confidence in oneself and one's own values. It depends on taking time and slowing down to reflect, discuss, and discern. It succeeds when small goals are realized and celebrated. Transformational leaders create new processes, invite in those who are silenced, and enact new ways of being together. They trust and are trustworthy. They are honest and transparent, open about their own limitations and humanness. They take responsibility even as they empower others. They engage in long-term thinking and realistic, short-term, actionable changes.

When transformational leaders serve, they help others come alive and cultivate their own flourishing. They bring life to organizations with their attentive presence, insight, and compassion. The capacity to stay in the stuck places and wait; facilitate grieving; and pay attention to one another, oneself, and God is the spiritual work of religious leadership. It may not *save* the world, but it is the unique way religious leaders *serve* the world.

REFERENCES

Ancona, Deborah, and Elaine Backman. "It's Not All About You." *Harvard Business Review* (blog), April 26, 2020. https://hbr.org/2010/04/its-not-all-about-me-its-all-a.

Anderson, Derek W., and Jaco J. Hamman. *The Essence of Leadership: Maintaining Emotional Independence in Situations Requiring Change.* Chalice Press, 2024.

Armstrong, Lisa. "Have Faith." *Working Mother*, December 2007 / January 2008, 53–56. *Working Mother* (New York, 1981), 2007–12, Vol. 31 (1).

Artson, Rabbi Bradley Shavit. *God of Becoming and Relationship: The Dynamic Nature of Process Theology.* Jewish Lights Publishing, 2013.

Ashby, Homer U. "Pastoral Theology as Public Theology: Participating in the Healing of Damaged and Damaging Cultures and Institutions." *Journal of Pastoral Theology* 10, no. 1 (2000): 18–27.

Aspinwall, L. G., and S. L. Leaf. "In Search of the Unique Aspects of Hope: Pinning Our Hopes on Positive Emotions, Future-Oriented Thinking, Hard Times, and Other People." *Psychological Inquiry* 13, no. 4 (2002): 276–321.

Augsburger, David. *Pastoral Counseling Across Cultures.* Westminster Press, 1986.

Azevedo, Flavio, John T. Jost, Tobias Rothmund, and Joanna Sterling. "Neoliberal Ideology and the Justification of Inequality in Capitalist Societies: Why Social and Economic Dimensions of Ideology Are Intertwined." *Journal of Social Issues* 75, no. 1 (2019): 49–88.

Barentsen, Jack. "Pastoral Leadership as Dance: How Embodiment, Practice and Identity Shape Communities and Their Leadership." *Practical Theology* 12, no. 3 (2019): 312–322.

Barnes, Jonathan, ed. *The Complete Works of Aristotle: The Revised Translation.* Vols. 1 and 2. Bollingen Series 71: 2. Princeton University Press, 1984.

Barrett, Richard. *Liberating the Corporate Soul: Building Visionary Organizations.* Butterworth-Heinemann, 1998.

Barrett, Richard. *The Metrics of Human Consciousness.* Lulu Publishing Services, 2014.

Barrett, Richard. *The New Leadership Paradigm.* Fulfilling Books, 2011.

Barrett, Richard. *The Values-Driven Organization: Unleashing Human Potential for Performance and Profit*. Routledge, 2014.

Barsade, S. G. "The Ripple Effect: Emotional Contagion and Its Influence on Group Behavior." *Administrative Science Quarterly* 47, no. 4 (2002): 644–675.

Bass, Dorothy, Kathleen A. Cahalan, Bonnie J. Miller-McLemore, et al. *Christian Practical Wisdom: What It Is, Why It Matters*. Eerdmans, 2016.

Bauer, Jack J., and Dan P. McAdams. "Growth Goals, Maturity, and Well-Being." *Developmental Psychology* 40, no. 1 (2004): 114.

Beauregard, Andre. "Writing a Public Theology Within the Challenge of a Pluralistic Society." In *Dreaming the Land: Theologies of Resistance and Hope*, edited by Hans-Georg Ziebertz and Friedrich Schweitzer, 152–163. International Academy of Practical Theology, 2005.

Benjamin, Walter. "Capitalism as Religion." In *Walter Benjamin: Selected Writings, Volume 1: 1913–1926*, edited by Marcus Bullock and Michael W. Jennings, 278–281. Belknap Press of Harvard University Press, 1996.

Benner, David. *Human Being and Becoming: Living the Interpersonal Adventure*. InterVarsity Press, 2003.

Bennett, Nathan, and G. James Lemoine. "What a Difference a Word Makes: Comparing a VUCA World to a BANI World." *Journal of Business Strategy* 35, no. 2 (2014): 20–28.

Benzein, E., A. Norberg, and B. Saveman. "The Meaning of the Lived Experience of Hope in Patients with Cancer in Palliative Home Care." *Palliative Medicine* 15, no. 2 (2001): 117–126.

Benzein, E., and B. Saveman. "One Step Towards the Understanding of Hope: A Concept Analysis." *International Journal of Nursing Studies* 35, no. 6 (1998): 322–329.

Bernardo, A. B. I. "Extending Hope Theory: Internal and External Locus of Trait Hope." *Personality and Individual Differences* 49, no. 8 (2010): 944–949. https://doi.org/10.1016/j.paid.2010.07.036.

Bertrams, Alex, Roy F. Baumeister, and Chris Englert. "Higher Self-Control Capacity Predicts Lower Anxiety-Impaired Cognition During Math Examinations." *Frontiers in Psychology* 7 (2016): 1–10.

Blanchard, Kenneth, and Spencer Johnson. *The One-Minute Manager*. William Morrow, 1982.

Bland, R., and Y. Darlington. "The Nature and Sources of Hope: Perspectives of Family Caregivers of People with Serious Mental Illness." *Perspectives in Psychiatric Care* 38, no. 2 (2002): 61–68.

Blevins, John. "Hospitality Is a Queer Thing." *Journal of Pastoral Theology* 19, no. 2 (2009): 104–117.

Bloeser, C., and T. Stahl. "Hope." In *The Stanford Encyclopedia of Philosophy*, Summer 2022 ed., edited by Edward N. Zalta. 2017. https://plato.stanford.edu/archives/sum2022/entries/hope/.

Bloom, Matt. *Flourishing in Ministry: How to Cultivate Clergy Wellbeing.* Rowman & Littlefield, 2019.

Bloomfield, Paul. *Virtues of Happiness: A Theory of the Good Life.* Oxford University Press, 2014.

Blum, Dani. "The Other Side of Languishing Is Flourishing: Here's How to Get There." *New York Times,* May 4, 2021, updated June 23, 2023. https://www.nytimes.com/2021/05/04/well/mind/flourishing-languishing.html.

Bohm, David. *Wholeness and the Implicate Order.* Routledge, 1980.

Bolman, Lee G., and Terrence E. Deal. *Reframing Organizations: Artistry, Choice, and Leadership.* 6th ed. John Wiley & Sons, 2017.

Bridges, William, and Susan Bridges. *Managing Transitions: Making the Most of Change.* Da Capo Lifelong Books, 2016.

Brown, Wendy. *In the Ruins of Neoliberalism: The Rise of Antidemocratic Politics in the West.* Columbia University Press, 2019.

Brown, Wendy. "Neo-liberalism and the End of Liberal Democracy." *Theory and Event* 7, no. 1 (2003). https://doi.org/10.1353/tae.2003.0020.

Bschir, Karim. "Potentiality in Natural Philosophy." In *Physics and Speculative Philosophy: Potentiality in Modern Science,* edited by Timothy E. Eastman, Michael Epperson, and David Ray Griffin, 17–46. Walter de Gruyter, 2016.

Burck, J. R., and Rodney J. Hunter. "Pastoral Theology. Protestant." In *The Dictionary of Pastoral Care and Counseling,* edited by Rodney J. Hunter, 867–872. Abingdon Press, 1990.

Burge, Ryan. "Why It Is Unlikely US Mainline Protestants Outnumber Evangelicals." *Religion Unplugged,* July 12, 2021. https://religionunplugged.com/news/2021/7/12/why-its-unlikely-us-mainline-protestants-outnumber-evangelicals.

Burns, James MacGregor. *Leadership.* Harper Perennial Modern Classics, 2010.

Butler, Lee H. *Liberating Our Dignity, Saving Our Souls.* Chalice Press, 2006.

Byrnes, Sarah, and Chuck Collins. "The Equity Crisis: The True Costs of Extractive Capitalism." In *The Community Resilience Reader,* edited by Daniel Lerch, 95–109. Island Press, 2017. https://doi.org/10.5822/978-1-61091-861-9_6.

Cabrera, Victoria, and Stewart I. Donaldson. "PERMA to PERMA+4 Building Blocks of Well-Being: A Systematic Review of the Empirical Literature." *Journal of Positive Psychology* 19, no. 3 (2023): 510–529. https://doi.org/10.1080/17439760.2023.2208099.

Cadge, Wendy, and Shelly Rambo, eds. *Chaplaincy and Spiritual Care in the 21st Century: An Introduction.* University of North Carolina Press, 2022.

Cambridge University Press. "Hope." *Cambridge English Dictionary*. Accessed July 13, 2024. https://dictionary.cambridge.org/us/dictionary/english/hope.

Cameron, Kim. *Positive Leadership: Strategies for Extraordinary Performance*. 2nd ed. Berrett-Koehler Publishers, 2012.

Campbell, James D., Dong Phil Yoon, and Brick Johnstone. "Determining Relationships Between Physical Health and Spiritual Experience, Religious Practices, and Congregational Support in a Heterogeneous Medical Sample." *Journal of Religion and Health* 49 (2010): 3–17.

Capra, Fritjof. *The Web of Life: A New Synthesis of Mind and Matter*. Vol. 132. 1996.

Caputo, John D. *Hoping Against Hope: Confessions of a Postmodern Pilgrim*. Fortress Press, 2015.

Carriera, Jeff. *The Spiritual Implications of Quantum Physics*. Emergence Education, 2023.

Carson, V., K. L. Soeken, and P. M. Grimm. "Hope and Its Relationship to Spiritual Well-Being." *Journal of Psychology and Theology* 16, no. 2 (1988): 159–167.

Carstens, F. J., and Neil Barnes. "The Quality of Leader/Employee Relationship in Business Performance." *Journal of Human Resource Management* 4, no. 2 (2006): 10–19.

Carstensen, Laura L., Monisha Pasupathi, Ulrich Mayr, and John R. Nesselrode. "Emotional Experience in Everyday Life Across the Adult Life Span." *Journal of Personality and Social Psychology* 79, no. 4 (2000): 644–655.

Chamberlain, Linda. *Strange Attractors in Patterns of Family Interactions*. Psychology Press, 1995.

Charry, Ellen T. *God and the Art of Happiness*. William B. Eerdmans, 2010.

Chignell, A. "The Focus Theory of Hope." *Philosophical Quarterly* 73, no. 1 (2023): 44–63.

Ciarrocchi, J. W., G. S. Dy-Liacco, and E. Deneke. "Gods or Rituals? Relational Faith, Spiritual Discontent, and Religious Practices as Predictors of Hope and Optimism." *Journal of Positive Psychology* 3, no. 2 (2008): 120–136.

Clapp, Rodney. *Naming Neoliberalism: Exposing the Spirit of Our Age*. Fortress Press, 2021.

Clebsch, William A., and Charles R. Jaekle. *Pastoral Care in Historical Perspective*. 2nd ed. Jason Aronson, 1994.

Cobb, John, Jr., and David Ray Griffin. *Process Theology: An Introductory Exposition*. Westminster Press, 1976.

Collins, Jim. *Good to Great: Why Some Companies Make the Leap . . . and Others Don't*. HarperCollins, 2001.

Collins, Jim, and Jerry I. Porras. *Built to Last: Successful Habits of Visionary Companies*. HarperBusiness, 1994.

Cone, James H. *A Black Theology of Liberation*. Orbis Books, 2010.

Cone, Jeremy, and Thomas Gilovich. "Understanding Money's Limits: People's Beliefs About the Income–Happiness Correlation." *Journal of Positive Psychology* 5, no. 4 (2010): 294–301.

Cooper, John M. "Eudaimonism, The Appeal to Nature, and 'Moral Duty' in Stoicism." In *Aristotle, Kant and the Stoics: Rethinking Happiness and Duty*, edited by Stephen Engstrom and Jennifer Whiting, 275–278. Cambridge University Press, 1996.

Cooper-White, Pamela. *Using Self in Pastoral Care and Counseling: A Narrative Approach*. Fortress Press, 2004.

Couture, Pamela. "Rethinking Private and Public Patriarchy." In *Religion, Feminism, and the Family*, edited by A. Carr and M. S. Van Leeuwen, 249–274. Westminster John Knox Press, 1996.

Cox, Harvey. *The Market as God*. Harvard University Press, 2016.

Cushman, Philip. *The Empty Self: A Psychological Perspective on the Social Condition of Contemporary America*. Guilford Press, 1990.

Davies, Paul. *The Cosmic Blueprint: New Discoveries in Nature's Ability to Order the Universe*. Templeton Press, 2004.

Davis, Andrew M. *Mind, Value, and the Cosmos: On the Relational Nature of Ultimacy*. Lexington Books, 2020.

Day, David V., and Stanley M. Halpin. "Growing Leaders for Tomorrow: An Introduction." In *Leadership Development for Transforming Organizations: Growing Leaders for Tomorrow*, edited by David V. Day, Stanley M. Halpin, and Stephen J. Zaccaro, 1–13. Lawrence Erlbaum Associates, 2004.

Day, David V., and Charles E. Lance. "Understanding the Development of Leadership Complexity Through Latent Growth Modeling." In *Leadership Development for Transforming Organizations: Growing Leaders for Tomorrow*, edited by David V. Day, Stanley M. Halpin, and Stephen J. Zaccaro, 93–120. Lawrence Erlbaum Associates, 2004.

Day, David V., Stephen J. Zaccaro, and Stanley M. Halpin. *Leader Development for Transforming Organizations: Growing Leaders for Tomorrow*. Lawrence Erlbaum Associates, 2004.

Day, Keri. *Religious Resistance to Neoliberalism: Womanist and Black Feminist Perspectives*. Springer, 2016.

Deci, Edward L., and Richard M. Ryan. "The Support of Autonomy and the Control of Behavior." *Journal of Personality and Social Psychology* 53, no. 6 (1987): 1024–1031.

De Meuse, Kenneth P. "Learning Agility: Its Evolution as a Psychological Construct and Its Empirical Relationship to Leader Success." *Consulting Psychology Journal: Practice and Research* 69, no. 4 (2017): 267–295.

Doehring, Carrie, and Allison Kestenbaum. "Introduction to Interpersonal Competencies." In *Chaplaincy and Spiritual Care in the Twenty-First*

Century: An Introduction, edited by Wendy Cadge and Shelly Rambo, 129–133. The University of North Carolina Press, 2022.

Dolan, Simon, Simon Landau, Simon Garcia, and A. Auerbach. "Understanding and Managing Chaos in Organizations." *International Journal of Management* 20, no. 1 (2003): 23–35.

Drahos, P. "Trading in Public Hope." *Annals of the American Academy of Political and Social Science* 592 (2004): 18–38.

Dykstra, Robert C., ed. *Images of Pastoral Care: Classic Readings.* Chalice Press, 2005.

Dykstra, Robert C. *Finding Ourselves Lost: Ministry in an Age of Overwhelm.* Cascade, 2018.

Dweck, Carol S. *Mindset: The New Psychology of Success.* Random House, 2006.

Eastman, Timothy E., Michael Epperson, and David Ray Griffin, eds. *Physics and Speculative Philosophy: Potentiality in Modern Science.* de Gruyter, 2016.

Einstein, Albert. *The Born-Einstein Letters 1916–1955: Friendship, Politics and Physics in Uncertain Times.* Edited by Peter L. Rosen, translated by M. J. Kenney. Palgrave Macmillan, 2014.

Elliott, J. A., and I. N. Olver. "Hope and Hoping in the Talk of Dying Cancer Patients." *Social Science and Medicine* 64, no. 1 (2007): 138–149.

Epperson, Michael, and Elias Zafiris. *Foundations of Relational Realism: A Topological Approach to Quantum Mechanics and the Philosophy of Nature.* Lexington Books, 2013.

Erikson, Erik H. *Childhood and Society.* W. W. Norton, 1950.

Erikson, Erik H., ed. "Growth and Crises of the Healthy Personality." In *Identity and the Lifecycle*, 51–107. W. W. Norton, 1980.

Erikson, Erik H. *The Life Cycle Completed.* W. W. Norton, 1982.

Fanon, Frantz. *Black Skin, White Masks.* Translated by Charles Lam Markmann. Grove Press, 1967.

Fanon, Frantz. *A Dying Colonialism.* Translated by Haakon Chevalier. Grove Press, 1994.

Fanon, Frantz. *The Wretched of the Earth.* Translated by Richard Philcox. Grove Press, 2004.

Farazmand, Ali, ed. *Modern Organizations: Theory and Practice.* Praeger, 2002.

Farley, Edward. "Practical Theology. Protestant." In *The Dictionary of Pastoral Care and Counseling*, edited by Rodney J. Hunter, 934–936. Abingdon Press, 1990.

Feldman, D. B., K. L. Rand, and K. Kahle-Wrobleski. "Hope and Goal Attainment: Testing a Basic Prediction of Hope." *Journal of Social and Clinical Psychology* 28, no. 4 (2009): 479–497. https://doi.org/10.1521/jscp.2009.28.4.479.

Ferry, Luc. *What Is the Good Life?* Translated by Lydia G. Cochrane. University of Chicago Press, 2005.

Foucault, Michel, and Colin Gordon, eds. *Power/Knowledge: Selected Interviews and Other Writings, 1972–1977.* 1st American ed. Pantheon Books, 1980.

Frankl, Viktor E. *Man's Search for Meaning.* 4th ed. Beacon Press, 2006.

Fraser, Nancy. *Cannibal Capitalism: How Our System Is Devouring Democracy, Care, and the Planet, and What We Can Do About It.* Verso, 2022.

Fraser, Nancy. *The Old Is Dying and the New Cannot Be Born: From Progressive Neoliberalism to Trump and Beyond.* Verso, 2019.

Freedman, Paul. "Islands of Sanity and Spiritual Leadership in a Time of Crisis: Margaret Wheatley and Paul Freedman in Dialogue." *Holistic Education Review* 4, no. 1 (2024): 1–11.

Fretheim, Terence E. "God, Creation, and the Pursuit of Happiness." In *The Bible and the Pursuit of Happiness*, edited by Brent A. Strawn, 33–55. Oxford University Press, 2012.

Friedman, Edwin. *Generation to Generation: Family Process in Church and Synagogue.* Guilford Press, 1985.

Ganz, Marshall, Julia Lee Cunningham, Inbal Ben Ezer, and Alaina Segura. "Crafting Public Narrative to Enable Collective Action: A Pedagogy for Leadership Development." *Academy of Management Learning & Education* 22, no. 2 (2023): 169–190.

Garland-Thomson, Rosemarie. "A Cross-Cultural Neuroethics View on the Language of Disability." *AJOB Neuroscience* 10, no. 2 (2019): 91–92.

Garrett-Cobina, Laurie. "The Emotional Undercurrents of Organizations." In *Chaplaincy and Spiritual Care in the 21st Century: An Introduction*, edited by Wendy Cadge and Shelly Rambo, 239–257. University of North Carolina Press, 2022.

Geller, Shari M., and L. S. Greenberg. "Therapeutic Presence: A Theory of Relationship." In *Therapeutic Presence: A Mindful Approach to Effective Therapy*, 51–72. W. W. Norton, 2012.

Geller, Shari M., and L. S. Greenberg, eds. *Therapeutic Presence: A Mindful Approach to Effective Therapy.* W. W. Norton, 2012.

George, Bill. *True North: Discover Your Authentic Leadership.* Jossey-Bass, 2007.

George, Jennifer M. "Emotions and Leadership: The Role of Emotional Intelligence." *Human Relations* 53, no. 8 (2000): 1027–1055.

Gergen, Kenneth. *Relational Being: Beyond Self and Community.* Oxford University Press, 2009.

Gilstrap, Donald L. "Strange Attractors and Human Interaction: Leading Complex Organizations through the Use of Metaphors." *Complicity: An International Journal of Complexity and Education* 2, no. 1 (2005): 55. https://doi.org/10.29173/cmplct8727.

Glubb, John. *The Fate of Empires and Search for Survival.* William Blackwood & Sons, 1976.

Goleman, Daniel. *Leadership: The Power of Emotional Intelligence.* More than Sound LLC, 2021.

Graham, C., and J. R. Pozuelo. "Does Hope Lead to Better Futures? Insights from a Survey of Young Adults in Peru." 2018-038. 2018. https://humcap.uchicago.edu/RePEc/hka/wpaper/Graham_Pozuelo_2018_hope-for-the-future.pdf.

Graham, Larry Kent. *Care of Persons, Care of Worlds: A Psychosystems Approach to Pastoral Care and Counseling.* Abingdon Press, 1992.

Graham, Larry Kent. "Pastoral Theology as Public Theology in Relation to the Clinic." *Journal of Pastoral Theology* 10, no. 1 (2000): 1–17.

Greenleaf, Robert K. *Servant Leadership: A Journey into the Nature of Legitimate Power and Greatness.* 25th anniversary ed. Paulist Press, 2002.

Grefe, Dagmar, Pamela McCarroll, and Bilal Ansari. "Meaning Making in Chaplaincy Practice: Presence, Assessment, and Interventions." In *Chaplaincy and Spiritual Care in the Twenty-First Century*, edited by Wendy Cadge and Shelly Rambo. The University of North Carolina Press, 2022.

Grey, Donald P. *Quantum Theory and Quantum Mechanics for Beginners: The Introduction Guide for Beginners Who Flunked Math and Science in Plain English.* Bluesource, 2020.

Grier, Nicholas A. "Building Our Power to Care for the World: Integrating Pastoral Theology, Mental Health, and Community Organizing." *Journal of Pastoral Theology* 30, no. 3 (2020): 197–206.

Griesemer, James R. "Sharing Spaces, Crossing Boundaries." 2016. https://doi.org/10.7551/mitpress/10113.003.0012.

Griffin, David Ray. *Panentheism and Scientific Naturalism.* Process Century Press, 2014.

Griffin, David Ray. *Religion and Scientific Naturalism: Overcoming the Conflicts.* State University of New York Press, 2000.

Griffin, Graeme Maxwell. *Coming to Care: An Introduction to Pastoral Care for Ordained Ministers and Lay People.* Uniting Church Theological Hall, 1995.

Gunderson, Gary. *Deeply Woven Roots: Improving the Quality of Life in Your Community.* Fortress Press, 1997.

Habermas, Jürgen. "The Public Sphere." In *Jürgen Habermas on Society and Politics*, edited by Steven Seidman, 231–236. Beacon Press, 1989.

Hall, Brian. *The Development of Consciousness: A Confluent Theory of Values.* Paulist Press, 1976.

Hall, Brian. "The Omega Factor: A Values-Based Approach for Developing Organizations and Leadership." Servant Leadership Forum: Serving

Students and the Common Good, 29, 2003. http://www.valuestech.com/gui/omegafactor4.pdf.

Hall, Brian. *Values Shift: A Guide to Individual and Organizational Transformation*. Berrett-Koehler Publishers, 2008.

Harver Team. "Learning Agility: What It Is and How to Assess It." February 13, 2024. https://harver.com/blog/learning-agility/.

Havel, Václav. *The Art of the Impossible: Politics as Morality in Practice: Speeches and Writing, 1990–1996*. Knopf, 1997.

Havel, Václav. *The Power of the Powerless: Citizens Against the State in Central-Eastern Europe*. Knopf, 1990.

Heidegger, Martin. *On the Way to Language*. Translated by Harold Hofstadter. Harper & Row, 1971.

Heifetz, Ronald A. *Leadership Without Easy Answers*. Harvard University Press, 1994.

Heifetz, Ronald A., and Donald L. Laurie. "The Work of Leadership." *Harvard Business Review* 79, no. 11 (2001), 35–48.

Helsel, Philip Browning. *Pastoral Power Beyond Psychology's Marginalization: Resisting the Discourses of the Psy-Complex*. Palgrave Macmillan, 2015.

Herbert, Nick. *Quantum Reality: Beyond the New Physics*. Anchor/Doubleday, 1985.

Hiltner, Seward. *Preface to Pastoral Theology*. Abingdon Press, 1958.

Hinds, Jay-Paul Michael. *A Gift Grows in the Ghetto: Reimagining the Spiritual Lives of Black Men*. Presbyterian Publishing, 2022.

Hogue, David A. *Remembering the Future, Imagining the Past: Story, Ritual, and the Human*. Pilgrim Press, 2003.

Holifield, E. Brooks. *A History of Pastoral Care in America: From Salvation to Self-Realization*. Academic Renewal Press, 1983.

The Holy Bible: New Revised Standard Version. National Council of Churches, 1989.

Hunter, Rodney J. "The Future of Pastoral Theology." *Pastoral Psychology* 29, no. 1 (Fall 1980): 58–69.

Hunter, Rodney J. "Participation in the Life of God: Revisioning Lapsley's Salvation-Health Model." In *The Treasure of Earthen Vessels: Explorations in Theological Anthropology in Honor of James N. Lapsley*, edited by Brian H. Childs and David W. Waanders. Westminster John Knox Press, 1994.

Illouz, Eva. *Saving the Modern Soul: Therapy, Emotions, and the Culture of Self-help*. University of California Press, 2008.

Insole, C. J. "Kant on Christianity, Religion and Politics: Three Hopes, Three Limits." *Studies in Christian Ethics* 29, no. 1 (2016): 14–33.

Irwin, Terence. *Aristotle's First Principles*. Clarendon Press, 1988.

Isasi-Díaz, Ada María. *Mujerista Theology: A Theology for the Twenty-First Century*. Orbis Books, 1996.

Jackson, Bailey W. "Theory and Practice of Multicultural Organization Development." In *The NTL Handbook of Organization Development and Change*, edited by B. B. Jones and M. Brazzel, 139–154. Pfeiffer, 2014.

Jackson, Bailey W., and Evangelina Holvino. "Multicultural Organization Development." 1988. https://deepblue.lib.umich.edu/bitstream/handle/2027.42/51124/356.pdf?sequence=1.

Jantsch, Erich. *The Self Organizing Universe: Scientific and Human Implications of the Emerging Paradigm of Evolution.*" 1st ed. Pergamon Press, 1980.

Jennings, Willie J. *The Christian Imagination: Theology and the Origins of Race.* Yale University Press, 2011.

Jenson, David. *Responsive Labor: A Theology of Work.* Westminster John Knox Press, 2006.

Johnson, Cedric C. *Race, Religion, and Resilience in the Neoliberal Age.* Palgrave Macmillan, 2016.

Johnstone, Brick, and Dong Pil Yoon. "Relationships Between the Brief Multidimensional Measure of Religiousness/Spirituality and Health Outcomes for a Heterogeneous Rehabilitation Population." *Rehabilitation Psychology* 54, no. 4 (2009): 422.

Kadlac, A. "The Virtue of Hope." *Ethical Theory and Moral Practice* 18, no. 2 (2015): 337–354.

Kanter, Rosabeth Moss. "Ten Essentials for Getting Value from Values." *Harvard Business Review* (blog), June 14, 2010. http://blogs.hbr.org/kanter/2010/06/ten-essentials-for-getting-val.html.

Karp, Tom. "Transforming Organizations for Organic Growth: The DNA of Change Leadership." *Journal of Change Management* 6, no. 1 (2006): 3–20.

Kegan, Robert. *The Evolving Self: Problem and Process in Human Development.* Harvard University Press, 1982.

Kegan, Robert, and Lisa Laskow Lahey. *Immunity to Change: How to Overcome It and Unlock the Potential in Yourself and Your Organization.* Harvard Business School Publishing, 2009.

Kegan, Robert, and Lisa Laskow Lahey. *The Real Reason People Won't Change.* Harvard Business Review, 2001.

Kendi, Ibram X. *How to Be an Antiracist.* One World, 2023.

Kerr, S., and S. Landauer. "Using Stretch Goals to Promote Organizational Effectiveness and Personal Growth: General Electric and Goldman Sachs." *Academy of Management Executive* 18, no. 4 (2004): 134–138.

Keyes, Corey L. M. "The Mental Health Continuum: From Languishing to Flourishing in Life." *Journal of Health and Social Behavior* 43, no. 2 (2002): 207–222.

Klein, Naomi. *The Shock Doctrine: The Rise of Disaster Capitalism.* Henry Holt, 2007.

Klein, Naomi. *This Changes Everything: Capitalism vs. the Climate.* Simon & Schuster, 2014.

Korejan, M. Moradi, and Hasan Shahbazi. "An Analysis of the Transformational Leadership Theory." *Journal of Fundamental and Applied Sciences* 8, no. 3 (2016): 452–461.

Korn Ferry. "Fast Rising Talent: Highly Learning Agile People Get Promoted at Double Speed." Accessed November 11, 2024. https://www.kornferry.com/institute/820-fast-rising-talent-highly-learning-agile-people-get-promoted-at-double-speed.

Kornfeld, Margaret. *Cultivating Wholeness: A Guide to Care and Counseling in Faith Communities.* Continuum International Publishing, 2002. Originally published in 2000.

Kotter, John P. *Leading Change.* Harvard Business Review Press, 2012.

Kotter, John P., and James L. Heskett. *Corporate Culture and Performance.* The Free Press, 1992.

Kouzes, James M., and Barry Z. Posner. *The Leadership Challenge: How to Make Extraordinary Things Happen in Organizations.* 6th ed. Jossey-Bass, 2017.

Kuhn, Thomas S. *The Structure of Scientific Revolutions.* 4th ed. University of Chicago Press, 2012.

Kupperman, Joel J. *Six Myths about the Good Life: Thinking About What Has Value.* Hackett, 2006.

Kwong, J. M. C. "What Is Hope?" *European Journal of Philosophy* 27, no. 1 (2019): 243–254.

LaMothe, Ryan. *Care of Souls, Care of Polis: Toward a Political Pastoral Theology.* Cascade Books, 2017.

LaMothe, Ryan. *Pastoral Reflections on Global Citizenship: Framing the Political in Terms of Care, Faith, and Community.* Lexington Books, 2018.

LaPorte, Nicole. "Are You There, God? I'm at Harvard: Why on Earth Are a Bunch of Successful Midcareer Professionals Quitting Their Jobs and Applying to Harvard Divinity School? Hint: It Has Nothing to Do with Heaven." *Town and Country,* November 3, 2024. https://www.townandcountrymag.com/society/money-and-power/a62786069/harvard-divinity-school-career-change/.

Lapsley, James. *Salvation and Health: The Interlocking Processes of Life.* Westminster Press, 1972.

Lartey, Emmanuel Y. *In Living Color: An Intercultural Approach to Pastoral Care and Counseling.* 2nd ed. Jessica Kingsley Publishers, 2003.

Lartey, Emmanuel Y. *Postcolonializing God: New Perspectives on Pastoral and Practical Theology.* Hymns Ancient and Modern, 2013.

Lartey, Emmanuel Y., and Melinda A. McGarrah Sharp. "Entangled but Not Entrapped: Pastoral Practices of Resistance from Within Selves and Systems." *Journal of Pastoral Theology* 26, no. 1 (2016): 1–2.

Laszloffy, Tracy, and Monica McGoldrick. *You Can Go Home Again: Reconnecting with Your Family*. 3rd ed. W. W. Norton, 2024.

Lear, Jonathan. *Radical Hope: Ethics in the Face of Cultural Devastation*. Harvard University Press, 2006.

Leritz, Len. *Interpersonal Negotiations*. AMACOM Division of American Management Association, 1994.

Leritz, Len. *No-Fault Negotiating: A Simple and Innovative Approach for Solving Problems, Reaching Agreements and Resolving Conflicts*. Grand Central Publishing, 1990.

Leung, K. K., J. L. Silvius, N. Pimlott, W. Dalziel, and N. Drummond. "Why Health Expectations and Hopes Are Different: The Development of a Conceptual Model." *Health Expectations* 12, no. 4 (2009): 347–360.

Lin, Tom C. W. "Financial Weapons of War." *Minnesota Law Review* 100 (2015): 1377.

Lizardy-Hajbi, Kristina Isabel. "Frameworks Toward Post/Decolonial Pastoral Leaderships." *Journal of Religious Leadership* 19, no. 2 (2020): 100–130.

Lizardy-Hajbi, Kristina Isabel. *Unraveling Religious Leadership: Power, Authority, and Decoloniality*. Fortress Press, 2024.

Lorenz, Edward. "The Butterfly Effect." *World Scientific Series on Nonlinear Science Series A* 39 (2000): 91–94.

MacDonald, Nathan. "Is There Happiness in the Torah?" In *The Bible and the Pursuit of Happiness*, edited by Brent A. Strawn, 57–73. Oxford University Press, 2012.

Mager, Robert. "Do We Learn to Know God from What We Do?" In *Pathways to the Public Square: Practical Theology in an Age of Pluralism*, edited by Elaine Graham and Anna Rowlands, 191–201. Transaction Publishers, 2005.

Mallery, Suzanne T., and Paul Mallery. "Centers of Value and the Quest for Meaning in Faith Development: A Measurement Approach." *Frontiers in Psychology* 13 (2022): 975160.

Marshall, Joretta L. "Collaborating Hope: Joining the In-Between Spaces." *Journal of Pastoral Theology* 26, no. 2 (2016): 77–90.

Marshall, Joretta L. "Pastoral Theology and Lesbian/Gay/Bisexual Experiences." *Journal of Pastoral Theology* 4, no. 1 (1994): 73–79.

Martin, A. M. "Hopes and Dreams." *Philosophy and Phenomenological Research* 83, no. 1 (2011): 148–173.

Maslow, Abraham H. "A Dynamic Theory of Human Motivation." In *Understanding Human Motivation*, edited by C. L. Stacey and M. DeMartino. Howard Allen, 1958. https://doi.org/10.1037/11305-004.

Maslow, Abraham H., and Karen J. Lewis. "Maslow's Hierarchy of Needs." *Salenger Incorporated* 14, no. 17 (1987): 987–990.

Matsuoka, Fumitaka. *The Color of Faith: Building Community in a Multicultural Society*. United Church Press, 1989.

Mattingly, Cheryl. "Ethics, Immanent Transcendence and the Experimental Narrative Self." In *Moral Engines: Exploring the Ethical Drives in Human Life*, edited by Cheryl Mattingly, Rasmus Dyring, Maria Louw, and Thomas Schwarz Wentzer. Berghahn Books, 2017. https://doi.org/10.1515/9781785336942-003.

Mattingly, Cheryl. *Moral Laboratories: Family Peril and the Struggle for a Good Life*. University of California Press, 2014.

Mattingly, Cheryl. "Ordinary Possibility, Transcendent Immanence, and Responsive Ethics: A Philosophical Anthropology of the Small Event." *HAU: Journal of Ethnographic Theory* 8, no. 1–2 (2018): 172–184.

Mavelli, Luca. "Neoliberalism as Religion: Sacralization of the Market and Post-truth Politics." *International Political Sociology* 14, no. 1 (March 2020): 57–76.

Mayberry, Matt. *The Transformational Leader: How the World's Best Leaders Build Teams, Inspire Action, and Achieve Lasting Success*. John Wiley & Sons, 2024.

McClure, Barbara J. "Divining the Sacred in the Modern World: Ritual and the Relational Embodiment of Spirit." *Pastoral Psychology* 62 (2013): 727–742.

McClure, Barbara J. *Emotions: Problems and Promise for Human Flourishing*. Baylor University Press, 2019.

McClure, Barbara J. *Moving Beyond Individualism: Reflections on Theory, Theology and Practice*. Cascade, 2010.

McClure, Barbara J. "Pastoral Care." In *Wiley-Blackwell Companion to Practical Theology*, edited by Bonnie Miller-McLemore, 269–278. Blackwell Publishing, 2012.

McClure, Barbara J. "Pastoral Theology as the Art of Paying Attention: Widening the Horizons." *International Journal of Practical Theology* 12, no. 2 (2008): 189–210.

McFadyen, Alistair. *Bound to Sin: Abuse, Holocaust and the Christian Doctrine of Sin*. Cambridge University Press, 2000.

McGill, V. J. *The Idea of Happiness*. Praeger, 1967.

Merton, Thomas. *No Man Is an Island*. Harcourt, Brace, 1955.

Mesle, C. Robert. *Process-Relational Philosophy: An Introduction to Alfred North Whitehead*. Templeton Foundation Press, 2008.

Mesle, C. Robert. *Process Theology: A Basic Introduction*. Chalice Press, 1993.

Migliore, Daniel. *Faith Seeking Understanding: An Introduction to Christian Theology*. 2nd ed. Eerdmans, 2004.

Miguez, Nestor, Joerg Rieger, and Jung Mo Sung. *Beyond the Spirit of Empire: Theology and Politics in a New Key*. SCM Press, 2009.

Miller, David W. *God at Work: The History and Promise of the Faith at Work Movement*. Oxford University Press, 2006.

Miller, W. R. *8 Ways to Hope: Charting a Path Through Uncertain Times.* Guilford Press, 2024.

Miller-McLemore, Bonnie J. "The Human Web: Reflections on the State of Pastoral Theology." *The Christian Century*, April 7, 1993, 366–369. https://irbe.library.vanderbilt.edu/server/api/core/bitstreams/02752ee0-330d-4e18-a3ff-9e1a0c0c22e3/content.

Miller-McLemore, Bonnie, ed. *The Wiley-Blackwell Companion to Practical Theology.* Wiley-Blackwell, 2012.

Moschella, Mary Clark. "Affect in Narrative Spiritual Care." *Pastoral Psychology* 73, no. 2 (2024): 151–162.

Moschella, Mary Clark. *Caring for Joy: Narrative, Theology, and Practice.* Abingdon Press, 2016.

Muray, Lesley A. *An Introduction to the Process-Understanding of Science, Society, and the Self.* Edwin Mellen Press, 1988.

National Geographic. "Europe Burns Controversial Renewable Energy Trees." *National Geographic*, September 13, 2022. https://www.nationalgeographic.com/environment/article/europe-burns-controversial-renewable-energy-trees-from-us.

Nekolaichuk, C., R. Jevne, and T. Maguire. "Structuring the Meaning of Hope in Health and Illness." *Social Science and Medicine* 48, no. 5 (1999): 591–605.

Nelson, Sara Holiday. "Resilience and the Neoliberal Counter-Revolution: From Ecologies of Control to Production of the Common." *Resilience* 2 (January 2, 2014): 1–17.

Newman, David V. "Emergence and Strange Attractors." *Philosophy of Science* 63, no. 2 (1996): 245–261.

Nietzsche, Friedrich. *The Will to Power.* Edited by Walter Kaufmann and R. J. Hollingdale. Translated by Walter Kaufmann. Vintage Books, 1968.

Nouwen, Henri J. *Life of the Beloved: Spiritual Living in a Secular World.* Crossroad, 1992.

Nussbaum, Martha C., and Amartya Sen, eds. *The Quality of Life.* Oxford University Press, 1993.

Ogula, David. "Attractors, Strange Attractors, and Fractals." In *Encyclopedia of Administration and Public Policy*, 2nd ed., edited by Evan Berman. Routledge, 2007. https://doi.org/10.1081/e-epap2.

Oord, Thomas Jay. *Defining Love: A Philosophical, Scientific, and Theological Engagement.* Brazos Press, 2010.

Ott, Edward. "Strange Attractors and Chaotic Motions of Dynamical Systems." *Reviews of Modern Physics* 53, no. 4 (1981): 655–671.

Pak, Su Yon. "Through a Multi-Frame Lens: Surviving, Thriving, and Leading Organizations." In *Chaplaincy in the 21st Century*, edited by Wendy Cadge and Shelly Rambo, 219–238. Oxford University Press, 2022.

Pantheon Space Academy. *Quantum Physics for Beginners: Introduction to Essential Theories, the Behavior of Matter, and How It's Changing Our Lives.* Pantheon Space Academy, 2021.

Pembroke, Neil. *The Art of Listening: Dialogue, Shame, and Pastoral Care.* T&T Clark/Handsel, 2002.

Pennington, Jonathan T. *The Sermon on the Mount and Human Flourishing: A Theological Commentary.* Baker Academic, 2017.

Peters, Ted. "Clarity of the Part Versus Meaning of the Whole." In *Beginning with the End: God, Science, and Wolfhart Pannenberg*, edited by C. R. Albright and J. Haugen. Open Court, 1997.

Peterson, B. E., and L. E. Duncan. "Midlife Women's Generativity and Authoritarianism: Marriage, Motherhood, and 10 Years of Aging." *Psychology and Aging* 22, no. 3 (2007): 411–419.

Peterson, C., P. Nansook, N. Hall, and M. Seligman. "Zest and Work." *Journal of Organizational Behavior* 30, no. 2 (2009): 161–172.

Pink, Daniel H. *Drive: The Surprising Truth About What Motivates Us.* Riverhead Books, 2009.

Poling, James. *Render unto God: Economic Vulnerability, Family Violence, and Pastoral Theology.* Wipf and Stock Publishers, 2012.

Poling, James. "Recognizing the Congregation's Role as a Healing Community." *Brethren Life and Thought* 33 (1988): 122–130.

"Post-Truth Just Added to Oxford Dictionary." *Elite Daily.* Accessed June 28, 2017. https://www.elitedaily.com/news/post-truth-just-added-to-oxford-dictionary/2005066.

Pratt, Carl J. *Quantum Physics for Beginners: From Wave Theory to Quantum Computing, Understanding How Everything Works by a Simplified Explanation of Quantum Physics and Mechanics Principles.* Quantum Quill Press, 2021.

Prochaska, James O., and John C. Norcross. "Stages of Change." *Psychotherapy: Theory, Research, Practice, Training* 38, no. 4 (2001): 443–448.

Ramsay, Nancy J. "A Time of Ferment and Redefinition." In *Pastoral Care and Counseling: Redefining the Paradigms*, edited by Nancy J. Ramsay (Abingdon, 2004).

Ramsay, Nancy. "Where Race and Gender Collide: Deconstructing Racial Privilege." In *Women Out of Order: Risking Change and Creating Care in a Multicultural World*, edited by Jeanne Stevenson-Moessner and Teresa Snorton. Fortress, 2010, 331–340.

Rawls, John. *Justice as Fairness: A Restatement.* Edited by Erin Kelly. Harvard University Press, 2001.

Reeves, Gregory T., and Curtis E. Hrischuk. "Survey of Engineering Models for Systems Biology." *Computational Biology Journal* 2016, no. 1 (2016): 4106329.

Richardson, Ronald W. *Creating a Healthier Church: Family Systems Theory, Leadership, and Congregational Life*. 2nd ed. The Alban Institute, 2010.

Ricoeur, Paul. *Oneself as Another*. Translated by Kathleen Blamey. University of Chicago Press, 1992.

Ritchey, Tom. "Wicked Problems." *Acta Morphologica Generalis* 2, no. 1 (2014), 1–7.

Roberts, Ian G. *Parameter Hierarchies and Universal Grammar*. Oxford University Press, 2019.

Rogers-Vaughn, Bruce. *Caring for Souls in a Neoliberal Age*. Palgrave Macmillan, 2016.

Rogers-Vaughn, Bruce. "Powers and Principalities: Initial Reflections Toward a Post-Capitalist Pastoral Theology." *Journal of Pastoral Theology* 25, no. 2 (2015): 71–92.

Rogers-Vaughn, Bruce. "The Social Trifecta of Human Misery and Problematical Constructions of the Self: Implications for Formation and Supervision." 2012. https://ir.vanderbilt.edu/items/f2dcf313-d2cb-4f84-9f54-09c00edeb9c5.

Rogers-Vaughn, Bruce. "Soul Talk in a Neoliberal Age: Part 1." *Radical Discipleship*. Last modified August 21, 2020. https://radicaldiscipleship.net/2020/08/21/soul-talk-in-a-neoliberal-age-part-1/.

Rogers-Vaughn, Bruce. "Soul Talk in a Neoliberal Age: Part II." *Radical Discipleship*. Last modified August 28, 2020. https://radicaldiscipleship.net/2020/08/28/17418/.

Rogers-Vaughn, Bruce. "Soul Talk in a Neoliberal Age: Part III." *Radical Discipleship*. Last modified September 4, 2020. https://radicaldiscipleship.net/2020/09/04/soul-talk-in-a-neoliberal-age-part-iii/.

Rogers-Vaughn, Bruce. "Soul Talk in a Neoliberal Age: Part IV." *Radical Discipleship*. Last modified September 11, 2020. https://radicaldiscipleship.net/2020/09/11/soul-talk-in-a-neoliberal-age-part-iv/.

Rogers-Vaughn, Bruce. "Soul Talk in a Neoliberal Age: Part V." *Radical Discipleship*. Last modified September 18, 2020. https://radicaldiscipleship.net/2020/09/18/soul-talk-in-a-neoliberal-age-part-v/.

Rokeach, Milton. *The Nature of Human Values*. Free Press, 1973.

Russell, Robert. "Quantum Physics in Philosophical and Theological Perspective." In *Physics, Philosophy, and Theology: A Common Quest for Understanding*, edited by R. J. Russell, W. R. Stoeger, S.J., and G. V. Coyne, S.J., 35–50. Vatican Observatory, 1988.

Ryan, Richard M. *Self-Determination Theory: Basic Psychological Needs in Motivation, Development, and Wellness*. Guilford Press, 2017.

Ryan, Richard M., and Edward L. Deci. "Self-Determination Theory and the Facilitation of Intrinsic Motivation, Social Development, and Well-Being." *American Psychologist* 55, no. 1 (2000): 68–78.

Ryff, Carol D., and Burton H. Singer. "Know Thyself and Become What You Are: A Eudaimonic Approach to Psychological Well-Being." *Journal of Happiness Studies* 9 (2008): 13–39.

Safri, T. "Hope: A Psychological Perspective." *Indian Journal of Positive Psychology* 7, no. 1 (2016), 138–140.

Salovey, Peter, Brian T. Bedell, Jerusha B. Detweiler, and John D. Mayer. "Current Directions in Emotional Intelligence Research." In *Handbook of Emotions*, 2nd ed., edited by Michael Lewis and Jeannette M. Haviland-Jones, 504–520. Guilford Press, 2000.

Sanders, Cody J. *A Brief Guide to Ministry with LGBTQIA Youth*. Presbyterian Publishing, 2017.

Sashkin, Marshall. *Leadership That Matters: The Critical Factors for Making a Difference in People's Lives and Organizations' Success*. Berrett-Koehler Press, 2003.

Sassen, Saskia. *Expulsions: Brutality and Complexity in the Global Economy*. Belknap Press of Harvard University Press, 2022.

Savage, John. *Listening and Caring Skills: A Guide for Groups and Leaders*. Abingdon Press, 1996.

Schantz, Colleen. "I Have Learned to Be Content: Happiness According to St. Paul." In *The Bible and the Pursuit of Happiness*, edited by Brent A. Strawn, 187–202. Oxford University Press, 2012.

Schaubroeck, John, Simon S. K. Lam, and Sandra E. Cha. "Embracing Transformational Leadership: Team Values and the Impact of Leader Behavior on Team Performance." *Journal of Applied Psychology* 92, no. 4 (2007): 1020.

Scheib, Karen. *Attend to Stories: How to Flourish in Ministry*. Wesley's Foundry Books, 2018.

Scheib, Karen. *Pastoral Care: Telling the Stories of Our Lives*. Abingdon Press, 2016.

Schein, Edgar H. *Organizational Culture and Leadership*. 3rd ed. Jossey-Bass, 2004.

Schein, Edgar H. *Organizational Culture and Leadership*. 4th ed. Jossey-Bass, 2010.

Schein, Edgar H. *Organizational Culture and Leadership*. 5th ed. Wiley, 2017.

Schrank, B., G. Stanghellini, and M. Slade. "Hope in Psychiatry: A Review of the Literature." *Acta Psychiatrica Scandinavica* 118, no. 6 (2008): 421–433.

Scioli, Anthony, Michael Ricci, Than Nguyen, and Erica R. Scioli. "Hope: Its Nature and Measurement." *Psychology of Religion and Spirituality* 3, no. 2 (2011): 78–87.

Seidman, Dov. *How: Why How We Do Anything Means Everything*. John Wiley & Sons, 2011.

Seligman, Martin. "PERMA and the Building Blocks of Well-Being." *Journal of Positive Psychology* 13, no. 4 (2018): 333–335.

Seligman, Martin E. P. *Authentic Happiness: Using the New Positive Psychology to Realize Your Potential for Lasting Fulfillment*. Simon & Schuster, 2004.

Seligman, Martin E. P. *Flourish: A Visionary New Understanding of Happiness and Well-Being*. Atria Books, 2011.

Senge, Peter M. *The Fifth Discipline: The Art and Practice of the Learning Organization*. Doubleday, 1990.

Sheppard, Phillis. "Mourning the Loss of Cultural Selfobjects: Black Embodiment and Religious Experience after Trauma." *Practical Theology* 1, no. 2 (2008): 233–257. https://doi.org/10.1558/prth.v1i2.233.

Silva, J. M. *Coming Up Short: Working-Class Adulthood in an Age of Uncertainty*. Oxford University Press, 2013.

Sitkin, B. S., K. E. See, C. C. Miller, M. W. Lawless, and A. M. Carton. "The Paradox of Stretch Goals: Organizations in Pursuit of the Seemingly Impossible." *Academy of Management Review* 36, no. 3 (2011): 544–556.

Smith, Archie, Jr. "Certain Moral Challenges for Pastoral Care in Today's Early Twenty-First-Century World." *Pastoral Psychology* 69, no. 1 (2020): 69–76.

Smith, Ted A. *The End of Theological Education*. Eerdmans Publishing, 2023.

Snook, Scott A. "Imagine the Future of Leadership." *Harvard Business Review*, April 26, 2010. https://hbr.org/2010/04/imagine-the-future-of-leadersh.

Snyder, C. R. "Conceptualizing, Measuring, and Nurturing Hope." *Journal of Counseling and Development* 73, no. 3 (1995): 355–360.

Snyder, C. R. *The Psychology of Hope: You Can Get There from Here*. Free Press, 1994.

Spretnak, Charlene. *Relational Reality: New Discoveries of Interrelatedness That Are Transforming the Modern World*. Green Horizons, 2011.

Sprott, Julien C. "Strange Attractors: Creating Patterns in Chaos." *American Journal of Physics* 63, no. 5 (1995), 477

Steger, Manfred B., and Ravi K. Roy. *Neoliberalism: A Very Short Introduction*. 2nd ed. Oxford University Press, 2021.

Steinhoffsmith, R. "Infancy: Faith before Language." In *Human Development and Faith: Life-Cycle Stages of Body, Mind, and Soul*, edited by F. B. Kelcourse, 129–146. Chalice Press, 2004.

Steinke, Peter L. *Congregational Leadership in Anxious Times: Being Calm and Courageous No Matter What*. The Alban Institute, 2006.

Stone, Douglas, and Sheila Heen. *Thanks for the Feedback: The Science and Art of Receiving Feedback Well*. Penguin Books, 2014.

Storrar, William F. "Locating Public Theology." In *Pathways to the Public Square: Practical Theology in an Age of Pluralism*, edited by Elaine Graham and Anna Rowlands, 175–189. Transaction Publishers, 2005.

Strawn, Brent A., ed. *The Bible and the Pursuit of Happiness*. Oxford University Press, 2012.

Stroh, David Peter. *Systems Thinking for Social Change: A Practical Guide to Solving Complex Problems, Avoiding Unintended Consequences, and Achieving Lasting Results*. Chelsea Green Publishing, 2015.

Suchocki, Marjorie. *Divinity and Diversity: A Christian Affirmation of Religious Pluralism*. Abingdon Press, 2003.

Tanner, Kathryn. *Christianity and the New Spirit of Capitalism*. Yale University Press, 2019.

Thurman, Howard. *Jesus and the Disinherited*. 1st ed. Friends United Press, 1949.

Tillich, Paul. *Systematic Theology*. Vol. 1. University of Chicago Press, 1951.

Townes, Emilie, ed. *Troubling in My Soul: Womanist Perspectives on Evil and Suffering*. Orbis Books, 2015.

Treviño, Linda K., and Katherine A. Nelson. *Managing Business Ethics: Straight Talk About How to Do It Right*. John Wiley & Sons, 2010.

Tsoukas, Haridimos, and Stephen Cummings. "Marginalization and Recovery: The Emergence of Aristotelian Themes in Organization Studies." *Organization Studies* 18, no. 4 (1997): 655–683.

VanderWeele, Tyler J. "On the Promotion of Human Flourishing." *Proceedings of the National Academy of Sciences* 114, no. 31 (2017): 8148–8156.

Volf, Miroslav. *Flourishing: Why We Need Religion in a Globalized World*. Yale University Press, 2015.

Walker-Barnes, Chanequa. *Too Heavy a Yoke: Black Women and the Burden of Strength*. Fortress Press, 2014.

Webb, D. "Paulo Freire and 'the Need for a Kind of Education in Hope.'" *Cambridge Journal of Education* 40, no. 4 (2010): 327–339.

Weber, Max. *The Protestant Ethic and the Spirit of Capitalism*. Translated by Talcott Parsons. 5th ed. Routledge, 2002. Originally published in 1904–1905.

Wegter-McNelly, Kirk. *The Entangled God: Divine Relationality and Quantum Physics*. Routledge, 2012.

Wegter-McNelly, Kirk. "Quantum Mechanics." In *Religion Past and Present*, Online. Brill, 2011. https://doi.org/10.1163/1877-5888_rpp_SIM_124516.

Wegter-McNelly, Kirk. "Quantum Theory." In *Religion Past and Present*, Online. Brill, 2021. https://referenceworks.brill.com/display/entries/RPPO/SIM-124517.xml?language=en.

Weingarten, K. "Reasonable Hope: Construct, Clinical Applications, and Supports." *Family Process* 49, no. 1 (2010): 5–25.

Wheatley, Margaret J. *Finding Our Way: Leadership for Uncertain Times*. Berrett-Koehler Publishers, 2007.

Wheatley, Margaret J. "Islands of Sanity: A Prominent Organizational Leadership Author on How We Can Create and Nourish Places of Refuge and Possibility." *School Administrator*, September 2024, 32–37. https://margaretwheatley.com/wp-content/uploads/2024/08/Wheatley-School-Administratorpdf.pdf.

Wheatley, Margaret J. *Leadership and the New Science: Discovering Order in a Chaotic World*. Berrett-Koehler Publishers, 2006.

Wheatley, Margaret J. *Who Do We Choose to Be?: Facing Reality, Claiming Leadership, Restoring Sanity*. Berrett-Koehler Publishers, 2017 and 2023.

White, James D. *Anti-Racist Leadership: How to Transform Corporate Culture in a Race-Conscious World*. Harvard Business Review Press, 2022.

White, Nathan H. "Facilitating Resilience: Chaplaincy as a Catalyst for Organizational Well-Being." In *Chaplaincy and Spiritual Care in the 21st Century: An Introduction*, edited by Wendy Cadge and Shelly Rambo, 201–218. University of North Carolina Press, 2022.

White, Nicholas P. *A Brief History of Happiness*. John Wiley & Sons, 2008.

Whitehead, Alfred North. "Alfred North Whitehead." *Stanford Encyclopedia of Philosophy*. Last modified March 10, 2015. https://plato.stanford.edu/entries/whitehead/.

Whitehead, Alfred North. *Modes of Thought*. Free Press, 1968.

Whitehead, Alfred North. *Process and Reality: An Essay in Cosmology*. Free Press, 1978.

Whitehead, Alfred North. *Religion in the Making*. Cambridge University Press, 1926.

Wilber, Ken. *A Theory of Everything: An Integral Vision for Business, Politics, Science, and Spirituality*. Shambhala, 2001.

Wilkinson, Richard, and Kate Pickett. *A Convenient Truth: A Better Society for Us and for the Planet*. Bloomsbury Publishing, 2023.

Willen, Sarah S., Abigail Fisher Williamson, Colleen C. Walsh, Mikayla Hyman, and William Tootle. "Rethinking Flourishing: Critical Insights and Qualitative Perspectives from the US Midwest." *SSM—Mental Health* 2 (2022): 100057. https://doi.org/10.1016/j.ssmmh.2021.100057.

Willen, Sarah S. "Flourishing and Health in Critical Perspective: An Invitation to Interdisciplinary Dialogue." *SSM—Mental Health* 2 (2022): 100045. https://doi.org/10.1016/j.ssmmh.2021.100045.

Williams, Dean. *Real Leadership: Helping People and Organizations Face Their Toughest Challenges*. Berrett-Koehler Publishers, 2005.

Williams, Delores S. "Women's Oppression and Lifeline Politics in Black Women's Religious Narratives." *Journal of Feminist Studies in Religion* 1, no. 2 (1985): 59–71.

Williams, Jeremy L. *Criminalization in Acts of the Apostles: Race, Rhetoric, and the Prosecution of an Early Christian Movement.* Cambridge University Press, 2023.

Williams, Paul R., Anna Maria Tabernik, and Terry Krivak. "The Power of Leadership, Collaboration, and Professional Development: The Story of the SMART Consortium." *Education and Urban Society* 41, no. 4 (2009): 437–456.

Wilson, Samuel, and James McCalman. "Re-imagining Ethical Leadership as Leadership for the Greater Good." *European Management Journal* 35, no. 2 (2017): 151–154.

Wink, Walter. *Powers and Principalities.* Doubleday, 1984.

Wink, Walter. *Unmasking the Powers: The Invisible Forces That Determine Human Existence.* Fortress Press, 1986.

World Health Organization. "Constitution. Geneva, Switzerland," 1946, https://www.who.int/about/governance/constitution.

Yoon, Dong Pil, Patricia Bruininks, Erin I. Smith, et al. "The Relationships between Positive Character Traits, Virtues, and Health." *Social Work and Christianity* 49, no. 2 (2022), 135–163.

Young, Iris Marion. "Taking the Basic Structure Seriously." *Symposium: John Rawls and the Study of Politics* 4, no. 1 (March 2006): 91–97.

Zak, Paul J. "The Neuroscience of Trust." *Harvard Business Review* 95, no. 1 (2017): 84–90.

Zaleznik, Abraham. "Managers and Leaders: Are They Different?" *Clinical Leadership and Management Review: The Journal of CLMA* 18, no. 3 (2004): 171–177.

NOTES

PREFACE

1. Including the cultures of their organization, nation, and social milieu. Culture is "captured by the significant conversations in the organization and through its management and policy documents, which in turn reflect the values priorities held by the organization." Brian Hall, "The Omega Factor: A Values-Based Approach for Developing Organizations and Leadership," Servant Leadership Forum: Serving Students and the Common Good 29, 2003, http://www.valuestech.com/gui/omegafactor4.pdf.
2. Pastoral theologian Bruce Rogers-Vaughn argues that the culture of late capitalism (neoliberalism) has become globally hegemonic and is undermining social, interpersonal, and psychological well-being. Bruce Rogers-Vaughn, "Powers and Principalities: Initial Reflections Toward a Post-Capitalist Pastoral Theology," *Journal of Pastoral Theology* 25, no. 2 (2015): 71.
3. Wendy Brown, "Neo-liberalism and the End of Liberal Democracy," *Theory and Event* 7, no. 1 (2003), https://doi.org/10.1353/tae.2003.0020.
4. Pastoral theologian Nicholas Grier argues that there are five kinds of organizing for resistance: (1) power-based, (2) community-building, (3) civic, (4) women-centered, and (5) transformative. Nicholas A. Grier, "Building Our Power to Care for the World: Integrating Pastoral Theology, Mental Health, and Community Organizing," *Journal of Pastoral Theology* 30, no. 3 (2020): 197–206.
5. Wendy Brown, *In the Ruins of Neoliberalism: The Rise of Antidemocratic Politics in the West* (Columbia University Press, 2019).
6. Flavio Azevedo et al., "Neoliberal Ideology and the Justification of Inequality in Capitalist Societies: Why Social and Economic Dimensions of Ideology Are Intertwined," *Journal of Social Issues* 75, no. 1 (2019): 74.
7. Elon Musk, currently the richest man in the world, invested some of his massive resources in the 2024 presidential election to ensure he can amass even more.
8. Although he did not use the term *gilded cage* himself, German sociologist Max Weber's notion of the "iron cage" is a metaphor to describe the paradox of modern bureaucratic societies, particularly in relation to the development of rationalization and the increasing dominance of bureaucratic systems over social life. The gilded cage represents a situation where

individuals are technically free in terms of political rights, but they are constrained and controlled by impersonal, rationalized, and bureaucratic structures that limit their autonomy and agency through disinformation and other forms of deception. In other words, people are trapped in a system that offers them material security, efficiency, and comfort (the "gilding"), but they are also confined to and dehumanized by its rigid, impersonal rules and procedures (the "cage"). Max Weber, *The Protestant Ethic and the Spirit of Capitalism*, translated by Talcott Parsons, 5th ed. (Routledge, 2002; Originally published in 1930).

9. Mainline and progressive Christian denominations and mainstream and progressive Jewish and Islamic communities of faith are shrinking, while more conservative and triumphalist theologies are fueling growth, especially in the Global South. While I am convinced this can be traced, in part, to the effects of neoliberal pressures, it is beyond the scope of this project to explore that argument.
10. Harvey Cox, *The Market as God* (Harvard University Press, 2016). Not all values are explicitly religious, as we will see, but the highest-order values are consonant with religious virtues. Suzanne T. Mallery and Paul Mallery, "Centers of Value and the Quest for Meaning in Faith Development: A Measurement Approach," *Frontiers in Psychology* 13 (2022): 975160.
11. Ted A. Smith, *The End of Theological Education.* (Eerdmans Publishing, 2023).
12. My own Christology is informed by Howard Thurman's work in Howard Thurman, *Jesus and the Disinherited*, 2nd ed. (Friends United Press, 1976). See also Jeremy L. Williams, *Criminalization in Acts of the Apostles: Race, Rhetoric, and the Prosecution of an Early Christian Movement* (Cambridge University Press, 2023).
13. Paul Freedman, "Islands of Sanity and Spiritual Leadership in a Time of Crisis: Margaret Wheatley and Paul Freedman in Dialogue," *Holistic Education Review* 4, no. 1 (2024): 1–11; In his classic 1944 text *Children of Light / Children of Darkness*, Reinhold Niebuhr wisely reminds us that no political system "great enough or good enough to make itself the final end of human existence." When we elevate politics, ideology, or even theology to the level of ultimate truth, we displace God as the source of hope and redemption. Instead, religious, values-based leaders' calling is to be people of faith, hope, and love—even in (particularly in) times of heightened stress and strife.

CHAPTER 1: RELIGIOUS LEADERSHIP TOWARD HUMAN FLOURISHING

1. John P. Kotter and James L. Heskett, *Corporate Culture and Performance.* The Free Press, 1992). See also James M. Kouzes and Barry Z. Posner,

The Leadership Challenge: How to Make Extraordinary Things Happen in Organizations, 6th ed. (Jossey-Bass, 2017).

2. F. J. Carstens and Neil Barnes, "The Quality of Leader/Employee Relationship in Business Performance," *Journal of Human Resource Management* 4, no. 2 (2006): 11.
3. Scott A. Snook, "Imagine the Future of Leadership," *Harvard Business Review*, April 26, 2010, https://hbr.org/2010/04/imagine-the-future-of-leadersh.
4. This is one way to define a differentiated leader, often referred to in systems theory. Differentiated leaders can see what is and think clearly about it; they act on their own highest principles and values. They define themselves by taking a position and share it openly, they know themselves, they can regulate themselves and others, they can stay close to others, and they are willing to act rightly. For more details, see, for example, Peter L. Steinke, *Congregational Leadership in Anxious Times: Being Calm and Courageous No Matter What* (The Alban Institute, 2006).
5. Margaret J. Wheatley, *Finding Our Way: Leadership for Uncertain Times* (Berrett-Koehler Publishers, 2007), 292.
6. John P. Kotter, *Leading Change* (Harvard Business Review Press, 2012).
7. Kotter, *Leading Change*. Neither people nor organizations can change when they are stressed.
8. Transformational leadership is a leadership style where leaders inspire and motivate their followers to achieve higher levels of creativity and growth to more effectively contribute to the good of the whole. Transformational leaders transform their organization for greater good by helping its members grow, focusing on developing emotional intelligence (EQ), creating a vision, and enlivening their passions and values. By focusing on people rather than solely on tasks and goals, transformational leaders foster trust, respect, and loyalty among their followers. See, for example, Matt Mayberry, *The Transformational Leader: How the World's Best Leaders Build Teams, Inspire Action, and Achieve Lasting Success* (John Wiley & Sons, 2024).
9. Erik Erikson H., *The Life Cycle Completed* (W. W. Norton, 1982), 67. Erikson believed that the strengths gained from the six earlier stages are essential for the generative task of cultivating the strengths of the next generation.
10. Richard Barrett, *The New Leadership Paradigm* (Fulfilling Books, 2011), xv. Barrett argues that values-based organizations will be the ones that survive and even thrive. As he puts it, "In the 21st century, the rat race will be replaced by the values race," that the most successful organizations will care less about being "the best in the world" and focus on being "the best *for* the world." Richard Barrett, *The Values-Driven Organizations* (Routledge, 2014), xv.

11. B. E. Peterson and L. E. Duncan, "Midlife Women's Generativity and Authoritarianism: Marriage, Motherhood, and 10 Years of Aging," *Psychology and Aging* 22, no. 3 (2007): 411–419.
12. Proverbs 29:18, *The Holy Bible: The New Revised Standard Version* (National Council of Churches, 1989).
13. Karen Scheib, *Attend to Stories: How to Flourish in Ministry* (Wesley's Foundry Books, 2018), 9.
14. Harver Team, "Learning Agility: What It Is and How to Assess It," February 13, 2024, https://harver.com/blog/learning-agility/.
15. Harver Team, "Learning Agility."
16. Agile learners make high-quality decisions in the moment with confidence and make connections without complete data. Leaders who practice agile learning can imagine innovative solutions when previous ways no longer work. They can see the big picture, beyond what they know, and incorporate other perspectives. They can adapt their approach given new information, be comfortable in unfamiliarity, and lean into new situations, continually adapting as needed while maintaining their values. The leadership consulting firm Korn Ferry estimates that people with high learning agility are promoted twice as fast as those without it. Korn Ferry, "Fast Rising Talent: Highly Learning Agile People Get Promoted at Double Speed," accessed November 11, 2024, https://www.kornferry.com/institute/820-fast-rising-talent-highly-learning-agile-people-get-promoted-at-double-speed. One challenge of leadership is that the higher up you go and the more formal authority you have, the less honest feedback you will get, and the less real leadership can happen because you don't know what needs to change, what is working, and what is not. A leader can only lead and is only a leader if they have their finger on the pulse of their organization, including those at the ground level, who can give them honest feedback without fear of reprisal. Leaders are not the experts, but they know how to generate a productive conversation. Leadership is a reciprocal relationship, one that can and should be distributed throughout an organization. Transformational leadership begins with understanding the vital role of organizations in human life.
17. Bill George, *True North: Discover Your Authentic Leadership* (Jossey-Bass, 2007).
18. Barrett, *New Leadership Paradigm*, 10.

CHAPTER 2: THE *WHY* OF RELIGIOUS LEADERSHIP

1. Genuine and life-giving communities are safe, inclusive, and just. Genuine communities allow people to communicate honestly and without fear;

they resolve conflicts with each other individually and within the group, and in them, members learn to love themselves so they can love each other and reach out to strangers. Genuine communities can be contrasted with pseudo-communities, which can seem friendly and have an emphasis on group identity and involvement but whose members feel pressure to conform to the group, often at the expense of their own experience and values. As pastoral theologian Margaret Kornfeld notes, "Pseudo communities are not places where members are safe to be different, to disagree, to question the program or the leadership of the group." Margaret Kornfeld, *Cultivating Wholeness: A Guide to Care and Counseling in Faith Communities* (Continuum International Publishing, 2002), 18–19.

2. "Quiet quitting" refers to a situation when employees do the bare minimum required to meet their job responsibilities but do not go beyond what is absolutely necessary. Quiet quitting does not mean literally quitting a job, but rather about disengaging from any extra efforts such as taking on extra tasks, working overtime, or doing much enthusiastically. The term gained popularity as a response to burnout, poor work-life balance, and dissatisfaction with work culture, particularly in the context of a more passive resistance to overwork.
3. Theologian John Thatamanil argues that religious communities "may be one of the last remainders of face-to-face communities that can serve as intermediaries between individuals and families, on the one hand, and corporations and governments on the other." In Bruce Rogers-Vaughn, *Caring for Souls in a Neoliberal Age* (Palgrave Macmillan, 2019), 219.
4. There is a saying in leader development coaching circles that people don't leave jobs; they leave managers and leaders. If you pause to consider that statement, you will understand: Employees will leave one company to take a job in another, often doing the same job with roughly the same pay if it means they might be able to have a supervisor who treats them well, cares for them as human beings, and is the kind of leader to whom people are willing to give their best.
5. For our purposes here, an organization refers to any intentionally gathered people who share a basic set of common values and a common purpose or mission.
6. It is my intention to write about religious leadership rather than specifically Christian leadership, though that happens to be the tradition out of which I come, because I understand religious leaders to be oriented to unique values informed by their own religious tradition, and they serve in a variety of organizational contexts.
7. The president of the United States is responsible for the well-being of US citizens and visitors, underscoring the importance of this perspective for those in that position as well.

8. I want to be clear that I do not think human flourishing is possible without planetary flourishing.
9. Barbara J. McClure, *Moving Beyond Individualism: Reflections on Theory, Theology and Practice* (Cascade, 2010). See also Barbara J. McClure, "Pastoral Theology as the Art of Paying Attention: Widening the Horizons," *International Journal of Practical Theology* 12, no. 2 (2008): 123–135.
10. Kornfeld, *Cultivating Wholeness*, 47.
11. Pastoral theologian Karen Scheib refers to this as being a story companion. Karen Scheib, *Attend to Stories: How to Flourish in Ministry* (Wesley's Foundry Books, 2018). Scheib refers to joining the individual person's story to God's story, however the care receivers understand that framing.
12. I use the word *God* as a placeholder for whatever the reader deems ultimate, sacred, divine, and holy. Readers will insert their own understanding of the term.
13. These are the guiding frames of the United Methodist tradition.
14. Philosophical theologian John Caputo calls this "hoping the impossible," in which hope persists along with stings of loss and mourning. Caputo argues that hoping for liberation and fulfillment is a fundamental mode of human existence. Hoping against hope "is the philosophical and theopolitical resistance against any form of control, domination, or fixation of being as the yet-to-be." John D. Caputo, *Hoping Against Hope: Confessions of a Postmodern Pilgrim* (Fortress Press, 2015), back cover. Pastoral theologians Emmanual Lartey and Mindy McGarrah-Sharp suggest that although religious leaders are entangled in the world, they are not entrapped. They support new "models of resistance and new forms of solidarity from within selves and systems." Emmanuel Y. Lartey and Melinda A. McGarrah Sharp, "Entangled but Not Entrapped: Pastoral Practices of Resistance from Within Selves and Systems," *Journal of Pastoral Theology* 26, no. 1 (2016): 2.
15. Suffering is distinguished from pain in that suffering is pain that does not make sense to a person. It is pain that people struggle to comprehend and make meaning of. It is pain that breaks the continuity of their life story. Suffering is often present when people cannot see or understand the sources of their distress and when they cannot name the oppressive systems that dehumanize them, creating their sense of being trapped and immobilized. Pastoral theologian Nicholas Grier argues, "To transform the world, we must first see it as it is." Nicholas Grier, "Building Our Power to Care for the World: Integrating Pastoral Theology, Mental Health, and Community Organizing," *Journal of Pastoral Theology* 30, no. 3 (2020): 199.

16. Grief includes loss of all kinds, of course. It also includes "negative cultural reflections" of Blackness and other underrepresented and marginalized persons that must be acknowledged as having a psychological and social impact. Phillis Sheppard, "Mourning the Loss of Cultural Self objects: Black Embodiment and Religious Experience After Trauma," *Practical Theology* 1, no. 2 (2008): 233–257, https://doi.org/10.1558/prth.v1i2.233.
17. David W. Miller, *God at Work: The History and Promise of the Faith at Work Movement* (Oxford University Press, 2006).
18. From the Latin *vocacioun*, meaning a particular *summons from God* to perform a particular task or function in life, especially a religious one. A vocation brings with it the sense of both divine calling and personal inclination toward a particular life path or occupation. Whether it's a religious calling or a strong desire to pursue a specific career that expresses one's values, the concept of *vocation* touches on one's purpose and direction in life.
19. My own professional experience for the last twenty-five years as an organizational and leadership consultant has given me some insight into the need for thoughtful theological reflection on the role and meaning of organizations in which our congregants (and probably even we ourselves) work. Religious leaders can be effective contributors to conversations about the aims and purposes of organizations (both religious and not). In my consultative role, I have been able to engage in conversations about the moral implications of an organization's official and unofficial policies and to think with the company's leadership about its purposes and ends. I have had many opportunities to hear employees at different levels of organizations talk about their experiences of the institutions in which they work. From these interviews, I know that inequities related to gender and racial equality, wage discrimination, sexual harassment, work/life balance, environmentally degrading policies, and the effects of hard-driving bottom-line business practices take a significant toll on individual people and the families and communities they seek to support. The individuals I have engaged are members of churches; they are clients in counseling centers; they are partners in marriages that the church had sanctified. Often the greatest impediment to their flourishing comes from the organizations within which they spent most of their day. For this reason and others, understanding organizations' roles in human life is crucial.
20. Miller, *God at Work*. Miller describes this gap as one in which people's religious values as expressed in worship on Sunday are compartmentalized and not operationalized at work on Monday. However, an increasing number of citations are made to work and religion, or

work and spirituality, in popular publications. See, for example, Lisa Armstrong, "Have Faith," *Working Mother*, December 2007/January 2008, 53–56. *Working Mother* (New York, 1981), 2007–12, Vol. 31 (1).

21. It is worth noting that many for-profit organizations are seeking to value more than the financial bottom line, seeing their business as an opportunity to create meaningful work, community, and a sense of purpose, but that is the subject for another book.
22. I am not naive that many religious organizations and traditions have done significant harm to people. I am calling out the best in religious traditions. As theologian Miroslav Volf argues, religious traditions, at their best, are important mediators of often countercultural commitments to love, justice, mercy, and inclusion. Miroslav Volf, *Flourishing: Why We Need Religion in a Globalized World* (Yale University Press, 2015).
23. McClure, "Pastoral Theology as the Art of Paying Attention."
24. James Lapsley, *Salvation and Health: The Interlocking Processes of Life* (Westminster Press, 1972).
25. See Lapsley, *Salvation and Health*. I want to say here that "participation in the Life of God" potentially has multiple meanings. In the broadest terms, I want to indicate that which is, ultimately, genuinely life-giving.
26. Larry Kent Graham, *Care of Persons, Care of Worlds: A Psychosystems Approach to Pastoral Care and Counseling* (Abingdon Press, 1992). See also Ryan LaMothe, *Care of Souls, Care of Polis: Toward a Political Pastoral Theology* (Cascade Books, 2017).
27. The word *pastoral* in this context refers to Jesus the Christ as the Good Shepherd, leading their flock from dry pastures where they could not flourish to the verdant pastures of life. Barbara J. McClure, "Pastoral Care," in *Wiley-Blackwell Companion to Practical Theology*, ed. Bonnie Miller-McLemore (Blackwell Publishing, 2012), 269–278. Pastoral theology derives its name from the image of shepherd and can be understood as a "theology of shepherding [or] a pastor's oversight of the people of God." See J. R. Burck and Rodney J. Hunter, "Pastoral Theology. Protestant," in *The Dictionary of Pastoral Care and Counseling*, ed. Rodney J. Hunter (Abingdon Press, 1990), 867–872. Pastoral theology formulates theories, theologies, and practices for ministers (broadly conceived) with the goal of healing. It is "a way of doing theology *pastorally*." Burck and Hunter, "Pastoral Theology." This is distinguished from practical theology, which addresses the whole range of responsibilities and activities of the minister. The subject of practical theology, in its ecclesial forms, usually includes attention to preaching, liturgics, church education, and church polity and administration. See Edward Farley, "Practical Theology. Protestant," in Hunter, *The Dictionary of Pastoral Care and Counseling*, 934–936. Practical theology can be widened even further into a theory

of experience, action, and practice, where practice can refer to public and world-transforming political activity. Practical theology attends to actual problems that profoundly shape lives and seeks to develop corollary transformative action that reflects the promise of God (Bonnie Miller-McLemore, ed., "Introduction: The Contributions of Practical Theology," in *The Wiley-Blackwell Companion to Practical Theology* (Wiley-Blackwell, 2012), 5–15. *Pastoral* theology is akin to practical theology in these ways, though it focuses on practices of care and seeks well-being normatively. Because this text focuses on practices explicitly designed to promote the flourishing of human lives, I will be primarily using the term *pastoral theology*, which integrates psychology, culture, and theology to understand and attend to people's suffering and healing. Because this term has its roots in Christian theology and practice, non-Christian religious leaders will want to explore the metaphors in their own traditions.

28. German philosopher Jurgen Habermas argued that the public sphere is "a domain of our social life in which public opinion can be formed." Jurgen Habermas, "The Public Sphere," in *Jurgen Habermas on Society and Politics*, ed. Steven Seidman (Beacon Press, 1989), 231–236. Cited in William F. Storrar, "Locating Public Theology," in *Pathways to the Public Square: Practical Theology in an Age of Pluralism*, ed. Elaine Graham and Anna Rowlands (Transaction Publishers, 2005), 176. See also Elaine Graham and Anna Rowlands, eds., *Pathways to the Public Square: Practical Theology in an Age of Pluralism* (Transaction Publishers, 2005), 175–189.
29. Seward Hiltner, *Preface to Pastoral Theology* (Abingdon Press, 1958), 16.
30. Hiltner, *Preface*, 20.
31. Hiltner, *Preface*, 28. An example Hiltner gives of these three functions is the parable of the good Samaritan: when he binds up the wounds of the man, he is healing. When he gives him a cup of water, he is sustaining him. When he takes the injured man to the hospital, he is guiding. Hiltner, *Preface*, 147.
32. Hiltner, *Preface*, 24.
33. Hiltner, *Preface*, 25.
34. Lee G. Bolman and Terrence E. Deal, *Reframing Organizations: Artistry, Choice, and Leadership*, 6th ed. (John Wiley & Sons, 2017); Su Yon Pak, "Through a Multi-Frame Lens: Surviving, Thriving, and Leading Organizations," in *Chaplaincy and Spiritual Care in the 21st Century: An Introduction*, ed. Wendy Cadge and Shelly Rambo (University of North Carolina Press, 2022), 219–238.
35. Hiltner, *Preface*, 25.
36. Pastoral theologian David Augsburger defines interpathy as "an intentional cognitive envisioning and affective experiencing of another's

thoughts and feelings, even though the thoughts rise from another process of knowing, the values frow from another frame of moral reasoning, and the feelings spring from another basis of assumptions." Pastoral theologian Emmanual Lartey argues that interpathy is more important than sympathy or empathy. David Augsburger, *Pastoral Counseling Across Cultures* (Westminster Press, 1986), 29, cited in Emmanual Lartey Y., *In Living Color: An Intercultural Approach to Pastoral Care and Counseling*, 2nd ed. (Jessica Kingsley Publishers, 2003), 93.

37. Bailey W. Jackson, "Theory and Practice of Multicultural Organization Development," in *The NTL Handbook of Organization Development and Change*, ed. B. B. Jones and M. Brazzel (Pfeiffer, 2014), 139–154.
38. Wholeness is defined here as the integration of body, mind, spirit, and soul. Both people and organizations can work toward wholeness. James Lapsley defined salvation as a kind of physical, spiritual, psychic, and communal health. See Lapsley, *Salvation and Health*.
39. Philosopher Ken Wilbur notes, "The Greeks had a beautiful word, *Kosmos*, which means the patterned Whole of all existence, including the physical, emotional, mental, and spiritual realms. Ultimate reality was not merely the cosmos, or the physical dimension, but the Kosmos, or the physical and emotional and mental and spiritual dimensions altogether. Not just matter, lifeless and insentient, but the living Totality of matter, body, mind, soul, and spirit." Ken Wilber, *A Theory of Everything: An Integral Vision for Business, Politics, Science, and Spirituality* (Shambhala, 2001), xi.
40. Rodney J. Hunter, "The Future of Pastoral Theology," *Pastoral Psychology* 29, no. 1 (Fall 1980): 69.
41. Hunter, "The Future of Pastoral Theology," 69.
42. I recognize that stewarding a community of faith's budget is an important facet of the organization's management and that churches need material resources to thrive. My point here is that numbers, whether financial or membership, cannot be the final measure of success or failure.
43. Transformational, generative religious leaders observe the behaviors of members in their organization, including their own. Practical theology has, at its heart, the commitment to learning about God through human experience. As practical theologian Roger Mager puts it, "Action may have results, but its essence is to be meaningful. It has to do with revelation: revelation of who people are—something that can only be told retrospectively from the point of view of those who witnessed the action and who can capture its meaning into words and texts." Robert Mager, "Do We Learn to Know God from What We Do?" in Graham and Rowlands, *Pathways to the Public Square*, 191–201.
44. William A. Clebsch and Charles R. Jaekle, *Pastoral Care in Historical Perspective* (Jason Aronson, 1994).

45. See, for example, Karen D. Scheib, *Pastoral Care: Telling the Stories of Our Lives* (Abingdon Press, 2016); and Gary Gunderson, *Deeply Woven Roots: Improving the Quality of Life in Your Community* (Fortress, Press, 1997).
46. Willie James Jennings explicitly uses the language of "seeing" to shift our perspectives from "above the ground" to what is happening on the ground. Willie J. Jennings, *The Christian Imagination: Theology and Its Origins of Race* (Yale University Press, 2011).
47. See James H. Cone, *A Black Theology of Liberation* (Orbis Books, 2010); Archie Smith Jr., "Certain Moral Challenges for Pastoral Care in Today's Early Twenty-First-Century World," *Pastoral Psychology* 69, no. 1 (2020): 69–76; Jennings, *Christian Imagination*; Delores S. Williams, "Women's Oppression and Lifeline Politics in Black Women's Religious Narratives," *Journal of Feminist Studies in Religion* 1, no. 2 (1985): 59–71; Keri Day, *Religious Resistance to Neoliberalism: Womanist and Black Feminist Perspectives* (Springer, 2016); Jay-Paul Michael Hinds, *A Gift Grows in the Ghetto: Reimagining the Spiritual Lives of Black Men* (Presbyterian Publishing, 2022); Emilie Townes, ed., *Troubling in My Soul: Womanist Perspectives on Evil and Suffering* (Orbis Books, 2015).
48. Emmanuel Y. Lartey, *Postcolonializing God: New Perspectives on Pastoral and Practical Theology* (Hymns Ancient and Modern, 2013); Lee H. Butler, *Liberating Our Dignity, Saving Our Souls* (Chalice Press, 2006); Chanequa Walker-Barnes, *Too Heavy a Yoke: Black Women and the Burden of Strength* (Fortress Press, 2014).
49. I hope readers will remember that these identities are not mutually exclusive and that care for human beings often involves needs at their intersections. See Rubem Alves, "Personal Wholeness and Political Creativity: The Theology of Liberation and Pastoral Care," *Pastoral Psychology* 26, no. 2 (1977): 124–136; Ryan LaMothe, *Pastoral Reflections on Global Citizenship: Framing the Political in Terms of Care, Faith, and Community* (Lexington Books, 2018); Cody J. Sanders, *A Brief Guide to Ministry with LGBTQIA Youth* (Presbyterian Publishing, 2017); Joretta L. Marshall, "Pastoral Theology and Lesbian/Gay/Bisexual Experiences," *Journal of Pastoral Theology* 4, no. 1 (1994): 73–79; John Blevins, "Hospitality Is a Queer Thing," *Journal of Pastoral Theology* 19, no. 2 (2009): 104–117.
50. McClure, *Moving Beyond Individualism*.
51. Pastoral counselor Margaret Kornfeld argues that health is not just the opposite of illness: health is the consciousness of one's wholeness, which means "accepting one's limitations as well as one's strengths." Kornfeld, *Cultivating Wholeness*, 8.
52. Graham, *Care of Persons, Care of Worlds*, 75.
53. Graham, *Care of Persons, Care of Worlds*, 37.

54. Graham, *Care of Persons, Care of Worlds*, 92.
55. Andre Beauregard, "Writing a Public Theology Within the Challenge of a Pluralistic Society," in *Dreaming the Land: Theologies of Resistance and Hope*, ed. Hans-Georg Ziebertz and Friedrich Schweitzer (International Academy of Practical Theology, 2005), 152–163.
56. This is a paraphrase of Pamela Couture, "Rethinking Private and Public Patriarchy," in *Religion, Feminism and the Family*, ed. A. Carr and M. S. Van Leeuwen (Westminster John Knox Press, 1996), 249–274.
57. Historian E. Brooks Holifield names the variously narrowing and widening focus of religious concern across the history of religious practices. See E. Brooks Holifield, *A History of Pastoral Care in America: From Salvation to Self-Realization* (Academic Renewal Press, 1983).
58. Barbara J. McClure, "Divining the Sacred in the Modern World: Ritual and the Relational Embodiment of Spirit," *Pastoral Psychology* 62 (2013): 727–742.
59. The faithful are enjoined to choose life, not death. Deuteronomy 30:15–20, *The Holy Bible*. The question in this project is how to do so.

CHAPTER 3: ENVISIONING A FLOURISHING WORLD

1. For example, New Testament scholar Jonathan Pennington argues that the question of what happiness, blessedness, or shalom is lies "at the core of the entire message of scripture." Jonathan T. Pennington, *The Sermon on the Mount and Human Flourishing: A Theological Commentary* (Baker Academic, 2017), 14. Hebrew Bible scholar Brent Strawn similarly argues that the Christian Bible has "profoundly" contributed to notions of happiness and the good life. Brent A. Strawn, ed., *The Bible and the Pursuit of Happiness* (Oxford University Press, 2012), 22. In the same edited volume, Hebrew Bible scholar Terence Fretheim argues that God is happy, and that divine happiness affects the created world and is, in turn, affected by it. Terence E. Fretheim, "God, Creation, and the Pursuit of Happiness," 33–55 in Strawn, *The Bible and the Pursuit of Happiness*. Another Hebrew Bible scholar, Nathan MacDonald, argues that there are important similarities between Aristotle and the Torah and that although the Torah is filled with much unhappiness, it also concerns itself with happiness or well-being. Nathan MacDonald, "Is There Happiness in the Torah?" in Strawn, *The Bible and the Pursuit of Happiness*, 57–73. Finally, professor of New Testament Colleen Schantz argues that the apostle Paul found in Jesus a meaningful way to live and so could face his own death "not only resolutely, but extraordinarily, with what might properly be called happiness." Colleen Schantz, "I Have

Learned to Be Content: Happiness According to St. Paul," in Strawn, *The Bible and the Pursuit of Happiness*, 200.

2. Ellen T. Charry, *God and the Art of Happiness* (William B. Eerdmans, 2010), 3.
3. Dani Blum, "The Other Side of Languishing Is Flourishing: Here's How to Get There," *New York Times*, May 4, 2021, updated June 23, 2023, https://www.nytimes.com/2021/05/04/well/mind/flourishing-languishing.html.
4. Dualistic cosmologies created either/or worldviews and opposing forces, as in good versus evil, spirit versus matter, and created versus creator.
5. In the early Greek view, this requires the objective confirmation of flourishing from a community. For example, if one were to assert that one is healthy because one feels good but was found to have an as-yet-undetected serious tumor, one would objectively not be healthy. Martin E. P. Seligman, *Flourish: A Visionary New Understanding of Happiness and Well-being* (Atria Books, 2011). One's community must affirm that one is well, defining what it means by the term. (For example, one might be deemed physically ill because of the tumor but spiritually and emotionally healthy by other measures). In addition, a historically (and religiously) developed understanding of what well-being entails must be included in the assessment.
6. John M. Cooper, "Eudaimonism, the Appeal to Nature, and 'Moral Duty' in Stoicism," in *Aristotle, Kant and the Stoics: Rethinking Happiness and Duty*, ed. Stephen Engstrom and Jennifer Whiting (Cambridge University Press, 1996), 275–278. Immanuel Kant would diverge from the understanding of happiness as the *telos* of life and focus on the importance of duty, although he did argue that it is everyone's duty to promote the happiness of other people. V. J. McGill, *The Idea of Happiness* (Praeger, 1967), 91, 183; Luc Ferry, *What Is the Good Life?* trans. Lydia G. Cochrane (University of Chicago Press, 2005), 201–206.
7. The Stoics invented the happiness quotient: Divide what you have by what you want. The higher that number, the happier you will be.
8. Raymond Angelo Belliotti, *Happiness Is Overrated* (Rowman & Littlefield, 2018), 22. Clearly, many contemporary appropriations of Epicurus's work misunderstand his philosophy.
9. In this, elements of the Epicureans and Stoics resemble certain aspects of Buddhism. Ferry, *What Is the Good Life?* 171. Indeed, one of the noble truths of Buddhism declares that life is suffering, and suffering comes from passion (desire), which is eliminable.
10. Psychologists call this cycle the *hedonic treadmill*: comparing many kinds of human pleasure-seeking to the activity of a hamster on its wheel, running hard but getting nowhere. That is, as soon as a person satisfies one desire, another arises to take its place, creating an unending cycle. Joel J.

Kupperman, *Six Myths About the Good Life: Thinking About What Has Value* (Hackett, 2006), 11.

11. Nicholas White, *A Brief History of Happiness* (John Wiley & Sons, 2008), 62–65.
12. The virtues are those mature capacities that seem to be ubiquitous across cultures, that generally do not hurt others, that are pursued for their own sake (rather than being a means to an end), and that are witnessed to or argued for in sacred texts. See, for example, Miroslav Volf's *Flourishing*, especially chap. 4, for a discussion of the important contributions of world religions to articulations of flourishing. Volf is not as critical as I would wish about the view of flourishing that some religions (and their followers) promote.
13. Belliotti, *Happiness Is Overrated*, 12.
14. Although Aristotle likely was thinking of biological families and their support, today we would include all manners of family forms, from chosen families to foster families and beyond.
15. Aristotle points out that the virtues of citizens are integral to the health of the state. "The polis, then, comprises a reciprocal relationship between the state and the citizen, each depending on and influencing the other … To live in the polis is to be caught in the drama of society and the state." Ryan LaMothe, *Care of Souls, Care of Polis: Toward a Political Pastoral Theology* (Cascade Books, 2017), 10. Unfortunately, Aristotle considered flourishing to be available to adult men, not those who are "inferior" such as enslaved people, women, or children. Transformational leaders, of course, will include these in their attempts to nurture flourishing.
16. Aristotle's first principles include the principle of non-contradiction, which claims that contradictory statements cannot both be true in the same sense at the same time. For example, something cannot both be and not be at the same time and in the same respect. The principle of identity asserts that each thing is the same as itself and different from another. It emphasizes the uniqueness and individuality of entities. Finally, the principle of the excluded middle maintains that a statement must either be true or false; there is no middle ground or third option. For any proposition, either it or its negation must be true. These principles constitute the foundation of Aristotle's philosophy of logic and metaphysics. They are the framework for his exploration of reality, causality, and the nature of existence. Terence Irwin, *Aristotle's First Principles* (Clarendon Press, 1988). As we shall see later in this chapter, the new science has disabused us of some of Aristotle's first principles.
17. Erik Erikson claimed Freud said this was his goal, but there seems to be no written record of it. See Erik H. Erikson, ed., "Growth and Crises of the Healthy Personality," in *Identity and the Lifecycle* (W. W. Norton, 1980), 102.

18. Seligman served as the president of the American Psychological Association in 1996.
19. Positive Psychology Center, https://ppc.sas.upenn.edu/.
20. Seligman, *Flourish*, 13; Corey L. M. Keyes, "The Mental Health Continuum: From Languishing to Flourishing in Life," *Journal of Health and Social Behavior* 43, no. 2 (2002): 210; Tyler J. VanderWeele, "On the Promotion of Human Flourishing," *Proceedings of the National Academy of Sciences* 114, no. 31 (2017): 8149.
21. PERMA refers to Positive emotions, Engagement, Relationships, Meaning, Accomplishment; Victoria Cabrera and Stewart I. Donaldson, "PERMA to PERMA+4: Building Blocks of Well-being: A Systematic Review of the Empirical Literature," *Journal of Positive Psychology* 19, no. 3 (2023): 1. PERMA+4 offers a "more holistic framework" for predicting a subjective sense of well-being. Cabrera and Donaldson, "PERMA to PERMA+4 Building Blocks," 2.
22. Cabrera and Donaldson, "PERMA to PERMA+4 Building Blocks," 2.
23. Seligman, *Flourish*.
24. While PERMA has been repeatedly measured, there is not as much research on PERMA+4. Cabrera and Donaldson, "PERMA to PERMA+4 Building Blocks," 10.
25. Sarah S. Willen et al., "Rethinking Flourishing: Critical Insights and Qualitative Perspectives from the US Midwest," *SSM—Mental Health* 2 (2022): 100056.
26. World Health Organization, "Constitution. Geneva, Switzerland," 1946, https://pmc.ncbi.nlm.nih.gov/articles/PMC2567705/.
27. Other challenges include specifying the character of flourishing versus well-being, thriving, resilience, etc. The nuances among these terms, while important, will not be explored here.
28. Susan Leigh Star and James R. Griesemer, "Institutional Ecology, 'Translations,' and Boundary Objects: Amateurs and Professionals in Berkeley's Museum of Vertebrate Zoology, 1907–39," *Social Studies of Science* 19, no. 3 (1989): 393.
29. Carol D. Ryff and Burton H. Singer, "Know Thyself and Become What You Are: A Eudaimonic Approach to Psychological Well-Being," *Journal of Happiness Studies* 9 (2008): 14.
30. Cheryl Mattingly, *Moral Laboratories: Family Peril and the Struggle for a Good Life* (University of California Press, 2014), 12.
31. Sarah S. Willen, "Flourishing and Health in Critical Perspective: An Invitation to Interdisciplinary Dialogue," *SSM—Mental Health* 2 (2022): 100045. https://doi.org/10.1016/j.ssmmh.2021.100045.
32. Rosemarie Garland-Thomson, "A Cross-Cultural Neuroethics View on the Language of Disability," *AJOB Neuroscience* 10, no. 2 (2019): 201.

33. Garland-Thomson, “Cross-Cultural Neuroethics,” 24.
34. Ian G. Roberts, *Parameter Hierarchies and Universal Grammar* (Oxford University Press, 2019), 203.
35. Willen et al., “Rethinking Flourishing,” 100057.
36. Garland-Thomson, “Cross-Cultural Neuroethics,” 21. First emphasis added, second in the original text.
37. Willen et al., “Rethinking Flourishing,” 100057.
38. Willen et al., “Rethinking Flourishing,” 100057.
39. Willen et al., “Rethinking Flourishing,” 100057.
40. McGill, *The Idea of Happiness*.
41. Central to Augustine’s theology is his understanding of human sinfulness and that only Jesus Christ and adherence to his teachings can save. Those from other religious traditions will find their own equivalents.
42. Although I eschew Augustine’s dualistic understanding of God and the world, I appreciate his thinking on flourishing.
43. Pastoral theologian Karen Scheib, personal communication, October 8, 2024.
44. Thriving in this perspective does not mean a life without sorrow or difficulty but that God is amid the challenges of life. In fact, there is a connection between income and happiness, but it is smaller than most would think. See, for example, Jeremy Cone and Thomas Gilovich, “Understanding Money’s Limits: People’s Beliefs About the Income–Happiness Correlation,” *Journal of Positive Psychology* 5, no. 4 (2010): 294–301.
45. Religious leaders, then, might look for small signs of life by this definition. Besides the attendance numbers and financial challenges, what new life is emerging in the community? What fruits of being seen, valued, and cherished by God are emerging in the life of the congregation?
46. Pastoral theologian Bonnie Miller-McLemore suggested years ago that a metaphor for the interdependence of the global human family is the “human web.” Bonnie J. Miller-McLemore, “The Human Web: Reflections on the State of Pastoral Theology,” *The Christian Century*, April 7, 1993, 366–369. https://irbe.library.vanderbilt.edu/server/api/core/bitstreams/02752ee0-330d-4e18-a3ff-9e1a0c0c22e3/content.
47. Physics is the science that explains the mechanics of how the world works. Physicists study invisible forces such as gravity and thermodynamics, observing and analyzing patterns to define and understand the laws of nature. It provides the basis for understanding how everything works together to create the world as we experience it. Quantum physics pushes the boundaries of what science has assumed until very recently, and it is changing the fundamental understandings of what is true about reality.

48. I first encountered quantum patterns, cosmology, and their powerful metaphors for life together and implications for transformative leadership in the work of Margaret Wheatley. As I embarked on my own course of study in quantum physics, I realized that Wheatley's science was not as careful or nuanced as it could be.
49. Gregory T. Reeves and Curtis E. Hrischuk, "Survey of Engineering Models for Systems Biology," *Computational Biology Journal* 2016, no. 1 (2016): 4106329.
50. Fritjof Capra, *The Web of Life: A New Scientific Understanding of Living Systems* (Anchor, 1996), 81, quoted in Margaret J. Wheatley, *Leadership and the New Science: Discovering Order in a Chaotic World*, 3rd ed. (Berrett-Koehler Publishers, 2006), 34. Physicist David Bohm argues that at a level we cannot discern, there is an "unbroken wholeness." David Bohm, *Wholeness and the Implicate Order* (Routledge, 1980), cited in Wheatley, *New Science*, 42–43.
51. Lesley A. Muray, *An Introduction to the Process-Understanding of Science, Society, and the Self* (Edwin Mellen Press, 1988), 3.
52. Karim Bschir, "Potentiality in Natural Philosophy," in *Physics and Speculative Philosophy: Potentiality in Modern Science*, ed. Timothy E. Eastman et al. (Walter de Gruyter, 2016), 18.
53. In contrast to Newton's understanding, there is nothing (at least at the atomic level) that is stable or unchanging. However, the new science is based on the assertion (commonly demonstrated) that particles such as electrons and photons exhibit both wavelike and particle-like properties and only take one form or the other when observed or measured. This is also referred to as *superposition*, in which a quantum system can simultaneously exist in several states until observation collapses its wave function to a single state. See Kirk Wegter-McNelly, *The Entangled God: Divine Relationality and Quantum Physics* (Routledge, 2012), chaps. 3 and 4, for the mathematical formulae that explain this. In addition, physicists have mathematically demonstrated that a quantum system can exist in multiple states, challenging both the stability and the isolated character of things and, in fact, the world.
54. Muray, *An Introduction to the Process-Understanding*, 5. In process thought, anything actual is an instance of creativity, from the tiniest energy event to the most complex creatures we know of: human beings.
55. Wegter-McNelly, *Entangled God*, 120. "Physicists have never observed entanglement 'in the wild,' so to speak, but rather entangle and disentangle small numbers of particles in the highly controlled and artificial environments of their laboratories," Wegter-McNelly, *Entangled God*, 121. The fact that theories and interpretations are inevitably incomplete and susceptible to revision, even replacement, does not preclude a critical

but nonetheless realistic attitude toward theories we judge to be the best at describing some portion of reality. The same point has been cogently argued about theological theories, in which case the meaning of *best* must be carefully tuned to the "particular nuances of the experiential realm over and against those of the experimental realm." Wegter-McNelly, *Entangled God*, 106.

56. Heraclitus observed 2,500 years ago that a person cannot step into the same river twice. Indeed, as his student Cratylus argued, one can't even step in the same river once. The river changes even as a person steps into it, and so does everything else in the cosmos. As one process thinker puts it, "The world is not composed of things at all if a 'thing' is something that exists over time without changing. [Rather], the world is composed primarily of events and processes." C. Robert Mesle, *Process-Relational Philosophy: An Introduction to Alfred North Whitehead* (Templeton Foundation Press, 2008), 8.

57. Unlike Newtonian mechanics, though, the standard account of quantum theory—commonly referred to as the Copenhagen interpretation after Niels Bohr, its Danish originator—insists that physical objects, from subatomic particles such as electrons to macroscopic objects such as E. Schrödinger's famous cat, can exist not only in classical states such as will-appear-at-A or will-appear-at-B but also in curious nonclassical amalgams, or superpositions, of these states such as will-appear-at-A-and-will-appear-at-B. Although the empirical success of quantum theory stems from its use of superpositions, these strange realities are never actually observed in the laboratory. There, as in everyday life, things always appear only in one classical state or another. Standard quantum theory explains this difficulty by postulating that the act of observation, or measurement, "collapses" a superposition onto one of its components' (classically allowed) states. Kirk Wegter-McNelly, "Quantum Theory," in *Religion Past and Present*. ed. Hans Dieter Betz (Brill, 2011), https://doi.org/10.1163/1877-5888_rpp_SIM_124517. A "presumed feature" of quantum theory can be summed up in the phrase *causal indeterminism*, by which is meant the apparently random character of physical events at the quantum level (such as the decay of a radioactive atom). Wegter-McNelly, *Entangled God*, 15. The central thesis of the relational realist speculative philosophical program is that "the classical, conventional conception of the relationship between a 'physical object' as ontologically extant and 'the history of facts' as epistemic construct by which physical objects are characterized, must be reversed if quantum mechanics is to be coherently understood as an ontologically significant theory." Michael Epperson and Elias Zafiris, *Foundations of Relational Realism: A Topological Approach to Quantum Mechanics and the Philosophy of Nature*

(Lexington Books, 2013), xvi. As theological speech about God, the term *relationality* is frequently used to evoke "dynamism and mutuality, a unity that incorporates difference, an open and welcoming orientation toward 'the other.' As theological speech about humanity, it commonly signals the complex interactions people have with each other and the world around them, as well as their connections to the past and future." Wegter-McNelly, *Entangled God*, 29. For an exploration of ontological relationality in human experience (what I call a *synergistic relationship* between selves and world), see Barbara J. McClure, *Moving Beyond Individualism: Reflections on Theory, Theology and Practice* (Cascade, 2010).

58. This is often called the *doctrine of universal relativity*, which maintains that everything that exists does so on account of its relationships. Muray, *An Introduction to the Process-Understanding*, 6. Despite Einstein's early objections to the "spooky action-at-a-distance" of entanglement systems, John Bell argued in the 1960s, and numerous experiments have subsequently confirmed, that quantum nonlocality is indeed a striking feature of the world. Theologically, this suggests that creation is a place not only of immense times and distances but also one of deep and subtle connections. Kirk Wegter-McNelly, "Quantum Mechanics," in *Religion Past and Present*, ed. Hans Dieter Betz (Brill, 2011), https://doi.org/10.1163/1877-5888_rpp_SIM_124516.
59. Wegter-McNelly, *Entangled God*, 114.
60. Nick Herbert, *Quantum Reality: Beyond the New Physics* (Anchor/Doubleday, 1985), 19, cited in Wegter-McNelly, *Entangled God*, 102.
61. Ted Peters, "Clarity of the Part Versus Meaning of the Whole," in *Beginning with the End: God, Science, and Wolfhart Pannenberg*, ed. C. R. Albright and J. Haugen (Open Court, 1997), 299, cited in Wegter-McNelly, *Entangled God*, 139.
62. Wegter-McNelly, *Entangled God*, 139–140.
63. Mathematician and philosopher Alfred N. Whitehead described existence in terms of a process: He focused on the "becoming, the being, and the relatedness of 'actual entities.'" Whitehead argued that actual entities, or "occurrences," are the real things of which the world is made but are always perishing and reforming, constantly being reconstituted. Alfred North Whitehead, *Process and Reality: An Essay in Cosmology* (Free Press, 1978).
64. Muray, *An Introduction to the Process-Understanding*, 8. Whitehead argues, "Existence . . . is activity ever moving into the future." Alfred North Whitehead, *Modes of Thought* (Free Press, 1968), 169, cited in Andrew M. Davis, *Mind, Value, and the Cosmos: On the Relational Nature of Ultimacy* (Lexington Books, 2020), 199. Davis goes on to note that in Whitehead's work, "existence is not the other side of nothingness

but the outcome of a more fundamental process. This 'ever moving' is a creative process that is older than 'existence,' precisely because it is what existence presupposes . . . Coming into existence is older than existence; becoming is older than being; process is older than stasis; creative activity is older than 'creation'; it must be-come such that becoming is the necessary metaphysical condition of being." Davis, *Mind, Value, and Cosmos*, 200.

65. Even though atoms are popularly depicted in a solar system design with a central nucleus closely surrounded by electrons, there is "considerable space" between the nucleus and its surrounding "cloud" of electrons. One analogy suggests that "if the nucleus were the size of a marble in the center of a stadium, the electrons would be orbiting just outside the stadium." Donald P. Grey, *Quantum Theory and Quantum Mechanics for Beginners: The Introduction Guide for Beginners Who Flunked Math and Science in Plain English* (Bluesource, 2020), 30.

66. As one scientist puts it, "Since quantum physics reveals that nothing is fixed . . . and reality is only defined by observation, then you could say that reality is just a state of potential." Pantheon Space Academy, *Quantum Physics for Beginners* (Pantheon Space Academy, 2021), 53. This is sometimes referred to as *superposition*, defined as the possibility that multiple realities can exist at the same time at the quantum level. As noted, in quantum mechanics, a subatomic particle exists in multiple states at the same time until it is measured, when its position becomes fixed and singular. That is, a subatomic particle "chooses a single state or position" on observation or measurement. Grey, *Quantum Theory and Quantum Mechanics*, 64.

67. In a widely told story, meteorologist Edward Lorenz asked whether the flap of a butterfly wing in Tokyo could affect a tornado in Texas or a thunderstorm in New York. His research suggested that the answer is yes. Edward Lorenz, "The Butterfly Effect," *World Scientific Series on Nonlinear Science Series A* 39 (2000): 91–94.

68. This is Heisenberg's uncertainty principle, which states that it is impossible to simultaneously know the precise position and momentum of a particle with absolute certainty. The more accurately you know one of these properties, the less accurately you can know the other. This principle fundamentally limits our ability to predict the behavior of particles on large or even small scales. This also hints at quantum superposition, a phenomenon in which particles can exist in multiple states at one time until they are measured or observed, at which point the particle "collapses" into one of its possible states, usually the one being measured or observed.

69. Shapes, or forms of organization that correspond to a particular formula, are referred to as *fractals*, which are intricate, repeating patterns—the

shapes—that emerge around a strange attractor. Fractals are intricate, repeating patterns that look similar regardless of how closely one looks at the system or how far one distances oneself from it. Fractals are similar shapes that emerge at different levels of magnification, exhibiting the same shape, the same complexity, and the same detail, such as a head of broccoli or the pattern that emerges on a screen when a mathematical formula (the strange attractor) is entered into a computer designed to display the patterns that emerge from that formula. As one scientist puts it, "Fractals represent a beautiful intersection of mathematics, art, and nature, revealing the underlying order and complexity present in the universe." The science of fractals has been applied to physics, computer graphics, finance, and art and is used in the formation of natural phenomena such as coastlines, clouds, mountains, and biological structures. One group of researchers argues that "it is on the 'boundary of chaos' that the greatest creativity occurs. In the 21st century, [organizations] will no longer be effectively managed by rigid objectives or instructions. Their capacity for self-organization will be derived from how their members accept a shared set of values." Simon Dolan et al., "Understanding and Managing Chaos in Organizations," *International Journal of Management* 20, no. 1 (2003): 23. Strange attractors, then, are metaphorically described in organizational settings as "shared vision, team processes, and information flows used as positive feedback mechanisms." Donald L. Gilstrap, "Strange Attractors and Human Interaction: Leading Complex Organizations Through the Use of Metaphors," *Complicity: An International Journal of Complexity and Education* 2, no. 1 (2005): 55, https://doi.org/10.29173/cmplct8727.

70. According to one interpretation of the law of attraction, whatever we focus on will show in our lives. Pantheon Space Academy, *Quantum Physics for Beginners*, 53. Another interpretation is that what we notice what we care about, and by noticing it, those values come into being through our attention.

71. This is why "invasive species are destructive because they do not operate within this reality: They take everything for themselves and wreak havoc with their insatiable appetites. Likewise, predatory invaders destroy the delicate harmony and balance that an ecosystem has created for itself." Wheatley, *New Science*, 23.

72. This is language scientists use. For example, it is now widely accepted that particles, such as electrons and photons, exhibit both wavelike and particle-like behavior. This concept is known as wave-particle duality. It means that particles can exhibit wavelike properties, such as interference and diffraction, and particle-like properties, such as localized position and momentum. There is some suggestion that whether an energy source

takes the form of a wave or the form of a particle depends on whether one is looking for or studying waves or particles.

73. One physicist suggests that reality should not be defined by its physical properties but by its potential to create life. For example, oxygen would not be defined by its physical properties or chemical formula but by what it made possible. Jeff Carriera, *Spiritual Implications of Quantum Physics* (Emergence Education, 2023), 23.
74. Wheatley, *New Science*, 23.
75. It is important to note that the quantum theory of self-organization does not suggest that all particles, or energies, organize around strange attractors. The theory of strange attractors is a concept more akin to classical physics, but there do seem to be some probabilistic tendencies in organization and the patterns they follow.
76. Despite the dualistic thinking of early philosophers and theologians such as Socrates and Augustine, there were others who understood that reality is one—even before science caught up to them—and these philosophers and religious mystics developed philosophical and theological systems around this view. These principles have also been extended to other fields. For example, strange attractors, while originating in the realm of mathematics and chaos theories, have been applied to disciplines including philosophy, psychology, and cultural studies. Here, it will be applied to theology and transformational leadership. For example, one might say that in theology, the Sacred is the strange attractor; the Sacred is the ultimate value around which spiritual experiences and the beliefs that emerged out of them became organized into religions. The underlying principles of complexity, unpredictability, and emergence that strange attractors embody deeply resonate with human experience. Linda Chamberlain, *Strange Attractors in Patterns of Family Interactions* (Psychology Press, 1995). In philosophy, for example, existential themes of uncertainty, chaos, and the complexities of human existence are organized around themes of relationships, emotions, and a sense of purpose in existence. In psychology, the chaotic and unpredictable dynamics of human experience are organized around themes of such as cognition and behavior that organize into patterns over time, both within individuals and between them. In music, the complexities of myriad and chaotic notes are organized into chords, melodies, and rhythms. In organizational leadership, values and the identity/ies that develop around them are the strange attractors.
77. I have tried to develop a more socially adequate theological anthropology that accounts for the way human beings/selves are fluid and relational, coming into existence and evolving through interactions with different social contexts, coming into being in relation to their relational and

institutional environments. See McClure, *Moving Beyond Individualism*. For the ways emotions are "constructed" from components both within people and in their environments, see Barbara J. McClure, *Emotions: Problems and Promise for Human Flourishing* (Baylor University Press, 2019).

78. Whitehead believed that mathematics was the foundation of all science and that philosophical assertions about reality must be consistent with scientific formulations of reality. John Cobb Jr. and David Ray Griffin, *Process Theology: An Introductory Exposition* (Westminster Press, 1976), 14.
79. Cobb and Griffin, *Process Theology*, 8–9. The application of Whitehead's process thought to theology was not difficult. Whitehead understood religion as "the vision of something which stands beyond, behind, and within, the passing flux of immediate things; something which is real, and yet waiting to be realized; something which is a remote possibility, and yet the greatest of present facts; something that gives meaning to all that passes, and yet eludes all apprehension; something whose possession is the final good, and yet is beyond all reach; something which is the ultimate ideal, and the hopeless quest" (1925 [1967]), 191–192. Alfred North Whitehead, "Alfred North Whitehead," *Stanford Encyclopedia of Philosophy*, last modified March 10, 2015, https://plato.stanford.edu/entries/whitehead/.
80. Cobb and Griffin, *Process Theology*, 13.
81. Cobb and Griffin, *Process Theology*, 15.
82. A motion picture suggests an analogy of what Whitehead meant: The picture appears to be a continuous flow, but in reality, it is "constituted by a series of distinct frames." Cobb and Griffin, *Process Theology*, 14. What we call *human beings* are just a series of occasions, or events of concreteness (*concrescence*), that we experience as a consistent person. Individuals, organizations, societies, etc. are always in the process of becoming. In Whitehead's formulation, "the past is composed of those events that have occurred; the future is radically different, since it contains no occasions; and the present is the occasion that is now occurring. The present is influenced by the past and will influence the future." Cobb and Griffin, *Process Theology*, 15–16.
83. C. Robert Mesle, *Process Theology: A Basic Introduction* (Chalice Press, 1993), 8.
84. This is a phrase Aristotle used. In Aristotle's philosophy, the Unmoved Mover is a transcendent, eternal, and immutable being that serves as the ultimate cause of all motion and change in the cosmos. This entity, "God," is unmoved and unmovable because it exists outside the realm of the material world. It does not change and is not subject to external forces. Rather, the Unmoved Mover is the source of all motion and

change in everything else, the prime mover that sets the universe in motion. The concept of the Unmoved Mover has been highly influential in Western philosophy and theology, particularly in discussions about the nature of God or the ultimate principle behind the universe's existence and order. Theologians such as Thomas Aquinas incorporated it into Christian theology as part of the cosmological arguments for the existence of God; This might invite reflection on Paul Tillich's conviction that "God" is the "ground of all being" and "creative power." Paul Tillich, *Systematic Theology* (University of Chicago Press, 1963), III:283.

85. Wegter-McNelly, *Entangled God*. The leap to theology from science can only be metaphorical since both are provisional understandings, and there is no hard evidence (yet) of a quantum world through and through. Here I intentionally use non-anthropomorphized language for God. While some theologians argue that personalized language for God, including the use of personal pronouns—usually he/him/his but sometimes also she/her—is vital for understanding a personal God, I disagree (see, for example, Wegter-McNelly, *Entangled God*, 126). One can find ways to refer to God in non-anthropomorphized ways that are also deeply personal, for example, identifying the *imago dei* in each person as their unique life force, the "Goodness beyond Being" within (John D. Caputo, *Hoping Against Hope: Confessions of a Postmodern Pilgrim* [Fortress Press, 2015]), and the "Ground of Being." (Tillich, *Systematic Theology*, III: 283). Physicist and theologian Robert Russell characterized God in Tillichian fashion as the "kind of ground of being in which differences need not be contradictions, distinctions need not be isolations, separate entities need not produce alienation, and in which, even at the elementary physical level, distant and simultaneous events need not be ultimately unrelated." Robert Russell, "Quantum Physics in Philosophical and Theological Perspective," in *Physics, Philosophy, and Theology: A Common Quest for Understanding*, ed. R. J. Russell et al. (Vatican Observatory, 1988), 365–366. Cited in Wegter-McNelly, *Entangled God*, 135.
86. Wegter-McNelly, *Entangled God*, 126, 144.
87. Wegter-McNelly, *Entangled God*, 124.
88. Epperson and Zafiris, *Foundations of Relational Realism*. See also Davis, *Mind, Value, and the Cosmos*, 1. As one process philosopher states, "People are islands, but islands aren't what they appear to be. Deeper down, even islands, like waves, are merely faces of a deeper unity. If we cannot see that unity, we imperil the web in which we live." Mesle, *Process-Relational Philosophy*, 9.
89. Classical theologies include, for example, those of Karl Barth and Juergen Moltmann.
90. Muray, *An Introduction to the Process-Understanding*, 106.

91. Mesle, *Process-Relational Philosophy*, 83. Imagining God as a being, and using personal pronouns such as *he* for God, could be seen as an error of misplaced concreteness, a term Whitehead used to describe the misguided tendency to present the abstract as concrete. I understand God as love, that which connects and binds toward life.
92. Mesle, *Process-Relational Philosophy*, 5.
93. At present, there is no "empirically well-confirmed theory" within which it is possible to treat the universe as a quantum object (string theory and other possibilities are still untestable). Still, this quantum cosmology can serve as ground for a metaphor for the creative impulse of the universe. Wegter-McNelly, *Entangled God*, 123.
94. As Whitehead argued, "When we speak about God, we are saying something about the world . . . and when we speak about the world, we are saying something about God." Alfred North Whitehead, *Religion in the Making* (Cambridge University Press, 1926), 58, cited in Davis, *Mind, Value, and Cosmos*, 192.
95. Whitehead, *Process and Reality*, xiv, 7, 21, cited in Davis, *Mind, Value, and Cosmos*, 200.
96. Davis, *Mind, Value, and Cosmos*, 201.
97. I have put *knows* in quotes here because I do not believe God has a conscious mind (though others argue against me on this), as the word might suggest (and I have already resisted anthropomorphized terms for God above). In process theology, God is always seen as acting persuasively, not coercively, "luring" the world to its fulfillment with an ideal possibility offered in each moment. However, all actualities are free in how they respond to God's lure, whether they actualize it (to whatever degree), reject it, or fall somewhere on the spectrum. God is always inviting the world (and everything in it) to become more than what it has been, to greater realizations of value and beauty in interdependence with each other. And just as God has an active quality, God also has a receptive one; just as the past of the whole universe flows into the becoming of any actuality, the whole universe flows into God. Not only do all actualities (or concrete manifestations of creative processes) prehend the lure of God; God prehends all actualities. Thus, all experience becomes part of the divine "memory." In addition, creation, for many process theologians, is a mutual act. For example, Christian process theologian Marjorie Suchocki has argued that creation is never a result of unilateral production but rather a matter of divine call and creaturely response: "God calls; creation responds. God then responds to the creation's response, and building upon it, calls yet again. Through call and response, the creation comes into being as world. It is incremental, gradual, with creation participating in its own becoming." Marjorie

Suchocki, *Divinity and Diversity: A Christian Affirmation of Religious Pluralism* (Abingdon Press, 2003), 28–29.

98. The writings of A. N. Whitehead, C. Hartshorne, J. Cobb, C. Keller, and other process thinkers are full of the sense of the tragic character of existence—that is, the possibilities never actualized, the perpetual perishing, the resistance to the possibility of newness of life, and the ambiguity of all instances of creative freedom that can always be used for good or ill. This is one reason knowing how to grieve well is an important element of human flourishing.
99. This is referred to as *panentheism*. Process theologian David Ray Griffin outlines the panentheistic position as one in which "the world's causal patterns are part and parcel of that which exists necessarily, understood as not simply God (as traditional theism says), or simply as world (as atheism says), but God-and-the-world." Panentheism has a long history in both philosophical and theological traditions. It finds a central place, though, in the process metaphysics developed by Whitehead. David Ray Griffin, *Panentheism and Scientific Naturalism* (Process Century Press, 2014), 2. Process metaphysicians argue that God is also subject to the same process and duration that any other entity in the universe is. Didier Debaise, *Speculative Empiricism: Revisiting Whitehead* (Edinburgh University Press, 2017), 27. This process is a continual creative becoming. The universe, like God, is a creative advance into novelty. Whitehead, *Process and Reality*, 222.
100. Davis, *Mind, Value, and Cosmos*, 7.
101. Davis, *Mind, Value, and Cosmos*, 202.
102. Rabbi Bradley Shavit Artson argues that the many translations of the Bible that refer to God as the "Almighty" derives from a mistranslation of *El Shaddai*. He notes that the Torah has terms for great power and unsearchable strength (for example, Psalm 145: 3 and Job 9:10), but "it has neither the concept nor a term for omnipotence." Rabbi Bradley Shavit Artson, *God of Becoming and Relationship: The Dynamic Nature of Process Theology* (Jewish Lights Publishing, 2013), 4–5. As Whitehead puts it, "God is that actual entity from which each temporal concrescence receives that initial aim from which its own self creation starts," Whitehead, *Process and Reality*, 244. Hartshorne imagines the God-world relationship akin to the soul and the body. Hartshorne thinks of each cell in the brain at each moment as an individual subject that receives from others and in turns acts on others. Each cellular event or experience is also taken up into the unified experience of the human person. This experience is not just made up of all the cellular experiences added to one another. Instead, it integrates them into a single coherent experience with its own memories and anticipations. Similarly, all human

(and other material) experiences are taken up into the unified cosmic experience that is God. Hartshorne called his view *panentheism*. David Ray Griffin calls this view of God as the "mind" of the world *hierarchical dualism* rather than a metaphysical one. David Ray Griffin, *Religion and Scientific Naturalism: Overcoming the Conflicts* (State University of New York Press, 2000), 176, cited in Mesle, *Process-Relational Philosophy*, 39.

103. Wegter-McNelly, *Entangled God*, 134.

104. God's power is the power that "enables all of reality to continue its creative advance, that makes creatures free, that shares the experience of every creature and is experienced by every creature. God's creative power sustains the universe." Mesle, *Process Theology*, 14. Relational power has three vital elements: (1) the ability to be actively open to and affected by the world around us, (2) the ability to create ourselves out of what we have taken in, and (3) the ability to influence those about us by having first been affected by them. Mesle, *Process-Relational Philosophy*, 76.

105. Because there is no distance between God and the world, God cannot "intervene" from the "outside" to change things on earth. Scientist/theologian Robert Russell and others have specifically appealed to the idea of quantum indeterminism in their attempts to mount a theological argument for the possibility of noninterventionist, objectively special divine action in the world. Wegter-McNelly, *Entangled God*, 15.

106. Wegter-McNelly, *Entangled God*, 140.

107. Wegter-McNelly, *Entangled God*, 34.

108. This is a small part, on the creaturely side, of what it means for God to create "freely." Wegter-McNelly, *Entangled God*, 141.

109. Mesle, *Process Theology*, 13.

110. Years ago, I read a devotion that struck me as so powerful that I wrote it on an index card and have it taped to my computer to this day. It reads, "I am part of a web that is pure relationship, with energy that is available to me that has been around since the universe was born. God is the web, the energy, the space, the light, the life. God is not captured in any other concept but revealed in that singular, vast net of relationship that animates all that is." Unfortunately, the edges of the card are so frayed now that I cannot read the attribution, but I think it may have been from Roman Catholic priest and process theologian Richard Rohr.

111. This is often referred to as *panentheism*, or *everything in God*. That is a different perspective than pantheism (God is everything).

112. Thich Nhat Hanh, *Old Path, White Clouds: Walking in the Footsteps of the Buddha* (Parallax, 1991), 169.

113. See, for example, Ken Wilbur, *A Theory of Everything: An Integral Vision for Business, Politics, Science, and Spirituality* (Shambhala, 2001) and *Integral Psychology: Consciousness, Spirit, Psychology, Therapy* (Shambhala, 2001).

114. Kenneth Gergen, *Relational Being: Beyond Self and Community* (Oxford University Press, 2009), 372.
115. McClure, *Moving Beyond Individualism.*
116. For how human beings develop in synergistic relationship to what is in their environments, see McClure, *Moving Beyond Individualism*, especially chap. 5, and *Emotions*, especially chaps. 6 and 7.
117. Richard Barrett, *The Values-Driven Organization: Unleashing Human Potential for Performance and Profit* (Routledge, 2014), 15.
118. The nature of these components will vary by circumstance, of course.
119. Laura L. Carstensen et al., "Emotional Experience in Everyday Life Across the Adult Life Span," *Journal of Personality and Social Psychology* 79, no. 4 (2000): 644–655.
120. Pastoral theologian Mary Clark Moschella suggests joy as an important outcome of caring work, for both the caregiver and the care receiver. See Mary Clark Moschella, *Caring for Joy: A Pastoral Theology of Hope and Healing* (Brill Academic Publishers, 2016).
121. In fact, studies show that when people are flourishing, they are more resilient and are more likely to engage.
122. "Love" is the word some cosmologists are bold enough to use to describe the attractional force that holds planets in orbit and provides the glue that holds atoms together. Thomas J. Oord, ed., "Love and Cosmology," in *Defining Love: A Philosophical, Scientific, and Theological Engagement* (Brazos, 2010), 137–72. Christian theologians would likely agree. For example, scientist and theologian Teilhard de Chardin called the attraction at the heart of the universe "Love," or more frequently, "God-Omega." In de Chardin's understanding, all of creation is oriented toward the integral wholeness that is achieved through unity in love. See also Brian P. Hall, *The Genesis Effect: Human and Organizational Transformation* (repr., Resource Publishing/Wipf and Stock, 2000), for a description of the values that express and work toward such wholeness.
123. Process theologian Thomas Jay Oord defines love as actively working toward the well-being of another. Thomas Jay Oord, *Defining Love: A Philosophical, Scientific, and Theological Engagement* (Brazos, 2010).
124. Caputo, *Hoping Against Hope*, 61.
125. McClure, *Emotions*, 172–175.
126. Caputo, *Hoping Against Hope*, 79.
127. Margaret J. Wheatley, *Finding Our Way: Leadership for Uncertain Times* (Berrett-Koehler Publishers, 2007), 39.
128. Caputo, *Hoping Against Hope*, 108.
129. The Christian tradition asserts that Jesus of Nazareth responded fully to the sacred insistence and so was recognized by his community as the Christ. See Paul Tillich's discussion of this Christology in his *Systematic*

Theology, vol. II (University of Chicago Press, 1957), and Mesle, *Process Theology*, 104–109. To the extent that religious traditions support and encourage the ideals and practices of love, care, inclusion, diversity, beauty, goodness, and justice, they are worthy of our engagement. To the extent that they do not, they invite our resistance.

CHAPTER 4: CONSTRAINTS ON HUMAN FLOURISHING

1. In an ongoing debate between Pope Francis and Michael Novak (who openly supports neoliberal capitalism), the pope has decried the ways neoliberalism has taken over church life and leadership. Francis argues that we have not analyzed the problems of contemporary society and the appropriate Christian response. Instead, Christian churches, he fears, have adopted neoliberal values and systems, making neoliberalism a crypto religion. Luca Mavelli, "Neoliberalism as Religion: Sacralization of the Market and Post-truth Politics," *International Political Sociology* 14, no. 1 (March 2020): 57–76, https://doi.org/10.1093/ips/olz021.
2. Ryan Burge, "Why It's Unlikely US Mainline Protestants Outnumber Evangelicals," *Religion Unplugged*, July 12, 2021, https://religionunplugged.com/news/2021/7/12/why-its-unlikely-us-mainline-protestants-outnumber-evangelicals.
3. Martha C. Nussbaum and Amartya Sen have argued this in their edited volume *The Quality of Life* (Oxford University Press, 1993).
4. Deuteronomy 30:15–20, *The Holy Bible*.
5. This is adapted from Barbara J. McClure, *Emotions: Problems and Promise for Human Flourishing* (Baylor University Press, 2010), chap. 7.
6. Self-actualization is psychologist Abraham Maslow's understanding of the highest goal of human development and of flourishing. Abraham Maslow and Karen J. Lewis, "Maslow's Hierarchy of Needs," *Salenger Incorporated* 14, no. 17 (1987): 987–990.
7. See Ryan LaMothe, *Care of Souls, Care of Polis: Toward a Political Pastoral Theology* (Cascade Books, 2017), especially chaps. 6 and 7 for a helpful discussion of this that takes neoliberalism into account.
8. Charlene Spretnak, *Relational Reality: New Discoveries of Interrelatedness That Are Transforming the Modern World* (Green Horizons, 2011).
9. The quantum view of the universe suggests that all life exists in an infinite series of nesting Russian dolls—from infinitesimally small subatomic ones that no existing technology allows scientists to see to the most expansive ones that exist at the cosmic level and are beyond scientists' present ability to observe. Everything that *is* exists within this nesting of life, from the smallest particle to the system of billions of galaxies into

uncountable universes. This organization has been described as the goal of evolution: a persistent pull toward increasing wholeness, complexity, and perhaps even consciousness. Human beings are just one part of this nested reality. David Benner, *Human Being and Becoming: Living the Interpersonal Adventure* (InterVarsity Press, 2003).

10. Spretnak, *Relational Reality*, 12–15. "God," then, is best understood as an urgent invitation, a restlessness hoping for (insisting on) love, and meaningful connection. It is an insistence that strains to exist in and as forgiveness, justice, mercy, and right relationship. John D. Caputo, *Hoping Against Hope: Confessions of a Postmodern Pilgrim* (Fortress Press, 2015), 61.
11. Paul Davies, *The Cosmic Blueprint: New Discoveries in Nature's Ability to Order the Universe* (Templeton, 2004). Cited in Benner, *Human Being and Becoming*, 29.
12. Frantz Fanon, *The Wretched of the Earth*, trans. Richard Philcox (Grove Press, 2021).
13. Rodney Clapp, *Naming Neoliberalism: Exposing the Spirit of Our Age* (Fortress Press, 2021), 23.
14. Clapp, *Naming Neoliberalism*, 3.
15. Clapp, *Naming Neoliberalism*, 19.
16. See Kathryn Tanner, *Christianity and the New Spirit of Capitalism* (Yale University Press, 2019); Sarah Byrnes and Chuck Collins, "The Equity Crisis: The True Costs of Extractive Capitalism," in *The Community Resilience Reader*, ed. Daniel Lerch (Island Press, 2017), https://doi.org/10.5822/978-1-61091-861-9_6; Naomi Klein, *The Shock Doctrine: The Rise of Disaster Capitalism* (Henry Holt, 2007); Nancy Fraser, *Cannibal Capitalism: How Our System Is Devouring Democracy, Care, and the Planet, and What We Can Do About It* (Verso, 2022); and Manfred B. Steger and Ravi K. Roy, *Neoliberalism: A Very Short Introduction*, 2nd ed. (Oxford University Press, 2021).
17. Steger and Roy, *Neoliberalism*, 13.
18. Bruce Rogers-Vaughn, "Soul Talk in a Neoliberal Age: Part 1," *Radical Discipleship*, last modified August 21, 2020, https://radicaldiscipleship.net/2020/08/21/soul-talk-in-a-neoliberal-age-part-1/.
19. Because of the variety of its manifestations, neoliberalism is best understood as "neoliberalisms." Steger and Roy, *Neoliberalism*, xviii.
20. Rogers-Vaughn, "Soul Talk in a Neoliberal Age: Part 1."
21. Clapp, *Naming Neoliberalism*, ix.
22. This discussion of rentiers is found in Rogers-Vaughn, "Soul Talk in a Neoliberal Age: Part 1."
23. Rogers-Vaughn, "Soul Talk in a Neoliberal Age: Part 1."
24. In just one example among many, Big Pharma has put millions into the development and marketing of Viagra, a medicine for the rich, while those

who wish to develop treatments for malaria, a disease that kills millions of people each year in the Global South, are hard-pressed to get funding.

25. Clapp, *Naming Neoliberalism*, 5. Proponents of neoliberal capitalist systems believe that when there is a wealth gap, those less advantaged will be motivated to work harder to get ahead, thus fueling the system of profit (which, it must be noted, rarely trickles down to the laborer, front line worker, managers, or even all executives).
26. Clapp, *Naming Neoliberalism*, 41. Clapp notes that the magisterial reformers, including Calvin, "unambiguously condemned avarice, acquisitive individualism, and any separation of economic behavior from biblical morality or the common good," 12.
27. Bruce Rogers-Vaughn, "Soul Talk in a Neoliberal Age: Part III," *Radical Discipleship*, last modified September 4, 2020, https://radicaldiscipleship.net/2020/09/04/soul-talk-in-a-neoliberal-age-part-iii/.
28. Clapp, *Naming Neoliberalism*, 43.
29. Theologian Fumitaka Matsuoka argues that sin is the "negation of relation." Racism negates the relation of mutual care and respect that creation in God's image describes and intends for humanity. Negation also rightly names the effect of choosing to look away, to lie about the humanity of another so that accountability for behavior can be avoided. Matsuoka asserts that racism "monopolizes the imagination" of whites so that we see only through the rationalizations or lies that are necessary to reproduce and sustain interlocking systems of dominance. Fumitaka Matsuoka, *The Color of Faith: Building Community in a Multicultural Society* (United Church Press, 1989), 59.
30. Tanner, *Christianity and the New Spirit of Capitalism*.
31. Tanner, *Christianity and the New Spirit of Capitalism*.
32. Walter Benjamin, "Capitalism as Religion," in *Walter Benjamin: Selected Writings, Volume 1: 1913–1926*, ed. Marcus Bullock and Michael W. Jennings (Belknap Press of Harvard University Press, 1996), cited in Clapp, *Naming Neoliberalism*, 57.
33. Neoliberal capitalism relies, too, on partial and in accurate information. Many organizations hide their goals and practices, lying about what they are doing to cover up the damage they do to communities, people, and the planet in the pursuit of profit. On common practices of deceptive accounting, see, for example, Sarah Gibbens, "Europe Burns a Controversial 'Renewable' Energy Source: Trees from the U.S.," *National Geographic*, November 11, 2021, https://www.nationalgeographic.com/environment/article/europe-burns-controversial-renewable-energy-trees-from-us.
34. Rogers-Vaughn, "Soul Talk in a Neoliberal Age: Part III."
35. Cedrick C. Johnson, *Race, Religion, and Resilience in the Neoliberal Age* (Palgrave Macmillan, 2016), cited in Bruce Rogers-Vaughn, *Caring for Souls in a Neoliberal Age* (Palgrave Macmillan, 2016), 23.

36. Clapp, *Naming Neoliberalism*, 7.
37. Bruce Rogers-Vaughn, "Soul Talk in a Neoliberal Age: Part IV," *Radical Discipleship*, last modified September 4, 2020, https://radicaldiscipleship.net/2020/09/04/soul-talk-in-a-neoliberal-age-part-iv/.
38. Rogers-Vaughn, "Soul Talk in a Neoliberal Age: Part IV."
39. Rogers-Vaughn, "Soul Talk in a Neoliberal Age: Part IV."
40. Tom C. W. Lin, "Financial Weapons of War," *Minnesota Law Review* 100 (2015): 1377.
41. Bruce Rogers-Vaughn, "The Social Trifecta of Human Misery and Problematical Constructions of the Self: Implications for Formation and Supervision," 2012, https://ir.vanderbilt.edu/items/f2dcf313-d2cb-4f84-9f54-09c00edeb9c5.
42. Rogers-Vaughn, "Soul Talk in a Neoliberal Age: Part III."
43. Bruce Rogers-Vaughn, "Powers and Principalities: Initial Reflections Toward a Post-Capitalist Pastoral Theology," *Journal of Pastoral Theology* 25, no. 2 (2015): 71–92.
44. As antiracist scholar Ibram Kendi argues, "Capitalism is essentially racist; racism is essentially capitalist. They are birthed together from the same unnatural causes, and [one hopes] they shall one day die together from unnatural causes. Or racial capitalism will live into another epoch of theft and rapacious inequity, especially if activists naïvely fight the conjoined twins independently, as if they are not the same." Ibram X. Kendi, *How to Be an Antiracist* (One World, 2023).
45. Rogers-Vaughn, "Soul Talk in a Neoliberal Age: Part III." See also Rogers-Vaughn, *Caring for Souls in a Neoliberal Age*.
46. The cover of Nancy Frasier's book *Cannibal Capitalism* is the image of an ouroboros, an ancient Egyptian image of a serpent or dragon eating itself by the tail. Fraser, *Cannibal Capitalism*.
47. As outlined in Margaret J. Wheatley, *Who Do We Choose to Be?: Facing Reality, Claiming Leadership, Restoring Sanity*, 2nd ed. (Berrett-Koehler Publishers, 2017), 40–42.
48. Tanner, *Christianity and the New Spirit of Capitalism*.
49. Sir John Glubb, *The Fate of Empires and Search for Survival* (William Blackwood & Sons, Ltd., 1976), cited in Wheatley, *Who Do We Choose to Be?* 2nd ed., 321.
50. "Wicked problems" are defined as complex, multifaceted issues that are difficult or impossible to solve because of their interconnectedness, uncertainty, and lack of a clear, definitive solution. Tom Ritchey, "Wicked Problems," *Acta Morphologica Generalis* 2, no. 1 (2013).
51. Wheatley, *Who Do We Choose to Be?* 1st ed., 11.
52. Wheatley, *Who Do We Choose to Be?* 1st ed., 11.
53. Steger and Roy, *Neoliberalism*.

54. *Post-truth* was the international word of the year in 2016, based on the political processes in the United States and the United Kingdom. The *Oxford Dictionary* defines *post-truth* as "relating to or denoting circumstances in which objective facts are less influential in shaping public opinion than appeals to emotion and personal belief," "Post-Truth Just Added to Oxford Dictionary," *Elite Daily*, accessed June 28, 2017, https://www.elitedaily.com/news/post-truth-just-added-to-oxford-dictionary/2005066. The dictionary added the word *gaslighting* in 2017, defined as "the process of making somebody believe untrue things in order to control them, especially that they have imagined or been wrong about what has really happened," "Gaslighting," *Oxford Learner's Dictionaries*, accessed January 11, 2025, https://www.oxfordlearnersdictionaries.com/definition/english/gaslighting.
55. Some scholars have even argued that "selves" no longer exist as meaningful entities. In the current situation, human beings have become empty shells, zombies wandering crowded streets. Philip Cushman, *Constructing the Self, Constructing America: A Cultural History of Psychotherapy* (Basic Books, 1995), and Rogers-Vaughn, *Caring for Souls*, 99.
56. Pastoral theologian Nancy Ramsay has argued that those in power suffer from this unjust and oppressive system too. Nancy Ramsay, "Where Race and Gender Collide: Deconstructing Racial Privilege," in *Women Out of Order: Risking Change and Creating Care in a Multicultural World*, ed. Jeanne Stevenson-Moessner and Teresa Snorton (Fortress Press, 2010), 331–340.
57. Third-order suffering is in Bruce Rogers-Vaughn, *Caring for Souls in a Neoliberal Age* (Palgrave Macmillan, 2019), 28.
58. Rogers-Vaughn, *Caring for Souls in a Neoliberal Age*, 131–162. In this case, Rogers-Vaughan argues, "its genius is that it has managed to do this while appearing 'progressive.' During the 1980s and 1990s, as neoliberalism was becoming the new normal, the academy embraced theories of postmodernity, critical race theories, gender and feminist studies, and postcolonial literature. These new intellectual movements analyzed and decried racism, sexism, heterosexism, and Western imperialism, and *yet did so virtually without any reference to capitalism or class.* (Class was occasionally cited but rarely theorized.) Ironically, the mention of class or capitalism is now imagined to be a distinguishing marker of a brand called 'old Marxist white men.'" Rogers-Vaughn, "Soul Talk in a Neoliberal Age: Part IV," emphasis in the original. Pastoral theologian Philip Helsel attempts to redress this when he argues, "Today people are working in worse conditions than ever before, often with less pay and fewer rights. They face frequent unemployment and carry heavy debts simply to survive. All of these factors have direct psychological

effects that are not described clearly by dominant medical frameworks for mental illness." Thus, class disparities are an appropriate focus of religious and spiritual care. Philip Browning Helsel, *Pastoral Power Beyond Psychology's Marginalization: Resisting the Discourses of the Psy-Complex* (Palgrave Macmillan, 2015).

59. Kendi, *How to Be an Antiracist*. As described by Nancy Fraser in her book *The Old Is Dying and the New Cannot Be Born* (2019), this is today's dominant hegemony, and it is a powerful alliance among social movements advocating diversity, multiculturalism, antiracism, environmentalism, and so on; the financial and "symbolic" sectors of the US economy (Wall Street, Silicon Valley, and Hollywood) will continue unchallenged. Generally, this alliance sees oppression (racism, sexism, etc.) as originating "inside the heads" of individuals. Nancy Fraser, *The Old Is Dying and the New Cannot Be Born: From Progressive Neoliberalism to Trump and Beyond* (Verso, 2019). See also Rogers-Vaughn, "Soul Talk in a Neoliberal Age: Part V."
60. Friedrich Nietzsche, *The Will to Power*, ed. Walter Kaufmann and R. J. Hollingdale, trans. Walter Kaufmann (Vintage Books, 1968).
61. Rogers-Vaughn, "Soul Talk in a Neoliberal Age: Part V."
62. Rogers-Vaughn, "Soul Talk in a Neoliberal Age: Part I."
63. Rogers-Vaughn, "Soul Talk in a Neoliberal Age: Part V."
64. Bruce Rogers-Vaughn, *Caring for Souls in a Neoliberal Age*. See also, for example, E. Illouz, *Saving the Modern Soul: Therapy, Emotions, and the Culture of Self-help* (University of California Press, 2008), and J. M. Silva, *Coming Up Short: Working-class Adulthood in an Age of Uncertainty* (Oxford University Press, 2013).
65. Rogers-Vaughn, *Caring for Souls in a Neoliberal Age*, 2.
66. Echoing Ephesians 6:12 in the *New Testament*, Walter Wink called these the "powers and principalities" of contemporary life. Walter Wink, *Powers and Principalities* (Doubleday, 1984).
67. One leadership scholar writes, "One thing that impedes effective change is being locked into rigid or restricted approaches to leadership." David V. Day et al., *Leader Development for Transforming Organizations: Growing Leaders for Tomorrow* (Lawrence Erlbaum Associates, 2004), 9.
68. Wheatley, *Who Do We Choose to Be?*, 2nd ed., 27.
69. I am not idealizing the ways religious communities and faith traditions can function. I am aware of the hurt that these traditions have wrought, and I am calling for religious leaders to help them find a different, more faithful way.
70. For more on this, see Cedric Johnson's book *Race, Religion and Resilience in the Neoliberal Age*, and theologians Nestor Miguel et al.'s text *Beyond the Spirit of Empire: Theology and Politics in a New Key* (SCM Press,

2009), sociologist Saskia Sasson's *Expulsions: Brutality and Complexity in the Global Economy* (Harvard University Press, 2014), feminist philosopher and activist Naomi Klein's *This Changes Everything: Capitalism v. the Climate* (Simon & Schuster, 2014), epidemiologists Richard Wilkinson and Kate Pickett's *A Convenient Truth: A Better Society for Us and for the Planet* (Bloomsbury, 2023), sociologist Luca Mavelli's "Neoliberalism as Religion," *International Political Sociology*, 14, no. 1(2020), and Black psychiatrist and decolonial scholar Franz Fanon's *A Dying Colonialism*, trans. Haakon Chevalier (Grove Press, 1994), *Alienation and Freedom*(Bloomsbury, 2018), and *The Wretched of the Earth*, trans. Richard Philcox (Grove Press, 2004).

71. Clapp, *Naming Neoliberalism*, 20; Miroslav Volf, *Flourishing: Why We Need Religion in a Globalized World* (Yale University Press, 2015).
72. These are adapted from Margaret Wheatley, *Who Do We Choose to Be?*, 1st ed., 114–115.
73. In family systems parlance, differentiated leaders can step outside the situation to see it objectively, to manage their own and others' emotions, to help reasonably name the problem, and to join others in solution seeking. When a crisis happens, religious leaders do well to notice whether people are able to stay calm and work through it together or whether they come undone. Ronald W. Richardson, *Creating a Healthier Church: Family Systems Theory, Leadership, and Congregational Life*, 2nd ed. (The Alban Institute, 2005).
74. I prefer the language of "kindom" rather than "kingdom," borrowed from Ada María Isasi-Díaz, *Mujerista Theology: A Theology for the Twenty-First Century* (Orbis Books, 1996).
75. Clapp, *Naming Neoliberalism*, 185–206.
76. Matthew 18:19–20, *The Holy Bible*.
77. Moschella constructs a theology of joy that embodies compassion, connection, justice, and freedom. She argues that care must be deep enough to hold human suffering and spacious enough to take in divine goodness, beauty, and love. Mary Clark Moschella, "Affect in Narrative Spiritual Care," *Pastoral Psychology* 73, no. 2 (2024): 151–162.

CHAPTER 5: CREATING A THRIVING ORGANIZATION

1. Margaret J. Wheatley, *Finding Our Way: Leadership for Uncertain Times* (Berrett-Koehler Publishers, 2007), 50–51.
2. Wheatley, *Who Do We Choose to Be?*, 1st ed., 64.
3. Wheatley, *Finding Our Way*, 86–88.
4. Wheatley, *Finding Our Way*, 37. Wheatley writes, "It is both sad and ironic that we have treated organizations like machines, acting as

though they were dead when all this time they've been living, open systems capable of self-renewal." She notes that many organizations are led to work like machines, deteriorating and losing capacity, predetermined to waste away because of the Second Law of Thermodynamics—the trajectory of heat energy from useful to useless. (The First Law of Thermodynamics states that the *quantity* of energy is always conserved, neither created nor destroyed as it changes form.) Margaret J. Wheatley, *Leadership and the New Science: Discovering Order in a Chaotic World* (Berrett-Koehler, 2006), 77.

5. Wheatley, *Finding Our Way*, 40.
6. Self-managed teams are far more productive than any other form of organization. There is a clear correlation between participation and productivity. In fact, productivity gains in truly self-managed work environments are *at a minimum 35 percent higher* than in traditionally managed organizations. Wheatley, *Finding Our Way*, 65. Emphasis in the original.
7. Wheatley, *Finding Our Way*, 40.
8. Wheatley, *Finding Our Way*, 45–54.
9. Wheatley, *New Science*, chap. 6.
10. As Wheatley describes it, living networks display incredible communicating power when information is meaningful to them. Meaningful information "lights up a network and moves through it like a windswept brush fire." Wheatley, *Finding Our Way*, 109. It is no wonder that employees frequently cite poor communication as one of their organizations' most significant problems. People are aware that information is critical to their ability to meaningfully engage. Wheatley notes that despite the barrage of information in the world in the twenty-first century, what people and organizations *really* need is knowledge, or information that is meaningful to them at the time they are receiving it. Meaningless information, in contrast, "smolders at the gates until somebody dumps cold water on it." The capacity of a network to communicate with itself is "truly awe-inspiring; its transmission capability far surpasses any other mode of communication." Wheatley, *Finding Our Way*, 109.
11. Stress deprives the human brain of its ability to see patterns. People become reactive and lose the capacity to understand their work as part of a larger system. People also have difficulty with memory and become forgetful. Then there are the physical manifestations of sleeplessness, restlessness, sudden anger, and unpredictable reactivity.
12. Wheatley notes that one organization began to think of information not as power but "as nourishment." Wheatley, *New Science*, 101.
13. Wheatley, *Finding Our Way*, 106.
14. Many studies show that when people belong to an organization or a community, they are healthier, both physically and mentally. People who

work together in groups are happier than those who are isolated, and the harder the work people are engaged in, the tighter the bonds since they must depend on each other to complete important tasks. Wheatley, *Finding Our Way*, 102–103. See also Barabara J. McClure, *Emotions: Problems and Promise for Human Flourishing* (Baylor University Press, 2019), chap. 7.

15. Authentic communities are places where people can be themselves and seek to understand one another rather than be right, attention is paid to differences and uniqueness is valued, there is less judgment and a positive understanding of conflict. Margaret Kornfeld, *Cultivating Wholeness: A Guide to Care and Counseling in Faith Communities* (Continuum International Publishing, 2002), chap. 2.
16. In Wheatley, *Finding Our Way*, 177.
17. Individual behaviors coevolve as individuals interact with system dynamics. If we want to change individual behaviors, we must pay attention to the dynamics of the system. Effective leaders can use what is going on in the system to understand individual behavior and explore it to learn about the whole.
18. In the Judeo-Christian tradition, this work is founded on belief in the *imago dei*, or the image of God in all people; Rabbi Bradley Shavit Artson, *God of Becoming and Relationship: The Dynamic Nature of Process Theology* (Jewish Lights Pub., 2013), chap. 2.
19. The word *encourage* comes from the Middle French *encourager*, which itself comes from *en-* (a prefix meaning *in* or *into*) and *courager*, derived from *courage* (meaning *heart* or *spirit*).
20. Václav Havel, *The Art of the Impossible: Politics as Morality in Practice: Speeches and Writing, 1990–1996* (Knopf, 1997), cited in Wheatley, *Finding Our Way*, 262. As Wheatley notes, "Havel seems to be describing not hope but hopelessness, a condition beyond hope or fear when we are liberated from results, when we give up outcomes. We choose our actions because they feel right even if they will not succeed in changing things. He helps me recall the Buddhist teaching that hopelessness is not the opposite of hope. Fear is. Hope and fear are inescapable partners. Anytime we hope for a certain outcome, and work hard to make it happen, then we also introduce fear—fear of failing, fear of loss. Hopelessness is free of fear and thus can feel quite liberating. I've listened to others describe this state. Unburdened of strong emotions, they describe the miraculous appearance of clarity and energy."
21. Daniel Migliore, *Faith Seeking Understanding: An Introduction to Christian Theology*, 4th ed. (Eerdmans, 2023).
22. Wheatley, *Finding Our Way*, 127. Rudolph Bahro writes, "When the forms of an old culture are dying, the new culture is created by a few

people who are not afraid to be insecure." Cited in Wheatley, *Finding Our Way*, 262. She suggests that feeling insecure, unattached to outcomes, even groundless, might be a good thing if it increases our ability to stay in the work.

23. For helpful texts on this, see Edwin Friedman, *Generation to Generation: Family Process in Church and Synagogue* (The Guilford Press, 1985) and Ronald W. Richardson, *Creating a Healthier Church* (Augsburg Fortress Press, 1996).
24. Bailey W. Jackson, "Theory and Practice of Multicultural Organization Development," in *The NTL Handbook of Organization Development and Change*, ed. B. B. Jones and M. Brazzel (Pfeiffer, 2014), 139–154.
25. Heidegger wrote that waiting/listening is the most profound way to serve God. Cited in Wheatley, *Finding Our Way*, 242. The quote is widely attributed to Heidegger, but I have not found where he actually said or wrote it.
26. Len Leritz, *Interpersonal Negotiations* (AMACOM Division of American Management Association, 1994).
27. Needs should not be confused with solutions: "I need to do X" is different from "I need X." Leritz, *Interpersonal Negotiations* and *No-Fault Negotiating: A Simple and Innovative Approach for Solving Problems, Reaching Agreements and Resolving Conflicts* (Grand Central Publishing, 1990).
28. Laurie Garrett-Cobina, "The Emotional Undercurrents of Organizations," in *Chaplaincy and Spiritual Care in the 21st Century: An Introduction*, ed. Wendy Cadge and Shelly Rambo (University of North Carolina Press, 2022), 239–257.
29. Edgar H. Schein, *Organizational Culture and Leadership*, 3rd ed. (Jossey-Bass, 2004): 84; Cf. Edgar H. Schein, *Organizational Culture and Leadership*, 5th ed. (Wiley, 2017), 343, cited in Nathan H. White, "Facilitating Resilience: Chaplaincy as a Catalyst for Organizational Well-Being," in *Chaplaincy and Spiritual Care in the 21st Century: An Introduction*, edited by Wendy Cadge and Shelly Rambo (University of North Carolina Press, 2022), 208.
30. Edgar H. Schein, *Organizational Culture and Leadership*, 4th ed. (Jossey-Bass, 2010), 218, cited in White, "Facilitating Resilience," 208.
31. Schein, *Organizational Culture and Leadership*, 4th ed., 365.
32. Wheatley, *Finding Our Way*, 83.
33. As Wheatley explains, "Strangely, we assert that it's a particular characteristic of the human species to resist change, even though we're surrounded by tens of millions of other species that demonstrate wonderful capacities to grow, adapt, and change. Our ideas and sensibilities about change come from the world of Newton. We treat a problematic organization as if it was a machine that had broken down. We use reductionism to diagnose the problem; we expect to find a simple, singular cause for our woes.

We sift through all the possible causes of failure, searching for that one broken part—a bad manager, a dysfunctional team, a poor business unit. To repair the organization, all we need to do is replace the faulty part and gear back up to operate at predetermined performance levels. This is the standard approach to organizational change. It is derived from the best engineering thinking. I believe this approach explains why many organizational change efforts fail." Wheatley, *New Science*, 138. CEO's report that up to 75 percent of their organizational change efforts did not yield the promised results. Wheatley, *Finding Our Way*, 83. Though everything changes over time, people often resist change. This is usually because they have competing commitments or values (e.g., stability versus creativity). If a leader can help the group identify what their competing values are, it can help move things forward. See Robert Kegan and Lisa Laskow Lahey, *The Real Reason People Won't Change* (Harvard Business Review, 2001).

34. Focusing on the bottom line, financial stability, monetary benefit is an error in reduction: it is a function on prioritizing one value (finances) over other meaningful and dynamic values.
35. These ethical concerns have been central to religious traditions for millennia, and religious leaders continue to speak powerfully on these topics. More recently, neoliberal critiques of capitalism have highlighted some significant concerns for ways in which ethical concerns for human beings may be subsumed by financial matters, even using seemingly positive constructs, such as resilience, toward this end. See, for example, Sara Holiday Nelson, "Resilience and the Neoliberal Counter-Revolution: From Ecologies of Control to Production of the Common," *Resilience* 2 (January 2, 2014): 1–17. Ethical leadership must be understood as leadership for the common good. Samuel Wilson and James McCalman, "Re-imagining Ethical Leadership as Leadership for the Greater Good," *European Management Journal* 35, no. 2 (2017): 151–154.
36. White, "Facilitating Resilience," 209.
37. Ethics have fast become an important aspect of the organizational recruitment process. It is becoming increasingly clear that young people want to work in organizations that make a difference, care, place renewed pressure on the leadership to attract new talent and maintain and grow existing customer bases. These leaders must lead in a way that communicates social responsibility, but it can only be done if they have a good understanding of what responsible leadership entails. One community established its ethical direction thus: "Take care of yourself, take care of each other, take care of this place." Wheatley, *Finding Our Way*, 51.
38. Margaret Kornfeld argues that religious leaders must decenter their own anxiety, reducing the "static" in their minds so that they can be present to

what is emerging in and between others. Margaret Kornfeld, *Cultivating Wholeness: A Guide to Care and Counseling in Faith Communities* (Continuum International Publishing, 2002), 47.

39. Wheatley, *Finding Our Way*, 196. Viktor Frankl argued that "meaning precedes being." Each member has a unique contribution that is necessary for the whole to thrive. In this leadership model, everyone's perspectives and gifts are required to succeed in the work at hand. Wheatley, *Finding Our Way*, 241.
40. Abraham H. Maslow, "A Dynamic Theory of Human Motivation," in *Understanding human motivation*, ed. C. L. Stacey and M. DeMartino (Howard Allen, 1958), https://doi.org/10.1037/11305-004.
41. Maslow, "A Dynamic Theory."
42. Every organization has emotions that move "like a current" through it. Grief is often a powerful undercurrent that needs to be addressed. Garrett-Cobina, "The Emotional Undercurrents of Organizations." One scholar agrees that "feelings (moods and emotions) play a central role in the leadership process." Jennifer M. George, "Emotions and Leadership: The Role of Emotional Intelligence," *Human Relations* 53, no. 8 (2000): 1027–1055.
43. Ecclesiastes 3:1, *The Holy Bible*.
44. This is why the models of leadership often must change if leaders are to be successful in meaningfully leading their organization with equitability, care, and sustainability.
45. If leaders wish to use power toward flourishing, they need an understanding of flourishing that is holistic and inclusive. Recent interest in happiness and how to achieve it illustrates the fact that people are seeking, in part, mental and emotional well-being, but the happiness of their organization's members cannot be enough for religious leaders. As noted in chapter 2, while happiness is largely an individual endeavor (though it often does include relationships with others), flourishing requires attention to the well-being of others in community, of the global community, and of the planet.
46. Wheatley, *Finding Our Way*, 71.
47. B. Collier, T. DeMarco, and P. Fearey, "A Defined Process for Project Post Mortem Review," *IEEE Software* 13, no. 4 (July 1996): 65–72, https://doi.org/10.1109/52.526833.
48. This process is outlined in Wheatley, *Who Do We Choose to Be?*, 1st ed., 130–132.
49. See Wheatley, *Finding Our Way*, 71.
50. It can be immensely helpful to have an outside, third-party facilitator of these processes, especially if there is conflict among members and opposing answers to the questions.

51. Garrett-Cobina, "The Emotional Undercurrents of Organizations." Su Yon Pak examines four frames through which to examine organizational structures and processes: the structural frame, which focuses on the architecture of the organization (its roles, responsibilities, policies, and procedures); the human resource frame, which focuses on the people within the organization, their needs, relationships, and motivations; the political frame, which focuses on the flow of power in the organization, conflicts, and coalitions; and the symbolic frame, which focuses on meaning, culture, and values within the organization and emphasizes rituals, stories, and shared beliefs that give the organization an identity. In applying a political frame, a religious leader will ask who will gain and who will lose as policies and/or structures are implemented, which coalitions of support and opposition to change there are, and whether compromise or mutual gain is a possibility. In the symbolic frame, leaders might ask what new meaning can be created, how people will interpret it, what they will do with it, whether it aligns with the current culture, and whether it strengthens or weakens the culture. Pak adds a white racial frame that recognizes the racialized hierarchies of power and uses them to analyze the ways white supremacy functions in organizations, processes, and procedures. Su Yon Pak, "Through a Multi-Frame Lens: Surviving, Thriving, and Leading Organizations," in *Chaplaincy in the 21st Century*, ed. Wendy Cadge and Shelly Rambo (Oxford University Press, 2022), 219–238, 233.
52. Transformative leaders look for patterns of behavior that seem to have little or no connection but that one suspects are deeply connected. At their core, racism, sexism, and classism are complex interconnected systems that "function as ubiquitous forces of the heart that support the maintenance of primarily affluent white males, and heteronormative power structures." Garrett-Cobina, "The Emotional Undercurrents of Organizations," 244. Because they persist as "socio-emotional constructs," transformational leaders are vigilant about routing them out.
53. Mandates for inclusion are beneficial to ensure representation, at least. However, representation is not enough: strong, resilient and long-lived organizations go beyond representation and include and listen to a wide spectrum of perspectives.
54. These questions come from Wheatley, *Finding Our Way*, 129.
55. Wheatley, *New Science*, 108.
56. Part of the responsibility of a leader is to keep the stress level in the organization at a sweet spot: high enough to motivate engagement and change but no so high that people become overwhelmed and shut down.
57. Bruce Rogers-Vaughn, "Soul Talk in a Neoliberal Age: Part 1," *Radical Discipleship*, last modified August 21, 2020, https://radicaldiscipleship.net/2020/08/21/soul-talk-in-a-neoliberal-age-part-1/.

58. Romans 8:22, *The Holy Bible*.
59. Wheatley, *Finding Our Way*, 55–57.

CHAPTER 6: LEADING ORGANIZATIONS

1. There is strong research that demonstrates the enduring strength and resiliency of companies that have strong values. Jim Collins and Jerry I. Porras, *Built to Last: Successful Habits of Visionary Companies* (Harper Business, 1994). There are several ways individuals, teams, and organizations can identify the most important values (implicit and explicit) that bind them together and motivate them, including using values inventories such as my preferred assessment, JustValues.
2. Albert Einstein is credited with saying, "No problem can be solved from the same level of thinking that created it." However, while this is often attributed to Einstein, no definitive source has been found. Cited in Margaret J. Wheatley, *Finding Our Way: Leadership for Uncertain Times* (Berrett-Koehler Publishers, 2007), 3.
3. The model of leadership being recommended here is often called *adaptive leadership* and *servant leadership*, and both are crucial qualities of transformational leadership. Transformational leaders are those who invite positive change in themselves, others, and the organization they lead and are willing to upend the existing structure, roles, habits, and flow of power. An element of transformational leadership, adaptive leadership is distinct from technical leadership, another name for mechanical leadership. Adaptive leaders lead change when the future is unclear. Adaptive leaders can intrinsically motivate others using their well-practiced emotional skills, communication skills, skills in managing conflict, and capacities to bring people together in collaborative and distributed leadership. Ronald A. Heifetz, *Leadership Without Easy Answers* (Harvard University Press, 1994). It is important to note, however, that leadership scholar Kristina Lizardy-Hajbi worries that transformational leadership upholds power and maintains control over laborers within the institution while giving only the appearance of agency through dialogue and other techniques, thus thwarting change that might disrupt systems and the bottom line and reinforcing modern/colonial ways of being and doing. Kristina Isabel Lizardy-Hajbi, *Unraveling Religious Leadership: Power, Authority, and Decoloniality* (Fortress Press, 2024), 185. Lizardy-Hajbi argues that "the actions of resistance, subversion, and reclamation by those harmed and abused by colonialism constitute the beginnings of postcolonial and decolonial practice." It is my hope that the approach I am suggesting in this text mitigates at least some of Lizardy-Hajbi's legitimate and important concerns, though the work might be undertaken

by allies as much as those most harmed. Kristina Isabel Lizardy-Hajbi, "Frameworks Toward Post/Decolonial Pastoral Leaderships," *Journal of Religious Leadership* 19, no. 2 (2020): 104. Yale theologian Katherine Tanner argues that religious- or values-based organizations are good sites for forming "resistant subjects" to the systemic oppressions people experience in the current age. Kathryn Tanner, *Christianity and the New Spirit of Capitalism* (Yale University Press, 2019).

4. The values and sense of purpose that bring people together in an organization, the *meaning* that brings people together, can be thought of as its strange attractors. According to Jewish Holocaust survivor Victor Frankl, people's primary motivator in life is not to gain pleasure or avoid pain but rather to see a meaning. Viktor E. Frankl, *Man's Search for Meaning*, 4th ed. (Beacon Press, 2006). No matter what is happening, human beings assign an explanation to it. When people organize around shared meaning, that meaning is a strange attractor that coordinates behaviors without control and coalesces around a vision for the future and a path toward it. As organizational scholar Margaret Wheatley puts it, "From witnessing how networks can communicate around the world with information they deem essential, I have come to believe that 'preaching to the choir' is exactly the right thing to do. If I can help those who already share certain beliefs and dreams sing their song a little clearer, a little more confidently, I know they will take that song back to their networks. [A leader] doesn't have to touch everybody; [they] just must support those first courageous voices and encourage them to put it out on their own airwaves. Soon large populations in diverse places will have heard the song because someone in their network had their voice amplified by meeting the choir. We gain courage from learning we're part of a choir. We sing better when we know we're not alone." Margaret J. Wheatley, *Leadership and the New Science: Discovering Order in a Chaotic World* (Berrett-Koehler Publishers, 2006), 152.

5. Leadership pioneer and Quaker Robert K. Greenleaf, *Servant Leadership: A Journey into the Nature of Legitimate Power and Greatness*, 25th anniversary ed. Paulist Press, 2002).

6. The first three terms are common in Christian theologies. In Judaism, the concept of salvation or redemption is often expressed using the Hebrew word גְאוּלָה (pronounced as "geulah"). This term encompasses the idea of deliverance, liberation, and redemption, particularly in a spiritual or national context. It is a central theme in Jewish theology, referring to the hope and belief in the eventual redemption of the Jewish people and the world as a whole.

7. Larry Kent Graham, *Care of Persons, Care of Worlds: A Psychosystems Approach to Pastoral Care and Counseling* (Abingdon Press, 1992).

8. E. Brooks Holifield, *A History of Pastoral Care in America: From Salvation to Self-Realization* (Academic Renewal Press, 2003).
9. Theologian David Jensen writes that meaningful human work has value because it "responds to the divine work that pulses at the heart of the universe. Though God's work is not dependent on ours, when our labors respond to the divine work, we also contribute to the life of the world." David Jenson, *Responsive Labor: A Theology of Work* (Westminster John Knox Press, 2006), ix. Work is elemental to human flourishing, and religious leaders' responses to God's work in the world through their own leadership have the potential to be sacred labor, if understood faithfully.
10. David W. Miller, *God at Work: The History and Promise of the Faith at Work Movement* (Oxford University Press, 2006), 79–80.
11. Nathan H. White, "Facilitating Resilience: Chaplaincy as a Catalyst for Organizational Well-Being," in *Chaplaincy and Spiritual Care in the 21st Century: An Introduction*, ed. Wendy Cadge and Shelly Rambo (University of North Carolina Press, 2022), 201–218.
12. Larry Kent Graham, "Pastoral Theology as Public Theology in Relation to the Clinic," *Journal of Pastoral Theology* 10, no. 1 (2000): 12.
13. Pastoral theologian Homer Ashby writes, "What we need more than anything else are [religious leaders] as public theologians who can help lead people in inclusive, thoughtful, spirited (and spirit filled), debate and conclusion drawing about the theological implications of life together in the realm of God." To that end, he argues, religious leaders "must make some very tough decisions regarding priorities and values. The identification of these priorities and values must be faith based. Pursue first that which reflects the highest values and commitments from the witness of your faith." Homer U. Ashby, "Pastoral Theology as Public Theology: Participating in the Healing of Damaged and Damaging Cultures and Institutions," *Journal of Pastoral Theology* 10, no. 1 (2000): 23, 25.
14. Laurie Garrett-Cobina, "The Emotional Undercurrents of Organizations," in *Chaplaincy and Spiritual Care in the 21st Century: An Introduction*, ed. Wendy Cadge and Shelly Rambo (University of North Carolina Press, 2022), 239–257.
15. Remember that people in formal leadership positions often conflate leadership and management and, as a result, end up managing rather than leading. Leading implies that others are willing to follow into unknown territory, enact change, and face the complex challenges of life together. Most simply, a leader is anyone who wants to help and is willing to step forward to create positive change in their world. People in all levels of an organization "need to cooperate with others to achieve the desired results." M. Moradi Korejan and Hasan Shahbazi, "An Analysis of the

Transformational Leadership Theory," *Journal of Fundamental and Applied Sciences* 8, no. 3 (2016): 452.

16. Garrett-Cobina, "The Emotional Undercurrents of Organizations," 245. Organizational systems are "so efficiently racist, sexist, and classist" in the ways some are advantaged and others disadvantaged that biases happen whether people within the organization wish them or not. Race, gender, and class preconceptions "regulate the psyche so effectively that isms are made to feel normal, which shields those in power from the sociopathic shock of becoming conscious of inflicting injury on another on such a pervasive scale. The normalization process is reinforced by the disconnection from one's feelings and the loss of the capacity for empathy." Garrett-Cobina, "The Emotional Undercurrents of Organizations," 245.
17. Life is about creation. This ability of life to create itself is captured in a strange-sounding word, *autopoiesis* (from Greek, meaning *self-production* or *self-making*). *Autopoiesis* is life's fundamental process for creating and renewing itself, for growth and change. A living system is a network of processes in which every process contributes to all other processes. The entire network is engaged together in producing itself. Fritjof Capra, *The Web of Life: A New Synthesis of Mind and Matter* (HarperCollins, 1996), 132:99, cited in Wheatley, *Finding Our Way*, 24–25. This process is not limited to one type of organism—it describes all life, from amoeba to human beings, to organizations. As described by systems scientist Erich Jantsch, any living system is "a never resting structure that constantly seeks its own self-renewal." Erich Jantsch, *The Self Organizing Universe: Scientific and Human Implications of the Emerging Paradigm of Evolution* (Pergamon Press, 1980), 10. This description defines a paradox that is important to note when we think about change: A living system produces itself; it will change to preserve that self. Change is prompted only when an organism decides that changing is the only way to maintain itself. Cited in Wheatley, *Finding Our Way*, 20.
18. Indeed, learning agility is one of the most important qualities and skills a leader can have. Peter M. Senge, *The Fifth Discipline: The Art and Practice of the Learning Organization* (Doubleday, 1990), 12.
19. Flourishing in today's world requires transformative leadership. As a reminder, flourishing is not something that is ever fully accomplished, however; rather, it is something that is pursued, cultivated, and nurtured, a by-product of living virtuously and engaging in meaningful work. As established, flourishing is a dynamic of activity rather than a static state. Flourishing is more a process than an accomplishment, and the journey is not a straight line.
20. White, "Facilitating Resilience," 201.
21. White, "Facilitating Resilience," 203.

22. Aristotle, *Politics* I.2, 1252b30. Quotations are from Jonathan Barnes, ed., *The Complete Works of Aristotle: The Revised Translation*, vols. 1 and 2, Bollingen Series 71:2 (Princeton University Press, 1984), cited in White, "Facilitating Resilience," 203. While Aristotle's comments are insightful, we must also acknowledge they come from a framework that only considered the rights of Greek citizens, thereby excluding foreigners, slaves, and women and denying the value and insights of these as full human beings. Transformative religious leaders will want to correct Aristotle's error on this.
23. Our society has assumed that culture of the dominant white group is the norm and standard by which everyone else should be judged. As one scholar writes, "White supremacy culture is reproduced in all institutions, including the media, education, and policies. This ideology, like the air we breathe, impacts us all, but it is hard to identify . . . It is important to recognize this dynamic, to name it, and to find antidotes that disrupt this culture with different organizational practices." Su Yon Pak, "Through a Multi-Frame Lens: Surviving, Thriving, and Leading Organizations," in *Chaplaincy in the 21st Century*, ed. Wendy Cadge and Shelly Rambo (Oxford University Press, 2022), 219–238.
24. Iris Marion Young, "Taking the Basic Structure Seriously," *Symposium: John Rawls and the Study of Politics* 4, no. 1 (March 2006): 94. Pastoral theologian Larry K. Graham argues that the "forces" that impinge on human well-being "are larger than individual persons and have cultural, ideological and systemic dimensions, which powerfully shape concrete persons and their options . . . To treat the individual in isolation from these forces is often to throw a straw into the wind. These very forces need challenge and modification along with the changes necessary in individual persons." Graham, *Care of Persons, Care of Worlds*, 11. John Rawls defines basic structures as "the way in which the main political and social institutions of a society fit together into one system of social cooperation, and the way they assign basic rights and duties and regulate the division of advantages that arise from social cooperation over time. The political constitution within an independent judiciary, the legally recognized forms of property, and the structure of the economy (e.g., as a system of competitive markets with private property in the means of production), as well as the family in some form, all belong to the basic structure. The basic structure is the background social framework within which the activities of associations and individuals take place." John Rawls, *Justice as Fairness: A Restatement*, ed. Erin Kelly (Harvard University Press, 2001), 10. As quoted in Iris Marion Young, "Taking the Basic Structure Seriously," *Symposium: John Rawls and the Study of Politics* 4, no. 1 (March 2006): 91.

25. Walter Wink, *Unmasking the Powers: The Invisible Forces That Determine Human Existence* (Fortress Press, 1986).
26. Organizations possess different moral cultures, some of which are more positive and others more negative; however, it is not the organization that carries moral weight but the individuals within it who hold attitudes and make decisions that nurture a specific moral orientation. To succeed in the long term (and to fulfill their appropriate religious moral function), organizations must be concerned about the well-being of their members and of the communities in which they are embedded. White, "Facilitating Resilience," 203.
27. Linda K. Treviño and Katherine A. Nelson, *Managing Business Ethics: Straight Talk about How to Do It Right*, 5th ed. (John Wiley & Sons, 2010), 151. Cited in White, "Facilitating Resilience," 204.
28. White, "Facilitating Resilience," 208–211. This is closely connected to the "symbolic frame" that Su Yon Pak describes in her chapter "Through a Multi-Frame Lens."
29. White, "Facilitating Resilience," 206.
30. White, "Facilitating Resilience," 205. These realities are also discussed, for example, in Garrett-Cobina's contribution, "The Emotional Undercurrents of Organizations."
31. Even families and neighborhoods are kinds of organizations.
32. Pak, "Through a Multi-Frame Lens," 233.
33. Organizational theorist Margaret Wheatley writes that the smallest of actions can, with repetition, "grow into powerful and unpredictable effects." She goes on to say that "the composite picture of those behaviors that emerges after countless iterations." We should note that these behaviors can be either positive and life-giving or negative and life-diminishing. Wheatley, *New Science*, 121–124. These dynamics have been described by scholars as diverse as social theorist Michel Foucault (who describes power dynamics as underlying all human relationships) and theologians Alistair McFadyen and Walter Wink, who identify a connection between structural sin and personal sin. Michel Foucault and Colin Gordon, eds., *Power/Knowledge: Selected Interviews and Other Writings, 1972–1977*, 1st American ed. (Pantheon Books, 1980); Alistair McFadyen, *Bound to Sin: Abuse, Holocaust and the Christian Doctrine of Sin* (Cambridge University Press, 2000); and Wink, *Unmasking the Powers*.
34. This example is found in White, "Facilitating Resilience," 206.
35. Organizations can be consistent in their identity, values, mission, and purpose even as the organizational form change.
36. White, "Facilitating Resilience," 207.
37. Paul Ricoeur's description of human identity in terms of a dialectic relationship between constancy and change over time could analogously be

applied to organizational identity. Cf. Paul Ricoeur, *Oneself as Another*, trans. Kathleen Blamey (University of Chicago Press, 1992), cited in White, "Facilitating Resilience," 207.

38. Many organizations that have failed were run by leaders who assumed that organizations are like machines—predictable, stable, and unchanging, needing to reach and maintain a state of equilibrium—and it was the formal leaders who were responsible for this achievement. Leaders once were expected to take on the responsibility of engineering efficient solutions to complex challenges directing followers to effect the instructions they were given rather than engaging the challenges cooperatively and creatively.
39. White, "Facilitating Resilience," 207.
40. Wheatley, *New Science*, 145.
41. Wheatley, *Finding Our Way*, 64–68.
42. Wheatley, *Finding Our Way*, 93.
43. Wheatley, *Finding Our Way*, 93.
44. Wheatley, *New Science*, 145.
45. Wheatley, *Finding Our Way*, 80–81.
46. These three themes are in Wheatley, *New Science*, 146.
47. Wheatley, *Finding Our Way*, 37.
48. Identity is both what we want to believe is true and what our actions show to be true about ourselves. Wheatley, *Finding Our Way*, 37.
49. Wheatley, *Finding Our Way*, 37–40.
50. Wheatley argues that clear alignment around principles and purposes allows for maximum autonomy. People use their shared sense of identity to organize their unique contributions. Wheatley, *Finding Our Way*, 38.
51. Wheatley, *Finding Our Way*, 26.
52. Wheatley, *Finding Our Way*, 26.
53. Wheatley, *Finding Our Way*, 26.
54. Wheatley, *Finding Our Way*, 27.
55. Wheatley, *Finding Our Way*, 33.
56. Wheatley, *Finding Our Way*, 41.
57. David V. Day and Stanley M. Halpin, "Growing Leaders for Tomorrow: An Introduction," in David V. Day et al., eds., *Leadership Development for Transforming Organizations: Growing Leaders for Tomorrow* (Lawrence Erlbaum Associates, 2004), 3–22; David V. Day and Charles E. Lance, "Understanding the Development of Leadership Complexity Through Latent Growth Modeling," in Day et al., *Leadership Development for Transforming Organizations*, 41–69. Values of both the leader(s) and members of an organization were shown to enhance the performance of their subordinates through transformational leadership. One recent empirical study indicates that "one enabling condition [for successful transformative leadership] is team values." John Schaubroeck et al.,

"Embracing Transformational Leadership: Team Values and the Impact of Leader Behavior on Team Performance," *Journal of Applied Psychology* 92, no. 4 (2007): 1027.

CHAPTER 7: LEADING OTHERS

1. James Poling, "Recognizing the Congregation's Role as a Healing Community," *Brethren Life and Thought* 33 (1988): 122–130. Organizational systems, such as those in neoliberalism, are created so that the powerful can stay in power. The brief introduction to neoliberalism in chapter 3 highlights this dynamic and the costs to people's lives, organizational integrity, and global ecosystems. When the goal is keeping power (and controlling decision-making levers), the outcome is suffering of everyone involved. Whether in an organization, a city, a country, or a multinational corporation, what is valued and practiced has a direct effect on those closest to the organization, living in the city, etc. In the case of a country or a multinational corporation, all the citizens except those at the very top of the power and financial strata suffer under neoliberal practices. While we might not expect the CEO of a multinational corporation to think of anything beyond stakeholder value (though we should expect that), religious leaders are called to more. Jesus of Nazareth was analyzing (and critiquing) systems of power during his ministry when he turned over the money-changer's table, when he invited the woman at the well to touch his garment, when he ate with lepers. Christian leaders are called to be loyal not to themselves or those with whom they have a special affinity; rather, they are called to be loyal to the religious values of Jesus the Christ as modeled during his life and in his practices. Followers of other religious traditions have their own models as well.
2. In organizational consulting and leadership coaching, it is commonly said that "the 'soft' stuff is the hard stuff." What is usually meant by this is that developing emotional intelligence (self-awareness, self-regulation, other-awareness, social skills, capacity to productively manage conflict) and interpersonal skills is much more difficult than learning to read a budget, create a spreadsheet, or read a text, all of which are more technical skills that are easier to learn and take less practice than EQ and people skills. Daniel Goleman, *Leadership: The Power of Emotional Intelligence* (More Than Sound LLC, 2021). To learn these well, it is often helpful to have a coach to help you build and deepen your capacities.
3. Carrie Doehring and Allison Kestenbaum, "Introduction to Interpersonal Competencies," in *Chaplaincy and Spiritual Care in the Twenty-First Century: An Introduction*, ed. Wendy Cadge and Shelly Rambo (The University of North Carolina Press, 2022), 129–133.

4. To gain trust, leaders must act with authenticity and behave with integrity. They must demonstrate that they care about people and the common good, that they are willing to set aside their own desires at least some of the time and do what they say they will do, living aligned with their most deeply held values. The amount of trust in an organization greatly influences how well the organization functions and its sustainability into the future. In his leadership classic *Good to Great*, Jim Collins calls leaders who can put the interests of their organization above their own self-interest "Level 5 Leaders." What distinguishes them is their ability to channel their ego needs away from themselves and toward the common good. Jim Collins, *Good to Great: Why Some Companies Make the Leap . . . and Others Don't* (HarperCollins, 2001). Collins writes that great organizations are led by quiet, "self-effacing" leaders who have a "paradoxical blend" of humility and will. They put their highest priority on surrounding themselves with great people, are willing to confront the often "brutal facts" of the situation they and the organization find themselves in, identify something they care about that they could do better than others, create a culture so rules are not necessary, and make changes in ways that make sense to their situation.
5. Values are often used as a shorthand way of describing what is important to people individually and collectively (as an organization, community, or nation) at any given moment in time. Richard Barrett, *The Values-Driven Organization: Unleashing Human Potential for Performance and Profit* (Routledge, 2014), 3.
6. Tom Karp, "Transforming Organizations for Organic Growth: The DNA of Change Leadership," *Journal of Change Management* 6, no. 1 (2006): 3–20.
7. These are important values that neoliberalism does not nurture—indeed, that it outright discourages—virtues and Christian values such as mutual and genuine relationship, compassion, cooperation, and tenderness. The values of a neoliberal capitalist society are incompatible with Christianity's values and with the vision of flourishing that religious leaders are called to nurture. Religious leaders ought to be particularly critical of neoliberal market capitalism. Capitalism's emphasis on individualism, competition, and consumerism is antithetical to a reading of sacred texts from the underside, a perspective from which Jesus calls for corporate accountability as well as mutual and reciprocal care. Thus, while pastoral theologian James Poling provides a critique of capitalism using economic theory, he also brings a critical biblical analysis to support his argument. James N. Poling, *Render unto God: Economic Vulnerability, Family Violence, and Pastoral Theology*. Wipf and Stock Publishers, 2012.

8. Peter Drucker, one of the best-known and most influential thinkers on leadership in the twentieth century, famously argued that "culture eats strategy for breakfast." (However, while Peter Drucker is often associated with the idea, Mark Fields, the former CEO of Ford Motor Company, is more directly tied to the phrase.)
9. For example, Ken Blanchard's bestselling books on the "One-Minute Manager" essentially advocate for command-and-control leadership. Kenneth Blanchard and Spencer Johnson, *The One-Minute Manager* (William Morrow, 1982). Blanchard's is a model of leadership that people no longer desire and will often move away from if they can. In a voluntary organization, this can be a death knell.
10. Some of the metaphors used for religious leadership include midwives, gardeners, and wise guides. Pastoral theologian Robert Dykstra argues that pastoral caregivers are leaders for whom these metaphors apply. See Robert C. Dykstra, ed., *Images of Pastoral Care: Classic Readings* (Chalice Press, 2005).
11. As leadership experts William Bridges and Susan Bridges argue, it's not the changes that do people and organizations in; it's the transitions. They are not the same thing. Change is situational: moving to a new place, hiring a new director of music, pivoting to using technology to expand worship. Transition is psychological: It is a three-phase process that people go through as they internalize and come to terms with the details of the new situation that the change brings about. The three phases of transition include letting go of the old ways and the old identities that people and the organization had, recognizing the endings, and helping grieve the losses. Second, people and organizations will go through an in-between time when the old is gone, but the new is not fully operational. Bridges and Bridges call this the "neutral zone," and it is when critical psychological realignments and "repatternings" take place. In the final phase, people and organizations come out of the transition and make a new beginning. This involves developing a new identity, both for individuals and for the organization, and both typically experience new energy and a new sense of purpose. William Bridges and Susan Bridges, *Managing Transitions: Making the Most of Change* (Da Capo Lifelong Books, 2016), 5.
12. Kim Cameron, *Positive Leadership: Strategies for Extraordinary Performance*, 2nd ed. (Berrett-Koehler Publishers, 2012).
13. Milton Rokeach, *The Nature of Human Values* (Free Press, 1973) and Brian Hall, *Values Shift: A Guide to Individual and Organizational Transformation* (Twin Lights, 1995).
14. Hall, *Values Shift*.
15. Barrett, *Values-Driven Organization*, 19.
16. Barrett, *Values-Driven Organization*, xi.

17. Barrett, *Values-Driven Organization*, xii.
18. Barrett, *Values-Driven Organization*, xii; Even successful professionals are seeking religious, values-driven, meaning-making, and caring organizations. See Nicole Laporte, "Are You There, God? I'm at Harvard: Why on Earth Are a Bunch of Successful Midcareer Professionals Quitting Their Jobs and Applying to Harvard Divinity School? Hint: It Has Nothing to Do with Heaven," *Town and Country*, November 3, 2024, https://www.townandcountrymag.com/society/money-and-power/a62786069/harvard-divinity-school-career-change/.
19. Scott A. Snook, "Imagining the Future of Leadership," *Harvard Business Review*, April 26, 2010. Harvard Business School professor and author Bill George once remarked, "Can't we all finally agree that the 'great man' is dead?" His point was that models of leadership need to be significantly revised. Snook, "Imagine the Future of Leadership."
20. Barrett, *Values-Driven Organization*, xv. As leadership scholar Richard Barrett argues, values-based organizations will be the ones that survive and even thrive. He writes, in the 21st century, the rat race will be replaced by the values race," and the most successful organizations will care less about being "the best *in* the world" and focus on being "the best *for* the world." Richard Barrett, *The New Leadership Paradigm* (Fulfilling Books, 2011), xiii, emphasis in the original.
21. Barrett, *Values-Driven Organization*, xx.
22. Brian Hall, *Values Shift: A Guide to Individual and Organizational Transformation* (Berrett-Koehler Publishers, 2008), 39.
23. Barrett, *Values-Driven Organization*, 13.
24. Hall, *Values Shift*, 39.
25. Values theory has its roots in the work of philosopher and psychologist Abraham Maslow, social psychologist Milton Rokeach, and psychosocial developmental theorists Erik Erikson, Lawrence Kohlberg, and others.
26. Hall, *Values Shift*, 40.
27. Hall, *Values Shift*, 40.
28. In the values model I find most illuminative and useful, the Hall-Tonna values model, researchers Brian Hall and Benjamin Tonna isolated and verified 125 priorities (values) that human beings express. Although the range of human values is limited, the forms these priorities can take are numberless. People express their values in incredibly diverse ways. Drawing on Milton Rokeach's distinction between terminal and instrumental values, Hall and Tonna divide the 125 values into two basic types, goal values and means values. Goal values are the priorities toward which humans aim their actions. Means values are the skills and capacities by which humans achieve their aims. Hall, *Values Shift*, 28, 45. Hall and

Tonna range the 125 values across eight developmental stages, based on their findings about the progression in which the values are expressed by individual human beings. Later-stage priorities build on earlier-stage priorities, expanding them and rendering them more complex, in a kind of cogwheel concept of development. The goal values of a specific stage can only be reliably achieved by building on the means values of a prior stage. The goals and means of each stage must be mastered before those of subsequent stages can be attained. The increasingly complex priorities (goal values) of each later stage require the person to master and combine the less complex capacities of the prior stages. Hall and Tonna's research led to the discovery of several important insights regarding human values. First, they discovered that although 125 values exist as possibilities and potentials for humans, an individual person only prioritizes about 10–20 values at any given point. Hall, *Values Shift*, 85. It appears that this limit in the number of values any one person can express is the result of the constraints imposed by limits of time, attention, and the individual's current stage of cognitive, emotional, and psychosocial development.

29. Ali Farazmand, "Introduction. The Multifaceted Nature of Modern Organizations," in *Modern Organizations: Theory and Practice*, ed. Ali Farazmand (Praeger, 2002), 17.
30. Brian Hall, *Values Shift. A Guide to Personal and Organizational Transformation* (Twin Lights Publishers, 1995), 21.
31. Paragons of generativity such as Nelson Mandela will forego their personal safety and comfort for a higher cause, a characteristic that is interpreted by Hall and Tonna as wisdom and generative maturity.
32. Hall, *Values Shift*, 84.
33. Hall, *Values Shift*, 21.
34. Hall, *Values Shift*, 21.
35. Hall, *Values Shift*, 21.
36. One of the first researchers to make the link among needs, values, and motivations was Abraham Maslow. Maslow (1908–70), a philosopher and one of the foremost spokespeople for humanistic and positive psychology, identified two basic types of human needs: basic needs—also known as deficiency needs (Hall and Tonna call these *foundational* needs or values), and growth needs—also known as being needs (Hall and Tonna call these *vision values*). Abraham Maslow, *Toward a Psychology of Being*, 2nd ed. (Van Nostrand Reinhold, 1968), 173. A basic, or foundational, need is something that is important to get, have, or have more of to feel safe, happy, and comfortable in one's existing physical and social environments. These categories describe the subset of the 10–20 values that an individual prioritizes in their own life from among the 125 available. Foundation values are priorities that reflect the human biological,

social, and psychological processes that ground human development and continue to form the basis of our mammalian, social existence across the span of our lives. Hall, *Values Shift*, 84. People feel anxious and fearful when they are unable to satisfy their basic needs, but once those needs are met, people no longer pay much attention to them—they become subconscious. The reason people feel anxious or fearful when these needs are not met is because we need to be able to satisfy these needs to ensure our physiological and emotional well-being. When people can satisfy their growth needs, those foundation needs do not go away; rather, they engender deeper levels of attention and commitment. The reason people feel motivated to satisfy their growth needs is because they allow them to become more fully who they are. Satisfying these needs is an integral part of the process of self-actualization. Someone who has learned how to master the satisfaction of their basic needs and their growth needs is a "full spectrum" person. Abraham Maslow described such people as "healthy human specimens." Barrett, *Values-Driven Organization*, 7–9. Barrett writes, "A full spectrum individual feels called to work towards the creation of a world where every human being can grow and develop so they can live their own unique self-story. By engaging with your unique self, you are called to live a values-driven and purpose-driven life."

37. Barrett, *Values-Driven Organization*, 5.
38. Barrett, *Values-Driven Organization*, 13. Values are derived from and are carried by cultural and religious traditions as well as the social-structural arrangements those traditions are embedded in; that is, faith-based organizations are embedded in communities, towns, and societies that might operate from very different sets of values.
39. A growth need is something a person would like to have to feel a sense of internal alignment—being at ease or at peace with themselves—and a sense of fulfilment about the contribution they are making in the world. This is true even when things are challenging or difficult. See Martin E. P. Seligman, *Flourish: A Visionary New Understanding of Happiness and Well-Being* (Atria Press, 2011).
40. Barrett, *Values-Driven Organization*, 11.
41. Barrett, *Values-Driven Organization*, 11. Having purpose and meaning in life increases overall well-being and life satisfaction and improves mental and physical health. It also enhances resilience and self-esteem and decreases the chances of depression. Seligman, *Flourish*. In a research study, nearly four hundred Americans aged 18–78 were asked whether they thought their lives were meaningful and/or happy. Examining their self-reported attitudes toward meaning, happiness, and many other variables such as stress, spending patterns, and children, the researchers found that a meaningful life and a happy life overlap in certain ways but are ultimately very

different. Happiness is mainly about satisfying one's basic needs; meaning comes from tapping into and expressing one's true nature and helping others satisfy their needs. Barrett, *New Leadership Paradigm*, 11.

42. Barrett, *New Leadership Paradigm*, 12.
43. Barrett, *Values-Driven Organization*; James MacGregor Burns, *Leadership* (Harper Perennial Modern Classics, 2010); and Hall, *Values Shift*.
44. Brian Hall, *The Development of Consciousness: A Confluent Theory of Values* (Paulist Press, 1976).
45. Hall, *Values Shift*, 143, 233.
46. Hall, *Values Shift*, 85. One's values inform one's beliefs, and one's beliefs inform one's feelings, and feelings give rise to behaviors. Negative or limiting beliefs at the survival level are about not having enough of what you need to feel safe and secure. These beliefs result in the display of potentially limiting values such as control, manipulation, greed, and excessive caution. Limiting beliefs at the relationship level are about not feeling loved enough to be accepted and protected. These beliefs result in the display of potentially limiting values such as blame, being liked, competition, and internal politics. Limiting beliefs at the self-esteem level are about not being enough to engender the respect or acknowledgment of the peers or authority figures in your life. These beliefs result in the display of potentially limiting values such as status-seeking, power-seeking, arrogance, and an overly strong focus on self-image. Barrett, *Values-Driven Organization*, 15. Every person and organization must make hundreds of decisions every day. The decisions we make, and the feelings that drive them, are the result of our values and beliefs. People's priority—or foundation—needs, which are determined by where they are in their psychological development, what their current life circumstances are, and the situation they currently find themselves in, are the primary drivers of their values. People's ability to get, have, or experience what they value at the most basic level, together with their subconscious fear-based beliefs, often drive their life-limiting thoughts, feelings, and emotions. Their thoughts, feelings, and emotions, which are all related to their values, determine their actions and behaviors.
47. This dynamic also helps explain the phenomena of psychological regression. Hall, *Values Shift*, 82.
48. Hall, *Values Shift*, 80–81. The future pulls people from an internal vision they have of wholeness as expressed by the values in phase IV (stages 7 and 8), which are a fuller and more holistic expression of the phases I–III (stages 1–6) values. Hall, *Values Shift*, 81. Hall and Tonna's testing revealed that the values of stages 6–8 begin operating as priorities in people's lives early in their development, appearing by about age fourteen.

Hall argues that these values that arise within the thoughts and actions generated by a person's current level of development and can only be resolved by developing a new level of consciousness that reconciles the contradictory elements and creates a new, more adequate equilibrium. To paraphrase developmental psychologist Robert Kegan, there is nothing as productive for one's development as the possession of a robust contradiction. Robert Kegan, *The Evolving Self: Problem and Process in Human Development* (Harvard University Press, 1982), 125, 140–145. The contradictions people experience that spur their growth to higher phases must be worked through to be resolved. Doing so is the work of development. Jack J. Bauer and Dan P. McAdams, "Growth Goals, Maturity, and Well-Being," *Developmental Psychology* 40, no. 1 (2004): 125. Other researchers in change theory posit that people don't change because they are committed to one value more than another. James O. Prochaska and John C. Norcross, "Stages of Change," *Psychotherapy: Theory, Research, Practice, Training* 38, no. 4 (2001), 143–154; and Ronald A. Heifetz and Donald L. Laurie, "The Work of Leadership," *Harvard Business Review* 79, no. 11 (2001), 35–48.

49. Hall, *Values Shift*, 153.
50. Differentiation is defined in family systems theory as the process by which individuals develop the ability to separate their thoughts and emotions and to maintain a sense of self while still being connected to others, especially in the family unit. Introduced by psychiatrist Murray Bowen, the key aspects of differentiation include the capacity to manage one's responses rather than reacting impulsively; the capacity to develop one's own values, beliefs, and goals different from others; and a balance between connection and autonomy so that one can be intimate with others without losing one's autonomy. There are many good resources on this, including Tracy Laszloffy and Monica McGoldrick, *You Can Go Home Again: Reconnecting with Your Family*, 3rd ed. (W. W. Norton, 2024); Hall, *Values Shift*, 57. Hall and Tonna capture the major shifts in this differentiation by dividing the eight stages of development into four phases.
51. Upholding human dignity, for example, requires that one separate one's emotional experiences from those of other people, enabling one to empathically enter the emotional experience of others without becoming swamped by or identified with any other person or group's experience. Socially, the higher-stage priorities cannot be achieved without the skills and capacities for self-conscious participation in complex, interdependent social systems.
52. Hall, *Values Shift*, 91.
53. Hall, *Values Shift*, 94.

54. Hall, *Values Shift*, 94. These patterns of behavior, known in ego-psychology as *defense mechanisms*, or *coping resources*, limit the growth and development of the individual, consigning their action to circular movements that do not expand their capacities or create outcomes that are more adequate.
55. The fact that every individual has, at any one point in their life, achieved a specific developmental point does not mean that people do not regress or fall back from their highest point of development. As noted earlier, life events, stress, pressure, and conflict can, in various ways, pull a person "backward." Kegan, *Evolving Self*.
56. Stagnation or regression are the choices and acts that prevent a person from achieving their vision (future) values. When we choose to act out of guilt about our failure to achieve our foundational needs and are anxious about ever being able to achieve them, let alone achieve our vision values, we create a dynamic of despair.
57. *Servant leadership* is Greenleaf's term. I prefer the more active *serving leadership*. Robert K. Greenleaf, *Servant Leadership* (Paulist Press, 1977).
58. Greenleaf, *Servant Leadership*, 13–14.
59. Greenleaf, *Servant Leadership*, 13.
60. Distributed leadership, or collaborative, shared, or complexity leadership, is a model in which leadership functions are spread across multiple individuals and teams, even those outside the organization. In this model, leadership can be taken on by those not in formal leadership roles, and change can be driven from the bottom up. Deborah Ancona and Elaine Backman, "It's Not All About You," *Harvard Business Review* (blog), April 26, 2020, https://hbr.org/2010/04/its-not-all-about-me-its-all-a.
61. Hall, *Values Shift*, 163.
62. Hall, *Values Shift*, 93.
63. Existentialist theory underscores the intensely active process of human valuing, a process that does not happen passively but that requires the full engagement of a person's beliefs, emotions, passions, and agency.
64. As one leadership scholar notes, "Mutual sharing of values builds trust because our positive human values—known as virtues—are shared by all human beings. A virtue is a positive trait or quality deemed to be morally excellent." Barrett, *Values-Driven Organizations*, 14. There are positive values and limiting values, which always arise from our fears.
65. Graeme Maxwell Griffin, *Coming to Care: An Introduction to Pastoral Care for Ordained Ministers and Lay People* (Uniting Church Theological Hall, 1995), 34.
66. Karen D. Scheib, *Pastoral Care: Telling the Stories of Our Lives* (Abingdon Press, 2016). Inviting care seekers to share their stories and explore their meanings is a primary means for spiritual assessment; it can also

function as a spiritual care intervention that is itself therapeutic. Dagmar Grefe and Pamela McCarroll, with Bilal Ansari, "Meaning Making in Chaplaincy Practice: Presence, Assessment, and Interventions," in Cadge and Rambo, *Chaplaincy and Spiritual Care in the Twenty-First Century*, 78.

67. Pastoral theologian Karen Scheib suggests that story companions come alongside others, helping them make sense of their experiences from a personal and theological perspective. Scheib, *Telling the Stories of Our Lives*.
68. Pastoral theologian Margaret Kornfeld suggests that to listen well, caregivers need to silence the "static" in themselves and be open to the experience of another. Margaret Kornfeld, *Cultivating Wholeness: A Guide to Care and Counseling in Faith Communities* (2000; repr., Continuum International Publishing, 2002), 47.
69. While seemingly simple, these steps are not easy and take intentionality, practice, and lots of feedback. It is helpful to have a coach to learn these critical practices. Other resources are also available, including books such as John Savage's *Listening and Caring Skills: A Guide for Groups and Leaders* (Abingdon Press, 1996) and Scheib's *Telling the Stories of Our Lives*.
70. The language of "story companion" is Karen Scheib's. See Karen D. Scheib, *Pastoral Care: Telling the Stories of Our Lives* (Abingdon, 2016), 14.
71. Affirming someone's emotions does not mean you agree with them or that you would feel the same way in the same situation. It simply means you understand that *they* feel a certain way.
72. Validation does not mean agreement. It only means that the listener can understand what the speaker is feeling and why they might be feeling it. It does not mean the speaker would necessarily feel the same way in the same situation.
73. See Scheib, *Telling the Stories of Our Lives*. Scheib presents five elements she considers essential to pastoral companionship: (1) seeing the connection between storytelling and identity, (2) reading the "narrative environment" in which the storyteller grew up, (3) knowing how narrative development occurs throughout a lifetime, (4) improving reading skills of one's own and others' stories, and (5) knowing the criteria of a good life story and assessing whether a particular story meets those criteria.
74. This is about resonance between the storyteller and the listener. Being a good story companion requires attention to the body language, voice, and other nonverbal cues of the meaning and emotions the storyteller is trying to convey. Shari M. Geller and L. S. Greenberg, "Therapeutic Presence: A Theory of Relationship," in *Therapeutic Presence: A Mindful Approach to Effective Therapy*, ed. Shari M. Geller and L. S. Greenberg (W. W. Norton, 2012), 51–72. S. M. Geller and L. S. Greenberg, "Therapeutic Presence: A

Theory of Relationship," in *Therapeutic presence: A mindful approach to effective therapy*, ed. S. M. Geller and L. S. Greenberg (American Psychological Association), 51–72, https://doi.org/10.1037/13485-003. As Scheib puts it, "The primary intent of narrative therapy is to deconstruct problem-saturated life-stories and construct healthier, more functional, and preferred stories." Scheib, *Telling the Stories of Our Lives*. Narrative therapy separates the person from the problem and helps people see that they can stand outside the problem and view it versus getting lost among the trees in the forest of the problem. Those who have experienced grief from a loss of any kind can benefit by revising their stories. Narrative therapy recognizes that every experience of grief is unique. There is no timeline or certain stage one should be in. People experience emotional healing when they can "restory" their lives in meaningful ways. This is an important skill to develop but cannot be explored further here. For more, see Scheib, *Telling the Stories of Our Lives*. Making meaning is essential to the restorying process. We can make meaning out of grief in four ways: (1) expand or thicken the plot, (2) develop a new or revised interpretation of a loss, (3) attend to the impact of narrative environments on interpretation and meaning-making, and (4) affirm and support a reconfigured continuing bond with the deceased.

75. Dov Seidman, *How: Why How We Do Anything Means Everything* (John Wiley & Sons, 2011). Organizations that are innovative, successful, and sustainable hold regular and widespread discussions about their values, exploring what they mean to the identity and vision of the organization as well as how it will accomplish its mission. Rosabeth Moss Kanter, "Ten Essentials for Getting Value from Values," *Harvard Business Review* (blog), June 14, 2010, http://blogs.hbr.org/kanter/2010/06/ten-essentials-for-getting-val.html. One author argues that leaders can only sustain strong positive results if they care about the common good. Richard Barrett, *Liberating the Corporate Soul: Building Visionary Organizations* (Butterworth-Heinemann, 1998). Although this message "still has not penetrated very far in the business community and hardly at all in business schools," religious leaders in faith-based organizations and other not-for-profit organizations are well suited to this values orientation. Barrett, *New Leadership Paradigm*, 5.

76. Values can be life-giving or potentially life-limiting, and they correspond to the level of human consciousness a person has achieved, which correlates to the level of psychological development they are operating from. Richard Barrett, *The Metrics of Human Consciousness* (Lulu Publishing Services, 2014). Examples of positive values include trust, openness, honesty, and integrity. Examples of potentially life-limiting values include blame, greed, and jealousy. Barrett, *New Leadership Paradigm*, 12. In the model of values theory and the inventory I prefer, values are identified

in a developmental spectrum, from the most basic values such as self-preservation, which is especially critical in our earliest years (and when we are under threat), to middle-level values such as self-actualization and self-worth, which take on particular importance in our young adult years, to the highest-order values including wisdom, community, and interdependence, which can only be achieved by the most mature people and communities. Hall, *Values Shift*, 143.

77. Scheib describes a preferred narrative as one that is revised and reframed to be more life-giving. Scheib, *Telling the Stories of Our Lives*, 136–139.
78. These tools are best used if there is a genuine interest and intent to understand and deepen a relationship. If misused, any tool can become mechanical and lack empathy or intention to lead the storyteller closer to themselves, others, and God.
79. Barrett, *Values-Driven Organizations*, 19.
80. Daniel H. Pink, *Drive: The Surprising Truth About What Motivates Us* (Riverhead Books, 2009), 90, cited in Barrett, *Values-Driven Organizations*, 20.
81. Barrett, *New Leadership Paradigm*, 20. People who act out of intrinsic motivations (e.g., to help others improve their lives, to learn, and to grow) rather than extrinsic motivations (e.g., to become wealthy or to achieve fame) had higher levels of satisfaction and subjective well-being than others. Religious communities can provide opportunities for growth and development, key determinants for happiness.
82. Barabara J. McClure, *Emotions: Problems and Promise for Human Flourishing* (Baylor University Press, 2019), 27.
83. By *more human*, I mean people become more aware of who they are in all their gifts and limitations, they become more aware of their relationship with the Sacred Creator who made them, and they are more deeply aware of their interdependence with others.
84. Developmental theorists Robert Kegan and Lisa L. Lahey identify three stages of psychological development: the socialized mind is dependent on others to meet its needs and know what to do, the self-authorizing mind is independent and seeks to pursue its own agenda and needs, and the self-transforming mind is interdependent and continually seeks more information and consult with others to find the best way forward. The self-transforming mind "is not a prisoner to its beliefs, agenda or position. It is open to thoughts and ideas of others and can integrate them into a more inclusive worldview. People with self-authoring minds tend to think of their work as a mission or purpose. They are well suited to handle complex situations. They are motivated by the ability to satisfy their higher-order growth needs [their higher-level values], to make a difference in their world and leave a legacy by serving humanity or the

planet." Robert Kegan and Lisa L. Lahey, *Immunity to Change: How to Overcome It and Unlock the Potential in Yourself and Your Organization* (Harvard Business School Publishing, 2009), 16–21.

85. One of the most significant challenges of leading others is to unlearn the golden rule. In leadership, the task is not to treat others the way one wants to be treated themselves but rather to get to know people well enough that they can lead each person they way *that person* wants to be led, not the way that is comfortable to the leader or the way the leader would want to be led.
86. Truly transformational leaders are also antiracist leaders who set the tone for the rest of the organization by taking a bold stance against racism and other forms of discrimination and marginalization. James D. White, *Anti-Racist Leadership: How to Transform Corporate Culture in a Race-Conscious World* (Harvard Business Review Press, 2022). Values allow us to transcend our ethnic and cultural belief structures by uniting people around shared basic principles: "In human group cultures, values unite, and beliefs separate." Barrett, *New Leadership Paradigm*, 12. As Black and antiracist scholar Laurie Garrett-Cobina writes, "Being able to imagine what it looks like for an organization to be dedicated to justice, equality, and moral integrity in practice and procedure is vital. Offering a race-relevant, gender-conscious, and class-aware understanding of organizations will aid in recognizing what is really happening within organizations and why it is happening to the people within them." Laurie Garrett-Cobina, "The Emotional Undercurrents of Organizations," in *Chaplaincy and Spiritual Care in the 21st Century: An Introduction*, ed. Wendy Cadge and Shelly Rambo (University of North Carolina Press, 2022), 239.
87. Email should only be used to share data: what time the meeting is, confirmation of an action item, etc. Other forms of communication that involve negotiation or potential conflict are best done in person.
88. Douglas Stone and Sheila Heen, *Thanks for the Feedback: The Science and art of Receiving Feedback Well* (Penguin Books, 2014).
89. People will have more in common with those who share their values and are in a similar cycle of development than with others who are at different levels. There is no easy way to resolve these conflicts except by working through them.
90. Len Leritz, *No-Fault Negotiating: A Simple and Innovative Approach for Solving Problems, Reaching Agreements and Resolving Conflicts* (Grand Central Publishing, 1990), 8.
91. Len Leritz, *No-Fault Negotiating: A Practical Guide to the New Dealmaking Strategy That Lets Both Sides Win* (Warner Books, 1987).
92. David Peter Stroh, *Systems Thinking for Social Change: A Practical Guide to Solving Complex Problems, Avoiding Unintended Consequences, and*

Achieving Lasting Results (Chelsea Green Publishing, 2015), 21. Stroh argues that effective systems thinking motivates people to change because they discover their role in exacerbating the problems they want to solve. Second, systems thinking catalyzes collaboration because people learn they can collectively create the results they desire. Third, systems thinking allows for better outcomes because it focuses people to work on a few key and agreed-on changes over time to achieve systemwide impacts that are significant and sustainable. Finally, systems thinking stimulates continuous learning, which is an essential characteristic of sustainable, thriving organizations. Stroh, *Systems Thinking for Social Change*, 21–22.

93. These steps are drawn from Indigenous peoples' communal problem-solving processes and are found in Margaret J. Wheatley, *Finding Our Way: Leadership for Uncertain Times* (Berrett-Koehler Publishers, 2007), 184–197. They are "developmental," whereby one stage creates the conditions for the next.
94. Wheatley writes that the circle is the form of equality, the "most common and enduring form of human meeting." She notes that circles have been found from "half a million years ago as early. Human ancestors sat around fires, trying to get warm. The equality of the circle was important even then. Had they sat in a rectangle or any other form, some of them would have frozen!" Wheatley, *Finding Our Way*, 185.
95. Wheatley, *Finding Our Way*, 186.
96. Some people find it difficult to be vulnerable and share what matters to them most and why. Others find it invigorating. Almost everyone will forge a stronger relationship with the people who have shared because they find values in common. They connect at a deeper level because they have been open and vulnerable with one another.
97. Stroh, *Systems Thinking for Social Change*, 74–75.
98. Stroh, *Systems Thinking for Social Change*, 31.
99. Peter M. Senge, *The Fifth Discipline: The Art and Practice of the Learning Organization* (Currency Publishing, 2006). Senge argues that at the heart of a learning organization is a shift of mind, from seeing ourselves as separate from the world to connected to the world, from seeing problems as caused by something "out there" to seeing how our own actions create the problems we experience. Senge, *The Fifth Discipline*, 12.
100. John P. Kotter, *Leading Change* (Harvard Business Review Press, 2012), 37–38. If complacency is high, few people will be willing to work on the problem, and any initiatives are bound to fail.
101. Wheatley, *Finding Our Way*, 188.
102. Wheatley, *Finding Our Way*, 190.
103. Wheatley, *Finding Our Way*, 191.
104. Wheatley, *Finding Our Way*, 193.

105. Wheatley, *Finding Our Way*, 193.
106. Wheatley, *Finding Our Way*, 193.
107. Stroh, *Systems Thinking for Social Change*, 75.
108. Wheatley, *Finding Our Way*, 194.
109. Wheatley, *Finding Our Way*, 193.
110. Wheatley, *Finding Our Way*, 195.
111. Kotter, *Leading Change*, 123.
112. Kotter, *Leading Change*, 126. Short-term wins have at least three characteristics. They are visible: Large numbers of people can see for themselves whether the result is real or just hype. The change is unambiguous: There can be little argument over the call. And the change is clearly related to the larger change effort, which is related to the larger goals. Short-term wins provide evidence that sacrifices are worth it, they reward effort, they can help fine-tune vision and strategies, they undermine cynics and resisters, and they build momentum. Kotter, *Leading Change*, 127.
113. Wheatley, *Finding Our Way*, 195.
114. Wheatley, *Finding Our Way*, 195.
115. Barrett, *Values-Driven Organization*, 12.

CHAPTER 8: LEADING SELF

1. Paul Freedman, "Islands of Sanity and Spiritual Leadership in a Time of Crisis: Margaret Wheatley and Paul Freedman in Dialogue," *Holistic Education Review* 4, no. 1 (2024), 6.
2. Sin is defined as the "negation of relation" by theologian Fumitaka Matsuoka in *The Color of Faith: Building Community in a Multicultural Society* (United Church Press, 1989).
3. Pastoral theologian and Jungian scholar Margaret Kornfeld suggests that wholeness (her word, which I take to mean *well-being*) entails acknowledging and even embracing one's limits and that by so doing one feels a sense of freedom and acceptance: "'Survival' is not synonymous with 'health,' any more than the 'absence of symptoms' is the same as 'wholeness.'" Margaret Kornfeld, *Cultivating Wholeness: A Guide to Care and Counseling in Faith Communities* (2000; repr., Continuum International Publishing, 2002), 35.
4. Morality is defined as valuing what is rightly valued. Paul Bloomfield, *Virtues of Happiness: A Theory of the Good Life* (Oxford University Press, 2014), 125. This includes valuing ourselves as well as others, the earth, and the Sacred. Pastoral theologian James Lapsley argues that participation in the life of God is a hallmark of flourishing and is something of a developmental achievement. See James Lapsley, *Salvation and Health: Interlocking Processes of Life* (Westminster Press, 1972).

Pastoral theologian Rodney Hunter added nuance to the ability to participate in the life of God, saying it involves active engagement but is also available for those who cannot actively participate: Those who "suffer the limitation or destruction of their vital capacities" participate by offering themselves, their presence, and their ability to receive love as a mark of their participation in the life of God rather than a particular creation or achievement. Rodney J. Hunter, "Participation in the Life of God: Revisioning Lapsley's Salvation-Health Model," in *The Treasure of Earthen Vessels: Explorations in Theological Anthropology in Honor of James N. Lapsley*, ed. Brian H. Childs and David W. Waanders (Westminster John Knox Press, 1994), 13. See also Barbara J. McClure, *Moving Beyond Individualism: Reflections on Theory, Theology and Practice* (Cascade, 2010), for my proposal of a synergistic anthropology that privileges participation in valuable, liberative activities rather than insight as the ultimate goal of psychotherapeutic, or healing, practices.

5. John D. Caputo, *Hoping Against Hope: Confessions of a Postmodern Pilgrim* (Fortress Press, 2015), 79.
6. Sometimes the flourishing of all means that I must sacrifice my immediate happiness or contentment for that of another. But to flourish, I must choose what to sacrifice, and for what, with careful discernment.
7. Wisdom is a kind of "practical rationality" or, in Greek, *phronesis—practical wisdom* to Aristotle; Bloomfield, *Virtues of Happiness*, 134. The authors of *Christian Practical Wisdom: What It Is, Why It Matters* argue that practical wisdom, the kind Aristotle thought was indispensable for *eudaimonia*, is the least understood and the most difficult to learn. See Dorothy C. Bass et al., *Christian Practical Wisdom: What It Is, Why It Matters* (Eerdmans, 2016).
8. *Phronesis* is a virtue insofar as acting rationally in practical contexts can be a well-developed character trait that aids and partly constitutes a well-lived life. Bloomfield, *Virtues of Happiness*, 224, 134. See also the exploration of *phronesis* in the Christian life in Bass et al., *Christian Practical Wisdom*, 1.
9. Bloomfield, *Virtues of Happiness*, 225. Wisdom includes the recognition that complexity is at the heart of life and allows one to manage paradox. Despite the fact that all one can really do is try, often and regularly, to do what is moral and virtuous in the moment, the wise rest in the knowledge that they could not have tried harder, could not have discerned more carefully in the moment, and could not have done better, given who they were at the time and the challenges they faced. See a discussion of this in Bloomfield, *Virtues of Happiness*, 230.
10. Leadership scholar Bill George writes that "*authenticity is seen as the gold standard for leadership*. No longer is leadership about developing

charisma, emulating other leaders, looking good externally, and acting in one's self-interest, as was so often the case in the late twentieth century." Bill George (with Peter Sims), *True North: Discover Your Authentic Leadership* (John Wiley & Sons, 2007), online, n.p. Emphasis in the original. Pastoral theologian Robert Dykstra argues that it is important that religious leaders find the courage and resources necessary to explore their own debilitating childhood shame. By engaging one's own shame and deep, difficult emotions, "they gain empathy and skill for assisting others in their pastoral care." Robert C. Dykstra, *Finding Ourselves Lost: Ministry in an Age of Overwhelm* (Cascade, 2018), 2–3.

11. Leadership scholar Abraham Zaleznik argues that leaders tolerate chaos and lack of structure and are willing to delay closure to more fully understand the issues. In this way, Zaleznik suggests, transformational leaders have much more in common with artists, scientists, and other creative thinkers than they do with managers. Organizations need both managers and leaders to succeed, but developing both requires a "reduced focus on logic and strategic exercises in favor of an environment where creativity and imagination are permitted to flourish." Abraham Zaleznik, "Managers and Leaders: Are They Different?" *Clinical Leadership and Management Review: The Journal of CLMA* 18, no. 3 (2004): 171–177. Remember that although we are all saturated with information, it is knowledge that people need. Unlike information, meaningful knowledge "involves us and our deeper motivations and dynamics as human beings," Margaret J. Wheatley, *Finding Our Way: Leadership for Uncertain Times* (Berrett-Koehler Publishers, 2007), 154. When people receive information, they filter it through their history, identity, values, habits, and beliefs to decide the meaning of the information. Through this process of filtering, information becomes knowledge that is meaningful to people and organizations. Wheatley, *Finding Our Way*, 154. It is important to note that when deciding how and when to communicate, some topics are best discussed in person, while others can be covered in an email. An effective communicator can discern which mode of communication is best for the issue at hand. In general, emails and texts should only be used to share information (when a meeting is called, what the topic will be), while in-person communications are best when a significant discussion is needed, conflict is possible, or various opinions are being collected.
12. Leadership skills take time and practice to improve. Not everyone will lead the same way. It can be helpful to learn about your own leadership style. Leadership is wonderfully unique but can only be improved with intentionality, practice, feedback, and support. Having effective role models to emulate and coaches and mentors to guide is invaluable as one learns effective leadership. Only you can decide to develop yourself,

but you cannot do it alone. Having a trained leadership coach keeps your growth on the front burner and is a source of clarity, guidance, and support. However, research shows that seeing yourself as a leader is a crucial first step on the path of leadership, whereas reluctance to identify as a leader can stunt growth and development. Marshall Ganz et al., "Crafting Public Narrative to Enable Collective Action: A Pedagogy for Leadership Development," *Academy of Management Learning and Education* 22, no. 2 (2023): 169–190.

13. The Center for Creative Leadership, "12 Essential Qualities of Effective Leadership," July 3, 2024. https://www.ccl.org/articles/leading-effectively-articles/characteristics-good-leader/. One researcher on thriving in ministry argues that there are sixty-four competencies that religious leaders must cultivate. This impossible task is moderated through the model of collaborative and distributive leadership being proposed here. Matt Bloom, *Flourishing in Ministry: How to Cultivate Clergy Wellbeing* (Rowman & Littlefield, 2019), 9. This is an unrealistic expectation, and denominations need to take responsibility for ministry standards.
14. People expect to be treated with dignity, respect, and attentiveness. They also expect leaders (especially religious leaders) to care for them and to create a just organization that seeks to nurture the thriving of all. They will not respect, dignify, or pay attention to a leader who does not do the same for them.
15. Of course, no one is infallible or perfect in practical reasoning; being practically wise, like all virtues, is an ideal that we may only approach with greater or lesser success.
16. Organizational scholars often refer to dynamic systems as VUCA: volatile, uncertain, chaotic, and ambiguous. This is opposed to BANI systems: brittle, anxious, noncomprehensible, incoherent. Naturally, these qualities make leadership even more difficult and also make collaborative leadership the only way to transform an organization. Nathan Bennett and G. James Lemoine, "What a Difference a Word Makes: Comparing a VUCA World to a BANI World," *Journal of Business Strategy* 35, no. 2 (2014): 20–28.
17. It can be helpful to have some training in understanding family systems and organizational systems as well as theories of human development, trauma, and the relationships among emotions, values, and behaviors. Many good books are available to help with this, as are consultants and coaches. One book I use in class is Ronald W. Richardson's *Creating a Healthier Church* (Augsburg Fortress Press, 1996), which uses family systems theory to understand dynamics in congregations. Richardson offers guidance for religious leaders as they engage the systems in their congregations.

18. Martin Heidegger, *On the Way to Language*, trans. Harold Hofstadter (Harper & Row, 1971).
19. Matthew 18:20, *The Holy Bible*.
20. Pastoral theologian Graeme Griffin argues that listening enhances people's awareness that they are beings before God. Graeme Maxwell Griffin, *Coming to Care: An Introduction to Pastoral Care for Ordained Ministers and Lay People* (Uniting Church Theological Hall, 1995).
21. Others' stories connect them to the leader, but leaders' stories are crucial, too, even if they do not share them in all spaces or with all people. Humans' natural state is to be in relationship. Theologians have argued that in the Christian tradition, the Holy Trinity typifies this. For example, see Kirk Wegter-McNelly, *The Entangled God: Divine Relationality and Quantum Physics* (Routledge, 2012).
22. There are many helpful books on effective listening, including John Savage's *Listening and Caring Skills* (Abingdon Press, 1996) and Karen Scheib's *Pastoral Care: Telling the Stories of Our Lives* (Abingdon Press, 2016). Many potential leaders view themselves as unprepared to serve in the role. Some may feel uncomfortable embracing a role traditionally associated with male dominance, while others worry that their leadership will not be taken seriously. There are real experiences that inform and support these fears, especially for those in underrepresented groups such as women and people of color. These fears can have a significant impact on how a leader views themselves. The good news is that leadership is a set of skills that can be learned, and there are coaches who can work with leaders to develop their self-confidence and teach effective tools to increase their effectiveness.
23. The cultivation of intellectual and character virtues makes up the highest good and leads to *eudaimonia*, or thriving, according to Aristotle. In other words, one can achieve flourishing if one cultivates as fully as possible the intellectual and character virtues. However, this is not an easy task. For Aristotle, acquiring virtues requires more than studying or habituation; it requires a kind of practical reason. This practical wisdom informs people so that their responses to circumstances are rational. Practical reason enables people to deliberate well about what to do in a situation based on the highest good and helps them articulate and justify a valid conception of the highest good. Aristotle understood the good life to require that people both live up to their own potential and find happiness, but he also argued that *eudaimonia* requires that each person contribute to a just and well-functioning community and society.
24. Kenneth P. De Meuse, "Learning Agility: Its Evolution as a Psychological Construct and Its Empirical Relationship to Leader Success," *Consulting Psychology Journal: Practice and Research* 69, no. 4 (2017): 267–295.

25. These are often called *SMART plans*. See, for example, Paul R. Williams et al., "The Power of Leadership, Collaboration, and Professional Development: The Story of the SMART Consortium," *Education and Urban Society* 41, no. 4 (2009): 437–456. There are also STRETCH goals that expand the horizon of desired change. STRETCH goals encourage people to be creative, innovative, and ambitious. However, STRETCH plans often reach too far out and demand too much, resulting in demotivation and reduced capacities for change. See S. Kerr and S. Landauer, "Using Stretch Goals to Promote Organizational Effectiveness and Personal Growth: General Electric and Goldman Sachs," *Academy of Management Executives* 18, no. 4 (2004), 134–138.
26. Many leaders feel overwhelmed and have a long list of tasks demanding their attention. It can be tempting to dive in and make quick decisions, taking immediate action. This is often a mistake. Action without careful deliberation and reflection on possible outcomes can lead to errors and mistrust. People will not follow a leader who is fickle or lacks confidence, but they will also lose trust in a leader who cannot admit mistakes and show they have learned from them. Transformative leaders will reflect and understand why they failed, find ways to remedy the situation, and invite others into post-action reviews to prevent it from happening again. Effective leaders will follow their own values and let their conscience be their guides. They also do not define themselves by wins and losses but define themselves by the processes they develop to handle them and help the organization stay true to itself. A recognition of one's own biases, ambiguities, and inadequacies can go a long way toward making one available to others in need. The shepherd, to return to Seward Hiltner's work on congregational leadership, need not be perfect, but they do need a certain attitude toward their imperfection and inadequacy. This attitude may begin with a gift and requires diligent cultivation through shepherding activity, self-criticism during that activity, and intellectual and spiritual reflection on what the shepherding contributes to understanding of faith. Seward Hiltner, *Preface to Pastoral Theology* (Abingdon Press, 1958), 31–32. Careful reflection is the practice that precedes intelligent actions. We pause long enough to look more carefully at a situation, to see more of its character, to think about why it's happening, and to notice how it is affecting us and others.
27. Frequent, small behavioral changes that build on people's strengths are more likely to produce continuous positive improvements. See B. S. Sitkin et al., "The Paradox of Stretch Goals: Organizations in Pursuit of the Seemingly Impossible," *Academy of Management Review* 36, no. 3 (2011): 544–556.

28. Leaders are significantly helped by having someone outside their organizational system who can listen and support them, are trained to see and explore patterns, and can offer guidance and tools for dealing with difficult situations.
29. Carol Dweck has studied leaders for decades and found that mindset is a significant indicator of success. Carol S. Dweck, *Mindset: The New Psychology of Success* (Ballantine, 2006). Mindset drives every decision, action, opinion, and feeling of people, including leaders, and leaders set the emotional tone and level of maturity of an organization. See S. G. Barsade, "The Ripple Effect: Emotional Contagion and Its Influence on Group Behavior," *Administrative Science Quarterly* 47, no. 4 (2002), 644–675. Barsade explores what happens when something goes wrong or the leaders feel under attack. In these moments, the organization's real values become startlingly visible. Do leaders panic and scramble to get out of a tough situation, forgetting principles and values? Or do they take the time to work with the crisis, fully engaging their members, relying on their history, values, and principles—that is, their identity? Only in the latter case is it possible to create the strong social fabric that enables an institution to move confidently into its desired future.
30. It may be helpful to remember that people (including leaders) grow more spiritually and developmentally by doing it wrong than doing it right. However, religious leaders should not primarily seek the support for their own growth or their care and support from those in their congregations. Leaders of all kinds need support from people outside their organization.
31. Being willing to name uncomfortable truths, advocating for those most vulnerable in their midst, and empowering others to succeed are all good ways to build trust. Leadership scholar Marshall Sashkin writes that "our instinctual need for power centers on personal survival, but for leaders a higher stage of development of this power need involves the ability to use power in positive, 'prosocial' ways." Marshall Sashkin, *Leadership That Matters: The Critical Factors for Making a Difference in People's Lives and Organizations' Success* (Berrett-Koehler Press, 2003), 11.
32. Leaders who are intimidated to lead or are afraid of getting things wrong tend to shirk accountability. Individuals who find themselves in leadership positions need to own their role or risk becoming a shadow in the background. Leaders who own their roles are willing to make hard decisions and admit to their mistakes. The truth is that failure and mistakes are inevitable and necessary. Leaders, especially religious leaders whose traditions value honesty, will be most effective when they admit their errors and find ways to rectify them and prevent making the same mistake in the future. There is evidence that we are currently in an ethically conscious awakening. One study found that ethics and the ability to trust

an organization and its leaders carry more weight than a generous salary, as 62 percent of those surveyed noted that they want to work for an organization that makes a positive difference in the lives of its members as well as those outside of it. People in high-trust environments experience less stress, more energy, fewer sick days, increased productivity, and a 76 percent increase in engagement. Paul J. Zak, "The Neuroscience of Trust," *Harvard Business Review* 95, no. 1 (2017): 84–90.

33. Remember that in an interconnected system, there is no such thing as simple cause and effect. There is never just one person to take credit or blame. Furthermore, people are quick to notice the signs of an untrustworthy leader and will behave accordingly. It is important that leaders speak plainly and honestly and address difficult situations head on rather than procrastinating or avoiding them. Transformative leaders are judged by their actions rather than the situations they faced. Leaders who model authenticity, trust in themselves and others, and a willingness to learn and inspire others and increase motivation, productivity, engagement, and retention.
34. George, *True North*.
35. Cited in Derek W. Anderson and Jaco J. Hamman, *The Essence of Leadership: Maintaining Emotional Independence in Situations Requiring Change* (Chalice Press, 2024), 43–49. As these leadership experts write, "Some leaders might argue who they are, and their personal lives have nothing to do with who they are as leaders. They are wrong. They are also defensive in ways that inhibit their leadership. How one lives, loves, and works are deeply intertwined." Anderson and Hamman, *Essence of Leadership*, 26.
36. Self-compassion is not to be confused with self-love of the common self-help variety. In self-compassion, people are not trying to pump themselves up so that they believe in themselves. They are committed to knowing themselves so they can benefit others. Yet even with that good intent, the self they encounter in reflection can be painful. People see the harm they have done, the situations they did not handle well, their jealousies, desires, and pettiness. In other words, when people come face to face with their humanness, they often beat themselves up for it. The challenge is to treat ourselves with as much kindness and love as we would extend to a good friend who is suffering. Karen Scheib, personal communication, October 8, 2024. As people learn to hold themselves with the same tenderness, curiosity, and gentleness they hold for others they care about, they are often able to find self-acceptance and are less anxious. They accept that they are like every other human being: trying hard, making mistakes, trying again, and failing; this is what it is to live life. The quiet and confident humility that can emerge from this work supports us as we care for others.

37. The capacity to distinguish one's own feelings, beliefs, needs, and responses from others is called *differentiation* in family systems theory. When people are well-differentiated, the feelings, beliefs, needs, and responses of others do not affect them as strongly as they might otherwise. It is sometimes said that differentiated people have their feelings; their feelings don't "have" them. We tend to learn how to manage emotions from our families of origin, and we replay those patterns as adults at work. For example, if you find it difficult to manage conflict in your personal life, you will struggle in similar ways in your leadership role. If you find it difficult to clearly state what you need and want at home, you will likely have difficulty expressing yourself at work. For more, see Len Leritz, *No-Fault Negotiating: A Simple and Innovative Approach for Solving Problems, Reaching Agreements and Resolving Conflicts* (Grand Central Pub., 1990).
38. Laurie Garrett-Cobina, "The Emotional Undercurrents of Organizations," in *Chaplaincy and Spiritual Care in the 21st Century: An Introduction*, ed. Wendy Cadge and Shelly Rambo (University of North Carolina Press, 2022), 239–257.
39. Well-differentiated leaders are principle-oriented, have an internal locus of control, are self-regulated and less anxious, are not rigid in their thinking or acting, have a realistic self-image and expectations, and are aware of their own limitations. While they welcome honest feedback, they are not affected by either praise or criticism and can stay connected to others, even those who disagree with them. They can tolerate intense feelings, are not overly responsible for others, and do no micromanage; they respect and value difference, embrace change by discarding old beliefs and patterns for new ones, do not engage in polarizing debates, adapt to stressful situations, and exercise good personal boundaries. Well-differentiated leaders "can lead others to new possibilities by remaining less anxious as opposite truths are explored," Anderson and Hamman, *Essence of Leadership*, 106. Well-differentiated leaders are highly sought after because they are compassionate, keep their commitments, hold power loosely, direct their energy wisely, and project a sense of serenity. Anderson and Hamman, *Essence of Leadership*, 115. On the other end of the scale, poorly differentiated people carry high levels of chronic anxiety. They are reactive, blame others, have difficulty maintaining longer-term relationships, are emotionally needy and highly reactive with poor boundaries, are almost entirely governed by emotional reactions to others and the environment, cannot distinguish between thoughts and feelings, and are either or compliant or oppositional. Poorly differentiated leaders often either fail or burn out. Anderson and Hamman, *Essence of Leadership*, 91–95. Differentiated leaders don't try to fix people

or systems; rather, they invite others into the process of discerning what is not working and finding ways to address it. Anderson and Hamman, *Essence of Leadership*, 97.

40. Anderson and Hamman, *Essence of Leadership*, 54.
41. See Richardson, *Creating a Healthier Church*, and Edwin Friedman, *Generation to Generation: Family Process in Church and Synagogue* (The Guilford Press, 1985),
42. Anderson and Hamman, *Essence of Leadership*, 58.
43. Garrett-Cobina, "The Emotional Undercurrents of Organizations"; Anderson and Hamman, *Essence of Leadership*, 61. Emotional processes can be recognized in a system's relational patterns ("who agrees, who stirs conflict, who resists, who distances"), whose voices are heard and whose are silenced, the lines of power and authority ("who has responsibility with little authority and who has authority with little responsibility"), decision-making processes ("how reactivity, collaboration, transparency and secrecy affect decision-making"), the ability to manage conflict and sustain difficult conversations, and the ability to "create a place of interdependent belonging," including who is invited and who is excluded. Anderson and Hamman, *Essence of Leadership*, 61–62. Leaders do well to remember that emotional processes are largely subconscious, though they can be discerned by a careful observer.
44. Anderson and Hamman, *Essence of Leadership*, 69.
45. Anderson and Hamman, *Essence of Leadership*, 69.
46. Related to distancing themselves from an organization, some will also underfunction, allowing others to take on responsibilities that are their own. Anderson and Hamman, *Essence of Leadership*, 70.
47. Anderson and Hamman, *Essence of Leadership*, 72–75.
48. Anderson and Hamman, *Essence of Leadership*, 74.
49. One way to define differentiation is "the ability to feel when others want you to think and to think when others want you to feel." However, containing emotion and not becoming reactive is "not a natural human stance." It can require intentional effort. Anderson and Hamman, *Essence of Leadership*, 86–87.
50. Anderson and Hamman argue that "no leader will flourish without the ability to notice emotional triangles" and effectively deal with them. Anderson and Hamman, *Essence of Leadership*, 239.
51. Anderson and Hamman, *Essence of Leadership*, 128.
52. Anderson and Hamman, *Essence of Leadership*, 244.
53. Anderson and Hamman, *Essence of Leadership*, 244.
54. Martin E. P. Seligman, *Authentic Happiness: Using the New Positive Psychology to Realize Your Potential for Lasting Fulfillment* (Simon & Schuster, 2004).

55. Working with someone certified on a credible values inventory can deepen a leader's understanding of their own values and how they shape their sense of purpose. One example is the Barrett values inventory. However, I prefer to use the Hall-Tonna JustValues assessment to identify and clarify both individual and organizational values.
56. Peter Salovey et al., "Current Directions in Emotional Intelligence Research," in *Handbook of Emotions*, 2nd ed., ed. Michael Lewis and Jeannette M. Haviland-Jones (Guilford Press, 2000), 504–520.
57. I usually advise my students and coachees to share their lessons from wounds that have healed, not the ones that are still open and bleeding. Sharing active wounds invites the members of your organization to care for you and can muddy the important boundaries of roles, making it more difficult to act as a differentiated leader.
58. Dweck, *Mindset*.
59. Kim Cameron, *Positive Leadership: Strategies for Extraordinary Performance*, 2nd ed. (Berrett-Koehler Publishers, 2012). A recent study shows that practicing virtues such as empathy, gratitude, and hope has significant benefits to one's mental health. Dong Pil Yoon et al., "The Relationships Between Positive Character Traits, Virtues, and Health," *Social Work and Christianity* 49, no. 2 (2022): 32.
60. Emotions invite exploration at all levels—from personal to systemic—for their life-giving or life-limiting aspects. See Barbara J. McClure, *Emotions: Problems and Promise for Human Flourishing* (Baylor University Press, 2019). For example, emotions such as guilt among those in power can indicate an unjust hierarchy, and depression, rage, or helplessness among members of an organization, those oppressed, or underrepresented groups can indicate the same. Garrett-Cobina, "Emotional Undercurrents of Organizations." 246.
61. Garrett-Cobina, "Emotional Undercurrents of Organizations," 246.
62. This happens through the process of countertransference, which involves the triggers and personal experiences that people bring to situations in response to another's transference. When others impose their own subconscious value judgments, reactions, and biases on others and assume they belong to the leader, that is called *transference*. When leaders take that on, it is *countertransference*. Leaders set the emotional tone of an organization and a situation. Because emotions are contagious, leaders can change the emotional tenor of a situation by managing their own emotions, but simply covering them up will not do: They must be able to hold their perspective and continue to be congruent with themselves. Being present to themselves, grounding and centering practices, and calming one's own nervous system are all helpful tools for this work. Religious or spiritual practices including reading sacred texts, praying,

participating in liturgy and worship, meditating, getting into nature, and practicing gratitude and awe in the face of beauty can support religious leaders' well-being and allow them to be more differentiated, empathic, and caring. Learning your own emotional patterns and what generates certain emotions can help you move from reactivity to responsiveness. You may still feel triggered, but you will create more spaciousness for self-management.

63. It is important that leaders not use another's suffering to bring in their own stories of hardship. The most effective practices of care can draw on the scars in one's own life rather than incorporating the unhealed, bleeding wounds. For this reason, leaders are urged to engage their own wounds, mortality, and grief so that they can better care for others. Pamela Cooper-White, *Using Self in Pastoral Care and Counseling: A Narrative Approach* (Fortress Press, 2004). It is not uncommon for people to turn to vices when they are stressed; these include procrastinating, playing computer games, numbing oneself with drugs or alcohol, eating more than is nutritionally necessary, or binge-watching TV. These behaviors are an attempt to distract oneself form the negative emotions people often experience when stressed. Though these behaviors are common, improving self-control, self-awareness and self-compassion can help reduce anxiety-related problems. Alex Bertrams et al., "Higher Self-Control Capacity Predicts Lower Anxiety-Impaired Cognition During Math Examinations," *Frontiers in Psychology* 7 (2016): 485.
64. McClure, *Emotions*.
65. See McClure, *Emotions*, chap. 7, for more. This implies, of course, that people's stories are significant entry points for understanding their emotions and feelings: Stories are epistemological tools. It also implies that each of us needs story companions who can listen for ways our feelings are related to our developmental processes, memories of our past experiences, contextual challenges, needs, goals, values, and so on. For a good discussion of this, see Scheib, *Telling the Stories of Our Lives*, and David A. Hogue, *Remembering the Future, Imagining the Past: Story, Ritual, and the Human* (Pilgrim Press, 2003). Australian pastoral theologian Neil Pembroke also writes about the exploration of emotions, particularly shame, in pastoral care. See Neil Pembroke, *The Art of Listening: Dialogue, Shame, and Pastoral Care* (T&T Clark/Handsel, 2002). Accompanying one another in this work engenders hope, it has been argued, which emerges in relationship as we explore these things together. See Joretta L. Marshall, "Collaborating Hope: Joining the In-Between Spaces," *Journal of Pastoral Theology* 26, no. 2 (2016): 77–90.
66. For more on the ways emotions are constructed, see McClure, *Emotions*, especially chap. 6.

67. In religious traditions, this often means being clear about one's relationship to God and all else. Being related to the Divine is at the heart of many religious understandings of the human being, and human beings are not fully themselves—whole—unless they are conscious of this. As St. Augustine put it, "Our hearts are restless until they rest in thee."
68. Garrett-Cobina, "Emotional Undercurrents of Organizations," 250.
69. Garrett-Cobina, "Emotional Undercurrents of Organizations," 241.
70. Garrett-Cobina, "Emotional Undercurrents of Organizations," 246.
71. "Hope," *Cambridge English Dictionary*, accessed July 13, 2024, https://dictionary.cambridge.org/us/dictionary/english/hope. Two necessary components of hope are desire and uncertainty about an outcome. A. M. Martin, "Hopes and Dreams," *Philosophy and Phenomenological Research* 83, no. 1 (2011): 148–173; C. Bloeser and T. Stahl, "Hope," *The Stanford Encyclopedia of Philosophy*, Summer 2022 ed., ed. E. N. Zalta, https://plato.stanford.edu/archives/sum2022/entries/hope/; A. B. I. Bernardo, "Extending Hope Theory: Internal and External Locus of Trait Hope," *Personality and Individual Differences* 49, no. 8 (2010): 944–949, https://doi.org/10.1016/j.paid.2010.07.036.
72. Hope is, "to an extent, about constructive thinking—that is, taking in information and actively using it to achieve goals." D. B. Feldman et al., "Hope and Goal Attainment: Testing a Basic Prediction of Hope," *Journal of Social and Clinical Psychology* 28, no. 4 (2009): 479–497, https://doi.org/10.1521/jscp.2009.28.4.479.
73. K. K. Leung et al., "Why Health Expectations and Hopes Are Different: The Development of a Conceptual Model," *Health Expectations* 12, no. 4 (2009): 347–360.
74. Bernardo, "Extending Hope Theory" reported research in which the researchers found that hope often had an "external locus," including family, friends, or a "supernatural/spiritual being." See also J. W. Ciarrocchi et al., "Gods or Rituals? Relational Faith, Spiritual Discontent, and Religious Practices as Predictors of Hope and Optimism," *Journal of Positive Psychology* 3, no. 2 (2008): 120–136. Optimism may better be considered a personality trait rather than a psychological concept. W. R. Miller, *8 Ways to Hope: Charting a Path Through Uncertain Times* (The Guilford Press, 2024). In his exploration of the way Plenty Coups, the "last great Chief of the Crow," saved his people, philosopher Jonathan Lear recounts how a significant dream that Plenty Coups had when he was nine, understood as a message from a spirit, functioned in operationalizing his hope. See Jonathan Lear, *Radical Hope: Ethics in the Face of Cultural Devastation* (Harvard University Press, 2006).
75. C. R. Snyder, "Conceptualizing, Measuring, and Nurturing Hope," *Journal of Counseling and Development* 73, no. 3 (1995): 355–360.

76. E. Benzein and B. Saveman, "One Step Towards the Understanding of Hope: A Concept Analysis," *International Journal of Nursing Studies* 35, no. 6 (1998): 322–329. Others argue that hope is about choosing to focus on the possible good that might happen, despite uncertainties. C. A. Kadlac, "The Virtue of Hope," *Ethical Theory and Moral Practice* 18, no. 2 (2015): 337–354.
77. C. R. Snyder, *The Psychology of Hope: You Can Get There from Here* (Free Press, 1994).
78. J. A. Elliott and I. N. Olver, "Hope and Hoping in the Talk of Dying Cancer Patients," *Social Science and Medicine* 64, no. 1 (2007): 138–149.
79. Leung et al., "Why Health Expectations and Hopes Are Different"; J. M. C. Kwong, "What Is Hope?" *European Journal of Philosophy* 27, no. 1 (2019): 243–254.
80. Elliott and Olver, "Hope and Hoping in the Talk of Dying Cancer Patients." The authors argue that when goals are not realized, hopers change what they hope for.
81. C. Nekolaichuk et al., "Structuring the Meaning of Hope in Health and Illness," *Social Science and Medicine* 48, no. 5 (1999): 591–605.
82. E. Benzein et al., "The Meaning of the Lived Experience of Hope in Patients with Cancer in Palliative Home Care," *Palliative Medicine* 15, no. 2 (2001): 117–126; R. Bland and Y. Darlington, "The Nature and Sources of Hope: Perspectives of Family Caregivers of People with Serious Mental Illness," *Perspectives in Psychiatric Care* 38, no. 2 (2002): 61–68. Religious virtues differ from cardinal virtues in that the latter are considered the principal virtues that guide ethical behavior and are fundamental to living a good life. They are often seen as the hinges from which other virtues flow. (There are four: prudence, justice, temperance, and fortitude.) Theological virtues are specific to Christian theology and are believed to be gifts from God that shape the soul and orient it toward God. They represent the virtues that are infused into the believer by divine grace. (There are three: faith, hope, and love.)
83. V. Carson et al., "Hope and Its Relationship to Spiritual Well-Being," *Journal of Psychology and Theology* 16, no. 2 (1988): 159–167. Some argue that without hope, people can become indifferent to all options and lose their sense of purpose in life. In fact, philosopher Immanuel Kant describes reasonable hope as a rational imperative, seeing it as a bridge between reason and existential questions that cannot be answered by experience. C. J. Insole, "Kant on Christianity, Religion and Politics: Three Hopes, Three Limits," *Studies in Christian Ethics* 29, no. 1 (2016): 14–33.
84. T. Safri, "Hope: A Psychological Perspective," *Indian Journal of Positive Psychology* 7, no. 1 (2016): 138.

85. L. G. Aspinwall and S. L. Leaf, "In Search of the Unique Aspects of Hope: Pinning Our Hopes on Positive Emotions, Future-Oriented Thinking, Hard Times, and Other People," *Psychological Inquiry* 13, no. 4 (2002): 276–321; B. Schrank et al., "Hope in Psychiatry: A Review of the Literature," *Acta Psychiatrica Scandinavica* 118, no. 6 (2008): 421–433; Benzein and Saveman, "One Step Towards the Understanding of Hope"; Anthony Scioli et al., "Hope: Its Nature and Measurement," *Psychology of Religion and Spirituality* 3, no. 2 (2011): 78–87.
86. This view obviously refers to the mental act of hoping and imagining, which provides a psychological resource for individuals. P. Drahos, "Trading in Public Hope," *Annals of the American Academy of Political and Social Science* 592 (2004): 18–38. See also D. Webb, "Paulo Freire and 'The Need for a Kind of Education in Hope,'" *Cambridge Journal of Education* 40, no. 4 (2010): 327–339.
87. Lear, *Radical Hope*. With the rise of psychoanalysis and human development theory at the beginning of the twentieth century, attention again swayed to the more positive side of hope as an expression of fundamental trust in others and a basic force of human psychology. For example, Erik H. Erikson *Childhood and Society* (W. W. Norton, 1950) related hope to the experience of trust in the first stage of life. For Erikson, trust more accurately captures the vulnerable state of the infant, the mutuality that must exist between the recipient and provider, and most importantly, the growing sense of separateness that brings the desire to try to reclaim a "paradise forfeited." According to Erikson, it is this basic trust that spawns an enduring belief in the attainability of the individual's deepest desires. While Erikson considered basic hope the most lasting human strength, he believed that it might acquire new qualities as the individual ascended to higher stages of the life cycle. Erikson, *Childhood and Society*, 250. See also R. Steinhoffsmith, "On Hope and Trust as Foundations for Faith," in *Human Development and Faith: Life-Cycle Stages of Body, Mind, and Soul*, ed. F. B. Kelcourse (Chalice Press, 2004), 129–146.
88. K. Weingarten, "Reasonable Hope: Construct, Clinical Applications, and Supports," *Family Process* 49, no. 1 (2010): 5–25.
89. Marshall, "Collaborating Hope," 77–90.
90. C. Peterson et al., "Zest and Work," *Journal of Organizational Behavior: The International Journal of Industrial, Occupational and Organizational Psychology and Behavior* 30, no. 2 (2009): 161–172. Victor Frankl is a well-known Jewish philosopher of hope, especially for the possibilities its holds for transforming or at least mitigating suffering. V. E. Frankl, *Man's Search for Meaning* (Simon & Schuster, 1985).
91. C. Graham and J. R. Pozuelo, "Does Hope Lead to Better Futures: Insights from a Survey of Young Adults in Peru," 2018, https://humcap

.uchicago.edu/RePEc/hka/wpaper/Graham_Pozuelo_2018_hope-for-the-future.pdf; The study of hope from a scientific perspective is part of the subjective experiences that are increasingly understood to be important drivers of individual behaviors. Hope is one of the domains of human experience that are relevant to behavior.

92. A. Chignell, "The Focus Theory of Hope," *Philosophical Quarterly* 73, no. 1 (2023): 44–63.
93. Chignall, "Focus Theory." What people hope for matters; the best goals are those that meet basic human needs of autonomy, competence, and relatedness to others. Edward L. Deci and Richard M. Ryan, "The Support of Autonomy and the Control of Behavior," *Journal of Personality and Social Psychology* 53, no. 6 (1987): 91.
94. Safri, "Hope," 138.
95. Lear, *Radical Hope*.
96. People often confuse hope with optimism or faith. They obscure real hope with their own dreams, and dreams with the urgings of their own desire to control. Letting go of hope and leaning into faith allows people to figure out what needs to be done, what is virtuous, and act accordingly.
97. Václav Havel, *The Power of the Powerless: Citizens Against the State in Central-Eastern Europe* (Knopf, 1990).
98. Thomas Merton, *No Man Is an Island* (Harcourt, Brace, 1955).
99. Henri J. Nouwen, *Life of the Beloved: Spiritual Living in a Secular World* (Crossroad, 1992).
100. This is a paraphrase of the questions Quaker leadership expert Robert Greenleaf suggested when he articulated the outcomes of servant leadership, a model he developed. Robert K. Greenleaf, *Servant Leadership: A Journey into the Nature of Legitimate Power and Greatness*, 25th anniversary ed. (Paulist Press, 2002).
101. Two biblical leaders, Moses and Abraham, had been given promises by their God for their own flourishing. Over time, however, and faced with multiple challenges, they had to abandon hope that they would see the fruition of their efforts in their lifetimes. They changed their orientation from hope to faith that God would continue the work through others in their absence. Being hopeless but not despairing can generate patience and deepen faith.
102. Pastoral theologian Karen Scheib recommends religious leaders shift their efforts from self-care (a task) to self-compassion (an orientation). She argues that self-care is a task one does by oneself, for oneself, whereas self-compassion can be more communal. Karen Scheib, personal communication, October 8, 2024.
103. When people ask themselves, "Who do I like to be around? Do I seek out angry or peaceful people? Do I find relief in noise or in quiet?" the

vision of the kind of leaders people need, even crave, becomes clear. As leaders, we need to find ways to help people work from a place of inner peace, even amid turmoil. Frantic activity and fear only take us deeper into chaos. In my classes, I always begin with five minutes of silent stillness. At the beginning of the semester, students are uncomfortable and find sitting quiet for that long arduous. By the end of the semester, they often say I should have made it ten or fifteen minutes. When meetings get heated, invite people to sit quietly for a minute or two. It allows their nervous systems to cool, gives them time to reflect, and might help them connect to the bigger picture and even the Sacred, allowing for a shift in perspective.

104. The rate of burnout among religious leaders is very high, often reported between 30 and 50 percent. Factors contributing to this burnout include the emotional and spiritual demands of their roles, isolation, the stress of managing congregational needs, and the impact of societal changes. Burnout is also attributed to not making and keeping good boundaries or practicing self-care.

105. If leaders are burned out, it may be that they are not prioritizing well or delegating enough. It may also be that they are driving themselves and others too hard. Take a step back, reflect on your experiences and how you feel in your body, and ask others how they are feeling. Building a culture of care and justice might mean scaling back on goals and initiatives.

INDEX